The Politics
of Independent
Kenya 1963–8

The Politics
of Independent
Kenya 1963–8

CHERRY GERTZEL

Reader in Politics
University of Zambia, Lusaka

NORTHWESTERN UNIVERSITY PRESS·EVANSTON 1970

ISBN 0 8101 0317 6

Printed in Great Britain by
Cox and Wyman Ltd, London
Fakenham and Reading

To
my friends
in Kenya

Contents

The Politics of Independent Kenya

Preface

These essays seek to describe the most significant events that influenced the emerging political system in Kenya in the first five years of that country's independence. During that period the country survived the successive threats to its stability presented first by the Army mutiny of January 1964 and second by a succession of political crises that led to the fragmentation of the ruling party, the Kenya African National Union, early in 1966. Despite early forebodings the Government remained in control and the country's economy expanded. During this period there were however considerable changes in both the country's institutional framework and its internal political alignments. The most significant political realignments were undoubtedly those consequent upon the resignation of the then Vice-President, Mr Oginga Odinga, in April 1966 and the formation under his leadership of a new Opposition party, the Kenya People's Union. This book is concerned primarily with the debate that led to that realignment and with the institutional changes so closely connected with it.

The greater part of this book was completed in 1967; but since delays ensued in its publication (responsibility for which lay primarily with myself) at a time when much was taking place on the Kenya scene, I have added a final chapter to bring the story up to the middle of 1968. Events move rapidly in most African states, and Kenya is no exception; and further important institutional changes have since August 1968 been introduced, which have only been alluded to briefly in this last chapter. One tragic event, which occurred after this book had gone to press, must be recorded here: the assassination, in July 1969, of Mr Tom Mboya, then Minister for Economic Planning and Development in the Kenya Government. Mboya had, in the seventeen years that had passed since his first entry into trade union activities in Nairobi in 1952, occupied an increasingly significant position in Kenya politics: first in the nationalist movement and then in the independent state. A gifted but controversial leader, he made a crucial contribution to the fight for independence, and then to the drive, after independence, to build a stable polity. His death marks a significant stage in Kenya's history because it removed from the political scene a leader who had for many years played such a central role in determining events. I have made no alterations to the text in the light of his death. Nevertheless perhaps the book will contribute something to the reader's understanding of Mboya's place in Kenya history.

These essays are part of the product of research into problems of government and administration carried out in Kenya over a period of years; they are based on material collected in the field, and on many interviews with political and other leaders in Nairobi and the country districts. Kenya is also fortunate in having rich documentary sources, particularly the parliamentary record on which I have drawn considerably. I have also been permitted the use of selected central and local government files, for which I am grateful.

Chapters 3 and 4, both of which are concerned with the by-elections of 1966 (generally referred to as the 'little general election') arose out of research undertaken as part of a joint project to study that election, set up in May 1966 by a small group of scholars, including myself, all then connected with the University of East Africa. Each of us worked on a particular group of constituencies; and the original intention was that the resulting case studies should be produced as a single volume. For a variety of reasons this subsequently proved impracticable; and it was therefore decided that each of us should publish his work independently. Chapter 3 of this volume is consequently adapted from the Introduction that I wrote originally for that proposed volume. Chapter 4, which is published here jointly with Dr John Okumu of University College, Nairobi, is the product of our joint field work during that election period in the then Central Nyanza district. I am grateful to Dr Okumu for his agreement to publication of this joint study in this volume.

In writing about these by-elections of 1966 I have endeavoured as far as possible not to draw on my colleagues' material which I hope will in some cases be published as separate case studies. This has meant the omission of any detailed account of the crucial Kandara campaign in which the candidacy of Bildad Kaggia, a fellow Kikuyu, challenged President Kenyatta's leadership; and of the Kamba campaign in Machakos, where the KPU Opposition victory challenged the long-standing pre-eminence of Paul Ngei. These two stories will, I hope, be told by Lionel Cliffe, of University College, Dar es Salaam, and Eliud Maluki, now of the Office of the President in Nairobi. Both of them however helped me greatly in acquiring a deeper understanding of those areas, and I must acknowledge with gratitude the many discussions we had at that time. I am also grateful to Lionel Cliffe and David Koff for many fruitful discussions on the significance of the campaign and its place in Kenya politics.

A slightly different version of Chapter 1 of this volume was first written as the Introduction to a volume of documents illustrating the working of government and politics in Kenya which will be published by the East African Publishing House later this year. That volume was edited jointly by myself and Professors Donald Rothchild and Maure Goldschmidt, over the academic year of 1967–8 when we were colleagues at University College, Nairobi. Again, I am much indebted to them for stimulating discussion which helped me to clarify ideas about the nature of Kenya politics; and for reading part of this manuscript. Chapter 5, on Parliament in Kenya, originally appeared in *Parliamentary Affairs*, in November 1966. I am grateful to the editor for permission to use it here.

The research on which this study is based was carried out over the period October 1963 to October 1968 when I held a Nuffield Foundation research appointment in the Department of Government at the University of Manchester. I am grateful to the Nuffield Foundation for financing that appointment, and to the Ministry of Overseas Development for financial assistance towards travelling and research expenses. Under the terms of that appointment I was seconded for two terms each year to teach at the University College, Nairobi. I am grateful to the College for the facilities accorded me while I was a visitor on their staff.

There are more people than can be named here to whom I am indebted for assistance over the past five years. Most of all I must thank Professor W. J. M. Mackenzie, whose original idea the appointment was, for his help and encouragement, and for his forbearance when I stayed longer in East Africa than had originally been anticipated. I am also grateful to Dr W. Tordoff of the University of Manchester, and Professor Colin Leys, presently of University College, Nairobi, for their kindness and encouragement, and for always being willing to read and comment on manuscripts; to Dr John Lonsdale of Trinity College, Cambridge, for many helpful discussions on Nyanza; and to Professor Carl Rosberg who has so generously shared his rich understanding of Kenya politics with me. In Kenya I am indebted to many people, especially Ministers and Members of Parliament and civil servants, who generously gave time and hospitality and helped me understand their country. In Nairobi

Mr Humphrey Slade, Speaker of the National Assembly, and Mr Leonard Ngugi, Clerk to the Assembly, were always ready to discuss parliamentary and constitutional matters with me, and made it possible for me to attend parliamentary debates at any time. In the country at large many Kenyans – administrators, politicians, councillors and others – have accepted and helped me. Needless to say I alone remain responsible for the interpretations reached. I am grateful to Mrs Marion Leyland who typed the manuscript and Mr John Nottingham, of the East African Publishing House, who first suggested that I should publish this part of my work in this form. Finally, the manuscript was completed while I was a member of the Institute of Commonwealth Studies in the University of London, to whose director, Professor Morris-Jones, I am grateful for the facilities and hospitality so generously given.

1
The Political Legacy

Introduction[1]

Every state that has moved from colonialism to independence has sought to shape its inherited institutions to the changing circumstances and ideas of that independence. Seeking to move away from the colonial past they are concerned with adapting their political system to the needs of the independent society. But new states often like to seem newer than in fact they can be, for they all have to work within an inherited framework which is more difficult to change than it might appear.

Kenya is no exception. She became independent in December 1963. A year later her leaders established a Republic with an executive president, because the monarchy inherited from Britain was believed to be out of keeping with her own political traditions. The declaration of a Republic was seen as part of the process of moving towards full independence.[2] But full independence did not mean a complete break with the past. The manner in whioh Kenya has tackled the problems of independence and set out to create a new political order has, to a considerable degree, been dictated by circumstances and institutions inherited from that past. The pattern of political and governmental activity since independence is better understood if considered not only against the perspective of post independence requirements and capabilities but also in terms of the legacies bequeathed the country by the colonial period. The most important of these legacies for our purposes

---

[1] I am grateful to a number of people who have kindly read and commented on this chapter, in particular: Professor Donald Rothchild of University of California, Davis; Professor Glen Brooks of Colorado College, both formerly colleagues at University College, Nairobi; Professor Carl Rosberg, Mr Lionel Cliffe and Mr Richard Stern, of University College, Dar es Salaam; Professor B. A. Ogot of University College, Nairobi; and Mr John Nottingham of the East African Publishing House.

[2] Republic of Kenya, *Official Report*, House of Representatives, First Parliament, Second Session, Vol. III, 27 October 1964, col. 3879.

are the nationalist movement and the governmental structure and machine. These two legacies have given Kenya a political tradition and an institutional framework from which her leaders have found it difficult to depart.

The Nationalist Movement

A great deal has been written about the racial background of Kenyan politics before independence. The existence of immigrant, economically differentiated racial communities, to whom the Government alienated land, resulted in a situation in which racial categories provided 'the decisive divisions' in the colonial situation.[1] The European settler minority entrenched in the 'White Highlands' enjoyed the dominant political influence until the late 1950s. Although they did not achieve the full control of government for which they always campaigned, their informal influence gained them most of what they demanded. Governmental policies on land, labour and the distribution of services favoured the European minority at the expense of the African majority. Thus the European presence created acute social and economic grievances which led Africans, as early as the 1920s, to demand a share of political power as the only sure method of removing those grievances. The nationalist movement in Kenya had consequently from its inception a strong economic basis. This was particularly the case among the Kikuyu, the largest tribe, who felt the impact of the Europeans most strongly and who suffered the greatest restrictions from their presence. After the Second World War the Kikuyu sense of economic and social grievance led to the growth of the militant 'Mau Mau' movement and to the outbreak of violence in 1952.

The dominant political influence of the entrenched European settler minority was shattered by that violence. Although the Government proved itself able to contain and finally destroy the Kikuyu movement in the forests, it was forced to speed up constitutional reform. In this respect 'Mau Mau' certainly hastened independence. The first step was taken with the Lyttelton Constitution of 1954 which provided for a 'multi-racial' form of government in which Europeans, Asians and Africans were to have a significant voice.[2] These changes modified, but did not destroy, the concept of European leadership in

[1] The most important study of pre-independence African politics in Kenya published up to date is Carl Rosberg and John Nottingham, *The Myth of Mau Mau* (London Pall Mall 1966). A brief but useful account of the colonial period will be found in G. Bennett, *Kenya. A Political History. The Colonial Period* (London Oxford University Press 1963).

[2] Cmnd. 9103 of 1954.

2

Kenya. The fundamental constitutional change was finally conceded by the British Government at the Lancaster House Conference of 1960, when the Secretary of State imposed the principle of majority rule and ultimate independence for Kenya as an African, not a 'White Man's' country.[1] The battle had therefore been won by 1960, although full executive power did not pass into African hands until independence on 12 December 1963, three years later.

The nationalist movement that swept Kenya into independence had overwhelming popular support. The pre-independence elections of 1961 and 1963 testified to this. But it was not a unified movement. Rather it was fragmented into distinctive groupings. The reason for this fragmentation is partly historical, relating to the uneven political development of the different Kenyan peoples of Kenya. The earliest and most politically conscious section of the African population were the Kikuyu. Although the first African political association in Kenya, the East African Association, was certainly trans-tribal in membership it was predominantly Kikuyu. And it was the Kikuyu who in 1924 formed the Kikuyu Central Association (KCA) to agitate for African representation and land reforms. In Western Kenya there were Luo and Luyia who also began to agitate in a similar manner in the 1920s; but their activities and organization took on a more parochial expression. This was also true of Swahili agitation at the coast where political activity was focused on obtaining political change at the local rather than the national level. There was some communication between Kikuyu, Luo and Luyia, but, for a variety of reasons, including official discouragement, the difficulties of communication, and the limited leadership available, no countrywide nationalist movement emerged in those years. Furthermore there was no similar activity among the pastoral peoples of the Rift Valley.[2]

The end of the Second World War saw renewed and increased African political agitation; but again the intensity of political consciousness and activity was very uneven. The Kikuyu spearheaded the movement, politically organized through the Kenya African Union

[1] The phrase is Elspeth Huxley's. The constitutional changes are in Cmnd. 960 of 1960. The 1960 Constitution provided for a common roll and a Legislative Council of 65 members with an effective African majority. Of the 65 members 33 were elected on open seats, on a wide franchise; 20 seats were reserved for minority communities (10 European, 8 Asians and 2 Arab), and there were also 12 National Members. The Governor still chose his Ministers. Responsible government followed in June 1963, under the Internal Self Government Constitution, with a fully elective bicameral legislature (with 131 members in the House of Representatives and 41 Senators) and a Cabinet headed by the Prime Minister, the leader of the majority party in the House.

[2] Rosberg and Nottingham, op. cit., covers this whole period so well that it would be superfluous to go into further detail here. The pastoral peoples of the Rift Valley, including Nandi, Kipsigis, Elgeyo, Marakwet, and Tugen have come to be known collectively as the Kalenjin.

3

(KAU) formed in 1944. KAU (in many respects the heir to KCA) established a populist tradition that has continued to influence Kenyan politics up to the present; it focused on land as the most fundamental political issue in the country. The party failed, however, to establish itself over the whole country. Jomo Kenyatta, who after his return from abroad became its President in 1947, had begun by the end of the forties to command countrywide respect as a leader; but KAU had no countrywide organization to back him up. Furthermore KAU's attention was directed primarily at Central Province, and at the increasing economic difficulties of the Kikuyu. KAU's leaders overcame organizational problems in that area by using a Kikuyu oath to weld the Kikuyu together. While this entrenched KAU in the Central Province, it was achieved at the price of isolation from the rest of the country.

The Emergency (during which KAU was proscribed) marked a significant dividing line in the growth of the nationalist movement. One of its effects was to reinforce the tradition of violence that had earlier crept into Kenyan politics (European and Kikuyu alike). A second effect was the manner in which it limited Kikuyu participation in political events for eight crucial years in the development of African politics. During those eight years national consciousness developed rapidly among other African peoples, enlarging and changing the scope of the nationalist movement far beyond that of KAU. A new style of organization emerged which established stronger inter-tribal links. In addition a new leadership group came to the fore which voiced the growing African political consciousness and eventually won the crucial constitutional concessions of 1960. But this leadership was not Kikuyu.

The first element in the new leadership emerged from the young trade-union movement. Trade Unionists quickly filled the political vacuum created by the proscription of KAU in June 1953. Every problem became a worker's problem, primarily because there was no other group capable of shouldering the burden. In particular the Kenya Federation of Registered Trade Unions took up the battle; its leaders questioned the Government about the conduct of the Emergency, the conditions in the detention camps, the justice of the screening methods, and the social implications of the large-scale arrests that took place. Within this Trade Union group the young Luo Unionist, Tom Mboya (who became acting General Secretary of the Federation in August 1953 and was elected General Secretary in October) rapidly emerged as the dominant personality. He was a major figure in the campaign for the redress of Emergency grievances, and was active in the battle for better labour

4

conditions.[1] As a result, by 1955 he had become a leading spokesman for Kenyan nationalism. Though he and his Trade Union colleagues represented, in the first instance, urban rather than rural grievances. The Trade Union leaders were not the only men to challenge the Government at this point. At the district level colonial rule was also questioned. Prominent was another Luo leader, Oginga Odinga, who had by the mid-1950s established himself as the most outspoken critic of the colonial authorities in his home district of Central Nyanza.[2] Although his platform was more restricted in scope and his appeal was to an essentially rural, rather than urban, audience, Odinga's nationalist demands were similar to Mboya's. Ronald Ngala, then a member of the Mombasa Municipal Board, spoke with a similar, if more muted, tone at the Coast.

There were others. But it was essentially Mboya and Odinga and their colleagues (and not the Africans then in Legislative Council) who assumed the leadership of Kenya African politics left vacant by the detention of KAU leaders. This became evident in the debate over the multi-racial Lyttelton plan. When this plan was proposed the African Members of the Legislative Council rejected what they saw as an entrenchment of European dominance; and Mboya and the Labour Movement backed them up.[3] However, when the former were persuaded to accept the Lyttelton proposals, the latter stood by their earlier rejection of multi-racialism. Odinga took a similar line in Nyanza. In October 1955 he publicly challenged Mr B. A. Ohanga (then the Legislative Council member of Nyanza) over the African members' support of the principle of multi-racial government. Opposing the idea 'on behalf of the opposition', he rejected multi-racial government in general and in particular the idea that Asians should play an executive part in the government of Kenya. He favoured a purely nationalist movement aimed at eliminating immigrants in the shortest time.[4]

The nationalist leaders kept alive the political demands of KAU's radical militant wing[5] and thereby provided continuity of purpose for the nationalist movement. But in their organizational ties they

[1] See T. J. Mboya, *Freedom and After* (London André Deutsch 1963), for his account of the period. See also Kenya Federation of Registered Trade Unions, Press Handout 9 November 1953, 'The Eastleigh Evacuation'.

[2] See O. Odinga, *Not Yet Uhuru* (London Heinemann Educational Books 1967), for his account of these years. See also J. M. Lonsdale, *A Political History of Western Kenya, 1883–1958* (forthcoming).

[3] Kenya Federation of Registered Trade Unions, Press Release, 12 March 1954. See also *The Times* (London) 10 January 1956.

[4] *East African Standard* 14 October 1955.

[5] Rosberg and Nottingham, op. cit., pp. 226 and 269. In June 1951 the radical wing of KAU had demanded political independence within three years.

provided few significant associations with KAU. Mboya joined KAU only at the beginning of the Emergency, in protest against the arrest of its leaders. By his own account he was very much on the periphery of that party.[1] Odinga had a much longer association with the party since he had joined the Kenya African Study Union at Maseno in 1944.[2] In his autobiography he describes attending his first KAU Central Committee meeting in Nairobi in 1952.[3] Nevertheless he had at that date scarcely entered KAU's leadership group, indeed his contacts with KAU in the intervening years had probably been narrow and indirect. The party's Nyanza activities were extremely limited and Odinga himself was not one of its local leaders. Moreover he was fully occupied with the organization of the Luo Thrift and Trading Corporation as well as the Luo Union. But Odinga provided something of a link between the old and new leaders, particularly through his close association with Achieng Oneko, a Luo politician intimately involved with KAU in Nairobi.[4] But by his own account of his activities in those years he belongs more properly with the new leaders who emerged after 1952 than with the men who had built KAU. This was generally true of all the men who challenged the colonial authorities after 1952. Some former KAU officials remained in the districts, but between 1953 and 1960 those who were not restricted were noticeably discreet and circumspect. In their place, the political initiative was seized by a new élite which had little direct connection with the earlier KAU leadership.

It was this élite which won the first direct elections for African members to the Legislative Council in March 1957. In Nyanza Odinga overwhelmingly defeated Ohanga. In Nairobi Mboya unseated the former nominated member for the area (as well as defeating a fellow Luo politician, Ardwings Kodhek,who had been a KAU Committee member in 1952). Ronald Ngala defeated the former member for the Coast. Similarly in Nyanza North, Nyanza South and Central Province the new representatives were younger and more educated men who had only recently emerged as local political leaders.[5]

---

[1] Mboya, op. cit., p. 34. He was, of course, too young to have been involved at an earlier date.

[2] Odinga, op. cit., p. 97.

[3] Ibid., p. 107.

[4] Oneko had been one of Odinga's pupils at Maseno and had also worked with him in the Luo Thrift and Trading Corporation. The ties of personal loyalty between them therefore went back a long way. See Odinga, op. cit., especially pp. 98–112.

[5] For an account of these elections, see G. Engholm, 'African Elections in Kenya', in *Five Elections in Africa* (Oxford 1960). Two of the eight, Arap Moi and Muimi, had been previously nominated members of Legislative Council, but for a short time only.

The Political Legacy

The March 1957 elections marked a major watershed in the development of the Kenya nationalist movement. The holding of the first direct elections for Africans, even though on a qualitative franchise, was a significant step forward. In addition, and more important for political development, their election gave the new African Elected Members a legitimacy they had not previously enjoyed. This was of crucial significance at a time when there were still considerable official restrictions on political activity. Although the Lyttelton Constitution had given Africans direct representation, it had not conceded the principle of majority (and therefore African) rule. The battle for 'one man, one vote' had still to be won. In the struggle for this vital objective which took place in the following three years, participation in the Legislative Council was of crucial advantage to these African political leaders. It gave them a public platform from which they could not be excluded. It also gave them a status that had to be recognized by colonial authorities in Kenya and in London, as well as by the African people of the country. Thus in this period they not only presented African demands to the British, but they also shaped public opinion. They greatly enlarged the nationalist movement. Those areas of Kenya that had lagged behind in political consciousness were now drawn into the nationalist movement, which by 1960 covered almost the entire country.

But now varying tribal attitudes towards the future prevented the emergence of a unified countrywide movement and divided it into separate groupings. Tribal groups became increasingly conscious of their separate and often conflicting interests. This awareness grew out of a combination of factors: unequal economic development, governmental emphasis since the 1920s upon district political associations, the restrictions imposed upon political organization in the 1950s and the land question.

Since the time that the colonial Government had first stabilized tribal units within administrative boundaries, their policy had tended to emphasize the district as a separate unit, and to isolate tribal groups from each other. Local government bodies with an elective element, based on the administrative district, were established as early as 1924. This meant that Africans had access to local government institutions through which they could voice political demands thirty years before they had access to the centre. Politically conscious Africans had used these Councils since the 1920s for that purpose, although more so in the Luo and Kikuyu districts than in others.[1] But this did not result in the growth of deep loyalties to district

[1] Rosberg and Nottingham, op. cit., p. 189. Also Lonsdale, op. cit., *passim.*

government institutions comparable, for example, to the loyalty of the Baganda to the Lukiko.[1] However, because of the emphasis in the Councils on local issues, it did tend to heighten a people's awareness of their identity as a tribal group.

More significant for the divisions within the nationalist movement after 1957 was the fact that the African Elected Members had in these years no national party machine to back them up. As a consequence of the Emergency, African political parties had been prohibited between June 1953 and June 1955. In June 1955 the Government again permitted Africa political organization but only at a district level and outside the Central Province. The Government hoped that District Associations would serve as useful advisory bodies to the then African Nominated Members of the Legislative Council, as well as produce a stabilizing element of 'moderate' African public opinion. Initially only a handful of such District Associations were formed. More emerged in 1958 after the first direct elections had stimulated greater political interest at local level. These District Associations were essentially parochial organizations that emphasized local issues. An attempt in 1958 to amalgamate them into a Convention of Associations was disallowed. So until national parties were again permitted in 1960, they became the only official means of communication by which the African Elected Members could reach the public.

This limitation should be considered in conjunction with the basis of African representation in the Legislative Council. The eight constituencies established in 1957 all included more than one district and so were not specifically tribal units. But between 1957 and 1960, despite the imposition of constituencies which cut across districts, the African Members were forced, in the absence of national party organizations, to build up the district associations. In practice, this strengthened local leadership and organization, which in turn strengthened the tribal unit. The district emphasis remained when the original constituencies were progressively divided by the electoral process itself into what amounted to tribal constituencies. District representation without a national machine proved crucial in dictating the patterns of political leadership and organization into which the fast growing nationalist movement settled in the latter 1950s; it both provided the district with a spokesman and emphasized the district as the basis for political support.[2] The Members went to the Legislative Council as 'individuals committed to political reform', not

[1] The most important reason for this was probably the system of direct rule. The Kenya Government at no time embarked upon the kind of Indirect Rule that built up a traditional authority. A second significant factor would seem to be the nature of the traditional political structure.

[2] Bennett and Rosberg, *The Kenyatta Election* (Oxford 1961), p. 354.

subject to any common policy or discipline, but to the demands of a local base that emphasized tribal interests and connections. Each of them, seeking to build up constituency support, had to translate nationalist demands for political change at the centre into local terms. This meant relating them to local issues.

This association of nationalist political demands with local issues has been made by nationalists in all African states. The difference in Kenya lay in the Members' limited opportunities to speak across district and tribal boundaries, and so counter-balance the local emphasis with a common nationalist front.

The Members themselves recognized the dangers to a genuine Kenyan nationalism implicit in this situation; but they did not secure any changes until 1960.[1] Their fears were justified in so far as they were unable to separate themselves from their own tribal bases. It is significant that just four months after their election the first eight Members were criticized for being united only on the issue of African representation.

District self-consciousness was heightened by the significant economic and social differences that existed between the tribal groups. This was particularly marked between the Kikuyu, the most economically developed and politically conscious people, on the one hand, and the economically less developed pastoral and coastal peoples on the other. The Kikuyu were settled in most parts of the country before 1952, and wherever they settled they established themselves as a cohesive, identifiable group. This aroused the suspicions of the resident tribes. The Elgeyo people, for instance, in the Rift Valley 'resented the presence of "foreigners" in their reserve' early in the fifties.[2] As the years progressed these strains became particularly strong among the Kalenjin peoples. They both asserted their claim to the European Highlands bordering their tribal areas and feared the possibility that the Kikuyu would override that claim. Land was therefore a dividing factor between Kikuyu and Kalenjin, emphasizing their different interests while increasing their political consciousness. At the end of the Emergency, as the former White Highlands were opened up to Africans, the question of who should own and settle in the Rift Valley areas in the future caused the Kalenjin peoples to become increasingly antagonistic towards the Kikuyu.

Fears about their future economic position were the source of a growing political consciousness among the coast people in the second half of the fifties. These years also saw the outburst of latent

---

[1] See, for example, *Legislative Council Debates*, Vol. LXXX, 23 and 24 July 1959, for a motion by Masinde Muliro on ending the Emergency, which raised the issue.

[2] Annual Report, Elgeyo – Marakwet District, 1957.

9

conflict over land between coastal Africans and Arab landholders. Moreover coast Africans developed a fear of economic domination by the 'up-country tribes' who formed the bulk of the coast labour force.[1] Fears of this kind thus created something of a community of interests among the Kalenjin and Coastal tribes against the larger, dominant ethnic groupings.

For their part the Luo and the Kikuyu found each other convenient allies in the circumstances of the late 1950s despite earlier differences. These differences included a record of conflict between members of the two tribes in urban areas such as Nairobi during the 1940s. Furthermore there had been some dissatisfaction in 1944 among educated Luo over the alleged preference given to the Kikuyu with the appointment of the first African Eliud Mathu, to the Legislative Council, and the Luo had also questioned Kikuyu dominance in KAU.[2] But these influences were countered by long-established associations between the two tribes. They had fought together in the First World War. Some of them had worked together for the same political objectives since the days of KCA. James Beauttah, one of the early KCA leaders, had worked at Maseno. The Luo had worked in Central Province and the Kikuyu in Nyanza. They had also come into contact with each other at the Jeanes School in Nairobi. Furthermore, their greater educational and economic advancement gave them a common political consciousness that made both groups more receptive to radical nationalist demands. Most important of all, the Luo could co-operate politically with the Kikuyu because they did not regard them as a threat to their land.

It is difficult to avoid the conclusion that the fundamental source of the divisions within the nationalist movement in 1960 was the land question. Tribal interests were based upon land and thus upon essentially economic interests. This situation seemed to dictate an alliance between the Kalenjin in the Rift Valley and the people at the coast, all of whom were suspicious of the objectives of the Kikuyu and their allies. This alignment of tribal and economic interest was probably the single most important factor leading to the division of the nationalist movement into the Kenya African National Union (KANU) and Kenya African Democratic Union (KADU) in 1960.[3]

---

[1] Cmnd. 1585, 1962, The Kenya Coastal Strip, *Report of the Commission* (London Her Majesty's Stationery Office 1962), paras. 40 and 41.

[2] B. A. Ogot, 'British Administration in the Central Nyanza District of Kenya, 1900–1960', in *Journal of African History*, IV, 2 (1963), pp. 249–73.

[3] The Kamba and a large section of the Abaluhya peoples also went with the Luo and Kikuyu into KANU. Political ambition may, for men like Ngala and Arap Moi, have played a part in their rejection of KANU; but the economic factor was no less important for their followers. Such economic interests were not, at that time, however, primarily class interests.

Later economic interests would promote different groupings; in 1960, however, they dictated the withdrawal of the minority tribes from the nationalist movement into a party of their own.

In the pre-independence elections the electorate in the urban areas, in contrast to the countryside, was prepared in some cases to vote for men of different tribes. The high-water mark of this non-tribal voting was the 1961 Nairobi election. On this occasion Mboya, a Luo, was able to win his Nairobi seat against a Kikuyu opponent, in a predominantly Kikuyu constituency. Ethnic appeal was not the dominant political influence at that moment primarily because in the Nairobi of the early 1960s tribe and economics did not obviously run a parallel course. Nairobi had undoubtedly been the greatest forcing ground for African political consciousness in Kenya. It was in Nairobi that the political movement had its beginnings and was strongest and most radical. But this radical political feeling did not fully supplant ethnic loyalties for a new intra-tribal nationalism. What distinguished the nationalism of the urban as opposed to the rural areas in the early 1960s was that economic distinctions did not obviously reinforce tribal ones.[1] The issue of independence was at that moment uppermost, and the man who could state this demand most simply and effectively held the greatest advantage.

At that moment in the nationalist movement, in 1961, the urban electorate could be dissuaded from a purely tribal vote by an appeal to the dominant political objective of independence. In this situation Mboya held the advantage over his Kikuyu opponent. His organizational skill, his oratory, his knowledge of the Kikuyu, and his political record, were all of more importance for him at that point in 1961 (and again in 1963) than a tribal appeal. After independence, as Nairobi became the 'county town' of the Kikuyu, his non-tribal outlook would perhaps prove a disadvantage; in 1961 and 1963 this was not so.

Notwithstanding the Nairobi elections of 1961, tribe was a divisive factor in the nationalist movement. This emphasis upon tribe, however, obscures the differences of interest that even then existed within most tribal communities. Such internal divisions, which were to become of considerable significance for subsequent political developments, can be briefly enumerated as follows. First divisions arose out of traditional loyalties, such as the clan divisions in Nyanza and Kamba country, or the sub-tribal divisions within the Luyia group.

[1] What is not clear is how Kikuyu loyalty to Kenyatta dictated the Nairobi vote. I am grateful to both Richard Stren and Mark Howard Ross, who have worked in Mombasa and Nairobi, respectively, for discussions on urbanization and the relationship between tribal and urban associations in these two cities.

Second in several districts, particularly Nyanza and Central Province, there was a conflict between Government servants, principally the chiefs, and the politicians over the pace and direction of political change. In Central Province the Emergency created the deeper and more crucial conflict between Loyalists and Freedom Fighters that persisted even after independence. Third there were embryonic economic divisions in many districts, primarily in terms of land ownership. Divisions based on ownership of property began to emerge in the fifties wherever the consolidation of land took place. Such economic divisions tended to overlap political divisions: official chiefs, for example, tended to become a propertied class.[1]

Such social, economic and political divisions within each district were significant. They provided a possible basis for future political alignments on an inter-tribal basis. Moreover they provided a basis for rival factions and leadership within districts. Before independence this had made the district an important level for competitive politics within the party as well as between the two parties. A good deal of attention focused upon the local government institutions as bodies within which the various interests in the district sought a dominant position. The result was a tradition of competitive politics in the District Councils which the political parties could not ignore. Many of the internal party conflicts that emerged after 1960 at district level, which were responsible for the phenomenon of party independents in both local and national elections, reflected the rival interests within the district which had to be accommodated within the party as the price of controlling a 'one party district'. This was true of KADU as well as KANU districts, although the phenomenon of party independents was more apparent in the latter.

When KANU and KADU were formed in 1960, however, attention was focused on the divisions between rather than within, tribal groups. Thus the three years preceding independence saw the tensions generated by the fears of the smaller tribes reaching alarming proportions. It was these fears and tensions that persuaded the minority-based KADU to demand a quasi-federal division of power that would leave an African majority Government less omnipotent than its colonial predecessor. The result was regionalism, which in Kenyan terms meant the devolution of certain powers upon newly created Regional Authorities; the vesting of control of Trust (African tribal) Land in the County (formerly African District) Councils; and the

---

[1] See Lonsdale, op. cit. Also K. Sorrenson, *Land Reform in the Kikuyu Country* (Oxford 1966).

setting up of a bicameral legislature of which the Senate was to be representative of district interests.[1]

KANU only accepted this regional structure of government as the price of independence; and the KANU Government abolished it as soon as they were politically able, just one year after independence had been gained.[2] The diversion from a unitary form of government therefore lasted a mere eighteen months, after which it did not take the Central Government long to restore the former structure. Nor did the new tier of regional government set up in 1963 arouse strong loyalties. Although the members of the Regional Assemblies protested against the attrition of their powers there was no strong public reaction when the first constitutional amendment deprived them of those powers in October 1964.[3] The public interest continued to focus on the County, not the Region, as the significant local arena; it also concentrated on the centre as the real source of governmental authority.

The nationalist movement that grew after 1957 suffered from another divisive influence: the personal rivalry that developed within the ranks of the African Elected Members of the Legislative Council, which was closely influenced by tribal identification. At the outset the most obvious rivalry was between Odinga and Mboya. Theirs was by no means the only rivalry that developed within the group of African leaders, but it was the most publicized; and it undoubtedly became a dominant feature of KANU politics. Moreover its consequences affected the other Members as well who were unable to remain detached from the resulting arguments that took place within the group as a whole.

For these reasons it is important to look briefly at the nature and origins of this particular dispute, though even in retrospect it is difficult to establish beyond doubt the reasons for its beginnings. Whether their rivalry was created by the circumstances of the fifties, after their entry into the Legislative Council, or whether those circumstances can be traced back to a rivalry that had already been born is not clear. Although both these leaders were inclined to authoritarianism they were otherwise very different in character and personality. Odinga, as the older man, perhaps assumed that the younger should defer to him more than Mboya was able. Mboya, on

[1] See the Independence Constitution, The Kenya Independence Order in Council 1963, 1963 of 1968, Schedule 2. Also D. Rothchild, 'Majimbo Schemes in Kenya and Uganda', *Boston University Papers on Africa, Transition in African Politics*, ed. Jeffrey Butler and A. A. Castagno (New York Praeger 1967).

[2] See below, p. 34.

[3] Nor when the Assemblies were finally abolished by a further constitutional amendment in February 1968. The County was in most instances the former District.

13

his side, acquired a reputation for arrogance, independent action and personal pride which alienated many people. Each had a very different political style. Mboya proved the more capable organizer and tactician, whose organizational ability frequently won him the day against considerable odds. His tactics were, by Western standards, much more subtle and sophisticated than Odinga's, and his Trade Union experience stood him in good stead with an important element in the population. But perhaps the most significant difference between them – certainly for the future – was in their public appeal. Odinga had an ethnic appeal that Mboya lacked. Odinga's base was essentially the Luo people. Mboya's was the cross-section of workers across the country whose battles he had fought for four years. He was essentially the non-tribal man, possessing no ethnic base. This different power base was reflected in their different approaches to political organization. Although Odinga used the Central Nyanza African District Congress (the District association) to further his political battle in Nyanza, his influence was derived essentially from his dominant role in his Luo Thrift and Trading Corporation, and the Luo Union which had close ties with the District Congress. Mboya, on the other hand, was dependent on the trade unions, and on his own Nairobi People's Convention Party, through which he established between 1958 and 1960 an organizational network across the country. Notwithstanding these differences, when they entered the Legislative Council in 1957 there was no difference in their basic political objectives. Both spoke the same uncompromising language of African nationalism. Both were inflexible on the ultimate political goal of independence. When in 1959 the African Elected Members divided politically, Odinga and Mboya stood together.

At the same time each was ambitious for national political leadership. When they moved into the Legislative Council Mboya was already at the centre – Nairobi was his constituency. In a real sense Kenya was his platform, for his Trade Union activities had already given him a national base and potential mass support that cut across tribe. The Kenya Federation of Labour (the successor to the Federation of Trade Unions) provided him with a countrywide organization. He had already established his competence as a leader and negotiator at the national level against the colonial authorities, particularly for the Mombasa Dock Workers and the Nairobi City Council workers in the first half of 1955. In addition he had established an international audience for himself, through his Trade Union connections and his successful tours in Britain and America in 1955 and 1956.

Odinga's base was at that time more restricted. He had established himself as a nationalist, but only in effect with his own people. His

14

victory in the 1957 elections was for him the beginning of a new political phase. From that date he had to enlarge his activities in order to claim leadership at the centre. Unless he and Mboya were able to agree as to their respective positions, such a claim meant a challenge to the latter.

No sooner were the African Members elected than public speculation arose as to their leadership. At the time the two chief contenders were recognized as Mboya and Odinga, each of whom had already established a considerable reputation as a nationalist. Odinga became Chairman and Mboya Secretary of the African Elected Members Organization which was set up immediately after the March 1957 election. Events quickly indicated, however, that the two men found difficulty in working together; and it was not long before there was public disagreement between them.[1] Their failure to reach any enduring agreement divided both the nationalist movement and KANU, since each of them sought support for his case among his political colleagues.

Until 1960 when national political organizations were again allowed, this rivalry was to a large degree played out within the African Elected Members Organization. All the African representatives came together in this organization, which became the springboard for personal rivalries and political bargaining. The resulting manœuvring for support had important consequences for the pattern of political organization, both at the centre and in the country at large. It meant that the political process occurred within the limitations imposed by government restrictions. In effect any leader seeking political support in a district other than his own had to have the support of the constituency Member and (if one existed) his District Association.[2] Personal rivalries were frequently reinforced by tribal backing. This accentuated the significance of the constituency Member's position as the district leader, and so a Kenyan version of boss politics emerged. The man with a strong district base or strong alliances with district leaders could not be ignored at the centre. These relationships persisted, notwithstanding Mboya's success in establishing, between 1958 and 1960, core groups of the Nairobi People's Convention Party outside Nairobi. Although

---

[1] *Uganda Argus*, 18 August 1957. Odinga and Mboya clashed over the question of a mission to London proposed by Argwings-Kodhek, the Nairobi Luo political leader of the Nairobi African District Congress, whom Odinga had supported against Mboya in the 1957 elections. See Engholm, op. cit.

[2] On 27 April 1957, the Government permitted Odinga to hold a meeting in Kisumu to which he was able to invite all the Members. The tone of some of the speeches on that occasion so frightened officials, however, that permits were subsequently more sparingly given to all Elected Members, but especially the three Luo leaders, to speak outside their own constituencies.

Mboya laid the foundations of a national network of his own (which enabled him to bargain his way into KANU leadership in 1960) he could not break the power of a 'district boss' as strong as Odinga.

Personal rivalries within the leadership group as a whole and the alliances resulting from these rivalries emphasized the significance of the district as a local base of power for the national leader. The importance of these local bases of power was increased as the area of conflict was enlarged within the leadership group; first with the enlargement of African membership of the Legislative Council in 1958, 1961 and 1963; second with Mboya's organizing efforts outside Nairobi; and third with the return of the Kikuyu to national politics after 1961. As these events broadened the scope of the leadership conflict, it became more intense and open. But it was played out within the organizational pattern already laid down, which stressed the importance of personal alliances between district leaders, and therefore their followers.

KANU, the party of the majority tribes and the dominant sector in the nationalist movement, suffered more than KADU from personal rivalries. This competition impeded the establishment of a centralized and unified party.[1] While Kenyatta, who was the only man with sufficient authority to unite the party, remained in restriction, internal party strife continued unchecked into 1961. It was then only the need for a united front to win the 1961 elections that prevented the constant politics of manœuvre from breaking the party into pieces. At that crucial point the return of the Kikuyu to national politics (as their leaders were released from detention) added a new source of party rivalry.

It is important to consider what had been happening to the Kikuyu during the 1950s. The restrictions on political activity in Central Province had prevented the majority of Kikuyu from participating in nationalist politics and had excluded them from national leadership for the crucial eight years after 1952. At the same time the events of the Emergency emphasized the elements which separated the Kikuyu from the rest of the country. Among these were the use of the oath by the men in the forest to maintain organizational control and to build a greater loyalty to their cause, their fighting, and their common suffering; all of which had welded the Kikuyu closer together. Thus when they returned to the main political stream in 1961 it was with a sense of identity so much stronger that would be difficult to subordinate to a larger nationalism.[2]

[1] Bennett and Rosberg, op. cit., p. 41.
[2] Rosberg and Nottingham, op. cit., p. 354.

16

During the Emergency, moreover, the relatively prosperous Central Province (with extensive British financial aid) advanced economically much faster than other parts of the country. Consequently the Kikuyu were in a much stronger economic position in the early 1960s than any other single group. They did not, however, in 1961 dominate the national Kenyan political leadership. This leadership had passed to the new political élite, led by Mboya and Odinga. The Kikuyu were bound therefore to fight with this élite for the leadership.

But which Kikuyu? The Kikuyu had been welded closer together by the 'Mau Mau' movement but there were still divisions among them. The land consolidation programme of the 1950s had enabled the small landed gentry that had begun to appear before the Emergency to obtain legal title and security to their property. Land consolidation did not create a landless class – this had been present before 1952 – but it defined it more sharply.[1] Thus there were demonstrable economic differences based on ownership of land. There were also strong divisions between those who had fought in the Emergency and those who had not; between Freedom Fighters and Loyalists, divisions which were reinforced in many cases by economic position.[2] Not all former detainees were landless; but a considerable number were. There were also the younger, educated Kikuyu, making their way in the Civil Service and increasingly in the business world; as well as younger men who had played no part in the Emergency anxious to assert themselves in politics. Finally, there was the long-established rivalry between the three Kikuyu districts of Kiambu, Fort Hall (Muranga) and Nyeri, which remained very much alive. Thus as the Kikuyu moved back into nationalist politics there were among them conflicting interests which were potentially an additional source of conflict for KANU. Although all groups recognized Kenyatta's leadership he had no obvious successor among the Kikuyu; and the unresolved question of future Kikuyu leadership left a major unresolved issue for the party as a whole. Each of these groups was bound to assert its right to leadership.

Against the internal divisions and organizational weaknesses in the national movement Kenyatta's unifying role was crucial. Long years in detention had established him as the undoubted father-figure of the nationalist movement. Moreover, his dominance among the Kikuyu was recognized and he was the only man with sufficient authority to unite KANU. While he was in detention his distant

---

[1] Sorrenson, op. cit., p. 227.
[2] On this aspect of Kikuyu divisions, see K. Sorrenson, *Counter Revolution to Mau Mau*, East African Institute of Social Research Paper, June 1963 (mimeo.).

17

influence was not enough to keep the leaders together. After he returned, however, and more so after he accepted the leadership of KANU, he was able to enforce co-operation among his warring factions. He could not hold the Kamba leader, Paul Ngei, who for a time took that tribe into a separate party.[1] But he did assert himself over the rest, to lead them to victory in the 1963 elections and so to full power. Kenyatta then went on in the first year of independence to impose unity on KANU and KADU. The acquiescence in 1964 of all groups in the Republic and the move to a *de facto* one-party state, testified to his ability, at that stage, to act as an inspirational leader who could bridge gaps of tribe and race. Nevertheless the fact that neither personal rivalries nor the existing social, economic and political divisions within the society had been overcome became clear in 1965 and 1966 when new party groupings emerged. In the immediate post-independence period, the party was demonstrably unable to impose unity on the nation.

The Legislature

The organizational weakness of the party and the governmental restrictions on party activity contributed to the growth of another significant and more positive legacy from the colonial period. This was a legislature that had become popularly acknowledged as an established institution with a tradition of lively, critical debate.

Representation in the legislature had been one of the reforms originally demanded by Africans as early as the 1920s.[2] The Government's rejection of that demand meant that African agitation was conducted outside the legislature. Even after Africans were appointed to the Council in 1944, African nationalist leadership lay outside that body, with KAU. After 1957 however, when Africans were directly elected to the Council for the first time, a significant change of emphasis took place. Those elections put the new African nationalist leadership inside the Council. Membership of the Council provided those leaders with two important assets: status *vis-à-vis* the British and the colonial governments as well as their own people; and a platform from which to speak their political mind at a time when the right to organize and speak publicly was still severely controlled.

Both Mboya and Odinga have described the way the African Elected Members deliberately exploited this platform to the full. As Odinga put it:

[1] Clyde Sanger and John Nottingham, The Kenya General Election of 1963, *Journal of Modern African Studies*, 2, 1 (1964).
[2] See a letter by Jomo Kenyatta to the *Manchester Guardian*, 1 May 1930.

18

We had gone into the Legislative Council with a clear set of aims. These were to make the Council a platform from which settlers and the governments of Kenya and Britain could hear African opinion . . . above all we could use the Legislative Council as a national forum to build national unity.[1]

Mboya wrote '. . . We knew we would never win the vote, but we wanted to use the legislature as a platform.'[2] Notwithstanding the fact that 'they could never win', the African Members of the Legislature pressed the Government hard to enact political reforms; and it was, in the event, they who could publicly claim the political victories of Lancaster House in 1960.

The fact that the African Members were the only legitimate channel of communication between Nairobi and the countryside in these years gave them (and so the Council) greater status and prestige. Furthermore, the district basis of representation ensured that districts could air their grievances and demands at the centre through their Elected Member. Members used the Council from the outset not only to attack the Colonial Executive but also to publicize their constituents' grievances and fears. In the three years between 1957 and 1960, the Council was vital for their activities as an alternative to the national party platform that was prohibited. Moreover, between 1961 and 1963, when KANU was in opposition, it used the Council Chamber as well as the hustings to attack its KADU rivals. In addition, KADU and KANU Members voiced their fears about the future within the Council as well as in public.

The Legislative Council had always been used by the Europeans as a platform from which to attack the Executive. They had shaped the legislature into a critical, active, hard-hitting body. African activity within the Council after 1957 not only sustained and enlarged this reputation, but also gave the legislature a greater legitimacy in the eyes of the politically conscious African public. It also went a long way to establish the tradition of public, political debate in the legislature and the right of the legislature to challenge the executive.

What the African Elected Members were doing between 1957 and 1960, when they had no national party forum was to use the Legislative Council as a substitute. As the Opposition in the Council they debated policy with the Government. Within their Members Organization they argued with each other. In doing so they established a significant precedent for the period after independence: that in the absence of a properly functioning party organ, the legislature was the

---

[1] Op cit., p. 119.
[2] Op. cit., p. 149.

legitimate place to carry on both intra as well as inter-party debate. In the immediate post-independence period, therefore, when KANU failed to establish a working machinery, it is not surprising that KANU Members of Parliament quickly learned to use the House of Representatives as an alternative platform from which to make demands upon the Government. The Opposition to the Government within KANU sought to capture control of the parliamentary party. The legislature remained a significant institution where party and sectional interests were vigorously debated. As a result the KANU Executive found itself faced with the same kind of hard-hitting attack from the legislature that it had itself offered the colonial Government. On the floor of the House, in the lobbies, and in the Parliamentary Group the Government had to bargain with its own party critics. Moreover, after the formation of the new Opposition, the Kenya People's Union, in April 1966, the National Assembly was the one public platform of which that party was assured.

The Executive

Whether early African membership of the legislature created a desire for parliamentary control rather than cabinet government is, however, another question. For, as Mboya said, they knew that in their capacity as an Opposition in the Legislative Council they could never win. Power lay with the Executive, and control of that body was the real objective of African leaders. The Executive that they wished to take over, furthermore, was a powerful one. The Government with which the nationalist leaders did battle was highly centralized and tightly controlled. This government machine was independent Kenya's other crucial legacy.

The executive institutions changed rapidly in the post-war years. An embryonic Ministerial system was introduced at the end of the Second World War by the Governor, Sir Philip Mitchell.[1] Formerly all branches of government activity had been concentrated in the hands of the Colonial Secretary. Mitchell grouped government departments under the responsibility of Members of the Executive Council. These might be unofficial or official, although when unofficial representatives became Members they had to resign their seats. The Lyttelton Constitution of 1954 replaced the Member system with a full Ministerial System and established a multi-racial Council of

---

[1] See Secretariat Circular 16, 13 September 1946, for the first arrangement of portfolios. On the member system, see 'The Member System in British African Territories, A Note by the Colonial Office African Studies Branch', *Journal of African Administration* (London 1949), pp. 54–55.

Ministers as the principal instrument of government. Thus a full ministerial organization, with twelve ministries, was established eight years before independence, and five years before national parties were allowed to function.

A natural corollary to the growth of a ministerial system was the development of parliamentary control over finance. The introduction of the member system in 1945 was followed in 1948 by the devolution of financial responsibility to the Legislative Council. But since the latter body did not have full control of finance under the existing procedure, the Government initiated a review of the whole question of financial responsibility and budgetary control. This led to changes in the budgetary procedure; to the establishment of the Public Accounts Committee of the Legislative Council; to the promulgation of the Audit Ordinance in March 1952; to the establishment of the Treasury in 1953, bringing financial policy and the accounting system under one department; and finally to the passing of the Exchequer and Audit Ordinance in 1955 and the introduction of a full exchequer system. Thus by 1955 Kenya had established the 'Westminster model' in internal financial control.[1]

At the same time the civil service was expanding. This expansion resulted partly from the growth of services beyond the level found in most colonial territories. A 'complex of administrative procedures and meticulous checks and controls' expanded to support this structure.[2] In addition Kenya's post-war constitutional progress entailing the growth of both the Ministerial and the Exchequer system necessitated considerable expansion in personnel, particularly in senior posts. The administrative machine expanded also in response to the changing concept of the developmental role of government that gathered momentum after the Second World War. The change had begun during the war, when Kenya's war effort was that of a major agricultural producer for the Allies' food supplies. At the end of the war Governor Sir Philip Mitchell's policy emphasized the importance of agriculture as the basis of Kenya's economy, and this underlined the necessity for its development in both European

---

[1] *A Summary of the Events leading up to the Introduction of the Exchequer System in 1955.* Nairobi: The Treasury, 1955. See also K. W. S. Mackenzie, 'The Development of the Kenya Treasury since 1936', in *East African Economic Review*, Vol. 8, No. 2, December 1961.

[2] *The Report of the Economy Commission*, December 1962. Nairobi: Government Printer. The Commission found that the average vote increase between 1949 and 1961–62 had been about 500 per cent, and suggested that the increase in administrative costs was a major contributor to the growth of all votes. I am extremely grateful to both Sir Michael Blundell and Sir Ernest Vasey, each of whom gave generously of their time to discuss governmental developments in the 1950s. Neither, of course, is responsible for any conclusions reached here.

and the African areas. Expansion and consolidation in the European sector followed very much along the lines proposed by the Troughton Report of 1952. For the African areas Mitchell's objective was the radical transformation of the subsistence sector and, in his own words, a 'massive forward thrust of economic development'. He hoped by such a development to create a stable African middle class to act as a bulwark against subversive agitators. Recognizing that the African people had grievances, he hoped to overcome those grievances by economic reform. This was to be followed, much more slowly, by political change.[1] Such a policy of agricultural development was accelerated under Governor Baring during the Emergency. Development went ahead under the Swynnerton Plan, financed primarily with a £5,000,000 grant from the British Government,[2] and land consolidation and agricultural reform became the order of the day.

The result was a considerable expansion in the functions and staff of the Central Government, and particularly those ministries concerned with development. This was especially true of the Ministry of Agriculture which greatly enlarged its scope and authority in the 1950s. Staff in the Agriculture Department increased at all levels from 298 in 1945 to 2,519 in 1958. The Veterinary Department staff increased from 291 to 892. The African Land Development Department, which was non-existent in 1945, employed 477 people in 1958. The decision to push ahead with land consolidation was responsible for the build up of a considerable Land Consolidation staff.[3]

The other crucial influence upon the expansion of the governmental machine in the fifties was the Emergency, the prosecution of which resulted in a large expansion in security staff. Another important outcome of the Emergency period was the enlargement of the idea of the omnipotence and authority of government and the further entrenchment of the power of the executive. This resulted not only from the use of the Armed Forces to re-establish government control in Central Province but also from the expansion of the Police and the Provincial Administration.

For several years before the outbreak of the Emergency discussion

---

[1] P. Mitchell, *The Agrarian Problem* (Nairobi, 1949). See also Rosberg and Nottingham, op. cit., pp. 198–203. Also Sorrenson, op. cit., Chapter XIV.

[2] *Legislative Council Debates*, 20 October 1953. Also, *A Plan to Intensify the Development of African Agriculture in Kenya*. Nairobi, Government Printer 1954.

[3] Ministry of Agriculture, *Three Year Report 1955–57*. This build up of staff meant an increase in expatriate technical officers in most parts of the country, which in turn contributed to the development of national consciousness. See Lonsdale, op. cit., for the way in which opposition to agricultural programmes contributed to the growth of national political consciousness. Also his 'Some Origins of Nationalism in East Africa', *Journal of African History*, IX, 1 (1968).

The Political Legacy

had taken place inside the Government on the improvements needed in organizing and expanding the Kenya Police to enable it to fulfil its functions adequately.[1] Between 1948 and 1952 such expansion was sanctioned to meet enlarged responsibilities, but the actual increase was slower than planned. When the Emergency was declared, however, radical changes quickly took place in the whole pattern of policing the Colony. The Special Branch was increased considerably. The General Service Unit was created consisting of a strong police striking force with military training, capable of moving quickly to any part of the country. The transfer of much of the responsibility for law and order in the African areas from the Tribal Police to the Kenya Police (a policy that had been decided upon some years earlier) was speeded up. Most important, there was an unprecedented expansion of the force in which uniformed ranks increased from 6,057 in 1957 to 12,232 in 1962–3.[2] Organizational changes were carried out at the centre in order to improve efficiency. In 1954 the Ministry of Defence assumed responsibility for internal as well as external security under a strong Civil Service Minister.

Although almost all of the Emergency cadres subsequently left the Kenya Police on the expiry of their contracts, the overall increase in the permanent establishment was retained up to independence. The Emergency thus left Kenya with a large, well-organized force, much larger than that of either of her neighbours, Uganda and Tanzania. Such an efficient force was a major asset for the Executive in exercising its control and asserting its authority over the country.

The Executive's other major agency for control was the Provincial Administration. Governor Baring deliberately expanded this Provincial Administration during the Emergency both in numbers and authority, giving it the dominant position over other government agencies as his agent in the field. Its dominant position is best illustrated by its relationship with the Police. The Police were subordinate to the Administration in matters concerning the maintenance of law and order, and Baring made it clear, early in the Emergency, that this would remain the case.

[1] For the overall development of the Police, see the *Report of the Kenya Police Commission 1953* (The Baker Report), Nairobi, Government Printer, 1954, and Sessional Paper No. 24 of 1954, *The Implementation of the Recommendations of the Kenya Police Commission*, 1953. Also, *The Origins and Growth of Mau Mau*, Sessional Paper No. 5 of 1959/60 (The Corfield Report), Chapters III and XIII.
[2] These figures are taken from the Economy Commission, December 1962. The Baker Report did not consider that the expansion which occurred in the first year of the Emergency was, overall, beyond the needs of the Colony; but it did point out that the speed with which it took place had created specific problems, particularly because of the inadequate training the new recruits received.

Government recognizes that the final responsibility for good government and preservation of order clearly lies with the Provincial and District Commissioners who represent the Governor in their areas. These officers are entitled to give general directions concerning the preservation of peace and order. In all such matters the Police Force is subordinate to government.[1]

It was the Administration, therefore, not the Police, which was ultimately responsible for law and order. The Provincial and District Commissioners chaired the Emergency Committees set up at Provincial and District level to deal with the day-to-day conduct of the Emergency; as well as the existing Security and Intelligence Committees. Provincial Commissioners were empowered by Baring to issue orders to departmental officers in their provinces if the needs of the Emergency demanded it. He delegated his powers of detention to them. They were responsible for issuing permits for most public meetings. The Administration therefore occupied a position of considerable power. Administrative officers were given the right to overrule the Police in such matters, on the principle that they were the better judges of the political needs of the situation. They occupied a crucial position as the agents of control for the Governor, which made them, in effect, political agents for the Executive.

Future control of the police forces was understandably a major issue in the successive constitutional conferences that preceded independence; and the relationship between the Police and the Executive changed with the regional constitution of December 1963. Elaborate precautions were taken to ensure the isolation of the Police from political influences, including the establishment of an independent Police Service Commission to make all police appointments. The republican constitution of 1964 abandoned the regional devolution of control, as well as the Police Service Commission. The office of Commissioner for Police remained a constitutional office, however, to secure the independence of the Police from the executive; and so provided that they were no longer subordinate to the Provincial Administration. The Provincial Administration, as the agent of the Executive, resumed responsibility for law and order, when law and order was returned from the Regional Authorities to the Central Government in December 1964.[2]

---

[1] Government of Kenya, Sessional Paper No. 24 of 1954. *The Implementation of the Recommendations of the Kenya Police Commission, 1953*. Nairobi, Government Printer, 1954, para. 6.

[2] Blundell, *So Rough a Wind* (London Weidenfeld and Nicolson 1964), has an interesting insight into the pre-independence situation. For the changes after Regionalism, see Chapter 2 below. Also Legal Notice 153 of 1965, Kenya *Gazette* Supplement No. 45, 8 June 1965, 'The Constitution of Kenya (Amendment of Laws) (Public Order)

It was primarily in response to the Emergency situation that the policy of closer administration was introduced. Exponents of the new policy assumed that security would be more effective if Officers were in closer touch with the people. District Officers were therefore posted to divisions, instead of touring from District Headquarters; and Divisional Headquarters were set up in order to get into 'close touch with the people and to communicate with them better'.[1] The number of officers at all levels was considerably increased, including chiefs, headmen and the Tribal Police; and in 1956 a new cadre of District Assistants (including some Africans) was established to free more senior officers for the work of communication. The result of this expansion can be seen in the figures. Where there had been 184 administrative officer posts in 1951 (costing £152,000), there were 370 in 1962–3 (costing £443,400).[2] As a result the administrative network was able to effect much closer control.

Nor did the Government hesitate to change administrative boundaries to ensure greater control. Examples of this were the creation of the Nairobi Extra-Provincial District in 1953 and the excision of the Masai and Kamba from the predominantly Kikuyu Central Province into a new Southern Province of their own.

The Administration was not limited in its functions to the maintenance of law and order, as is so often assumed to have been the case with a colonial administration. In the post-war period they became closely involved in the development process as well. This reflected the changing ideas about the role and functions of the Colonial Civil Service in Britain and the Colonial Office, where there was a new emphasis on economic development.[3] It also reflected Mitchell's ideas and plans on agrarian policy; moreover his successor Baring emphasized the role of the Administration in agricultural and overall economic development as the prime means (apart from the security operations) of combating the 'Mau Mau' threat.

The Government believed that closer administration would

---

[1] *Legislative Council Debates*, 20 October 1953 and 24 November 1953, for statements by the Governor and the Chief Secretary on the Policy of Closer Administration. See also, Estimates 1955–6, p. 984, for a full list of all new Divisional Stations set up by that date. There was only a limited further expansion at divisional level beyond that date, after which divisions remained largely unchanged until the regional reorganization of 1963.

[2] *Economy Commission*, p. 30.

[3] R. Heusslar, *Yesterday's Rulers* (London 1964).

Order 1965'. The powers of the Provincial Administration on the licensing of public meetings will be found in the Public Order Act, Laws of Kenya, Chapter 56. The Administration had extensive statutory powers over the control of movement and activities of the public under, *inter alia*: The Penal Code; The Native Authority Ordinance; The Agricultural Ordinance 1955, in addition to administrative rules and Governor's directives. These were retained after independence.

facilitate development, the primary responsibility for which must lie with the Administration. Administrative officers were responsible for stimulating local initiative and for ensuring the co-ordination of development at the local level. Thus while agricultural officers, veterinary officers and those technical officers concerned with the economic development of the district had their role to play, it was the Administration with whom the final responsibility lay for development. They were charged, as the senior executive officers in the field, with responsibility for the co-ordination of all departmental activity; Provincial and District teams of technical officers, chaired by the Administration, were established for this purpose.

All this further enhanced the powers and position of the Administration. In the later 1950s, as a result of Ministerial reorganization, the Ministry of African Affairs acquired additional functions including responsibility for African courts, collection of the local taxes and the conduct of elections. It is not therefore surprising that the Administration, believing itself to be indispensable, grew in self-assertiveness; or that the Minister for African Affairs (in charge of the Provincial Administration) should describe it as 'the keystone, the lynchpin of our government on the ground',[1] and assert that 'My Ministry and the Provincial Administration are responsible for six million people', forgetting the multitude of technical officers also working in the field.[2]

The Provincial Commissioner was the expert on African Affairs. He had direct access to the Governor and his own Minister, as well as close contact with the senior Civil Service Minister, the Chief Secretary. As a group the Provincial Commissioners exerted a significant influence on central government. Thus before independence it could be said that the Provincial Administration had power, authority and influence. They also had three major functions: control, co-ordination and mobilization of the public for development. In the exercise of all three they acted in an executive capacity as the agent of the Governor.

The Provincial Administration was a highly effective centralizing agency, which ensured the Governor direct communication with, and control over, the districts. Its existence contributed considerably in the 1950s to the further scope of executive power – but on the civil service rather than the political side of the executive. This became apparent after 1955 when the political Ministers assumed a full role in the Executive. The Governor, as the head of the Executive, still had the Administrative machine at his disposal. This ensured him and his

---

[1] *Legislative Council Debates*, Vol. LXIX, 25 May 1956, col. 643.
[2] Ibid., May 1957, col. 1035.

26

civil service ministers an important channel of communication outside the control of the Council of Ministers.

The Provincial Administration did not enjoy this authority unquestioned. In the fifties, as the ministerial system and the nationalist movement both took shape, the Administration was challenged from three directions. First, central government officers questioned the necessity for such an authoritarian Administration; many of them clashed with it as their ministries developed and they acquired their own areas of power and authority. The ministerial system led to a greater conflict between district and centre than had probably occurred under Secretariat control.[1] Second, the Administration and the political Ministers appointed from 1955 were frequently at loggerheads.[2] Third, the African political leaders who consolidated the nationalist movement in the fifties did so in the face of the opposition of the Administration, whose existence was, as the Minister for African Affairs suggested, 'the stiffest hurdle along their chosen path'.[3] Not surprisingly they challenged the necessity for this branch of the bureaucracy.

Throughout the 1950s African politicians constantly challenged the hegemony of the unofficial European element, both elected and nominated, in the Executive Council as well as in its successor, the Council of Ministers. Nevertheless the most striking feature of executive government at that time was the dominance in the executive not of the elected Europeans but of the civil servants.[4]

This dominant position derived in the first place from the authority of the Governor as the head of the Executive; the civil service were ultimately responsible to him. This was most clearly illustrated in the case of the Provincial Administration; but it applied equally to the permanent secretaries in Nairobi. In the 1950s the authority of the Governor as the head of the Executive (and so of his officers) was considerably enhanced by the Emergency, notwithstanding the establishment of the Council of Ministers, and the inclusion of political ministers in that body. Responsibility for the prosecution of the Emergency lay with the Governor, not the Council of Ministers. When the latter body was established in 1954 the much smaller War Council was also set up to assist him with Emergency business.[5] The

---

[1] *Pritchard Report on the Simplification of Government Procedures*, Nairobi, 1958 (unpublished).

[2] Blundell, op. cit., p. 173.

[3] *Legislative Council Debates*, Vol. LXXX, Part I, 20 May 1959, col. 997.

[4] Europeans recognized this. See, for example, *Legislative Council Debates*, Vol. 77, 15 October 1958, for European members' criticisms of the government machinery and officials' handling of it.

[5] For one member's account of the War Council, see Blundell, op. cit., Chapter 11.

27

bulk of Emergency business was dealt with by the War Council and by small executive committees responsible directly to the Governor.

It is important to remember that the Governor derived his authority from the British Government rather than the Council of Ministers; and was ultimately responsible to that Government, through the Colonial Office, which remained until independence, the ruler in the last resort. The Executive was therefore in a real sense independent of the system of representative government growing up in Kenya. The Governor and his senior civil servants could in the last resort by-pass that area of government, for their authority was independent of it. This was in effect the allegation made against the new Governor, Renison, and his civil service ministers, after elected Africans took office following the 1961 elections; and again after the formation of the Coalition (KANU/KADU) Government in 1962.

In addition the authority and influence of senior departmental civil servants increased with the growth of the ministerial system after 1954. The enlargement of the functions of government, the consequent expansion of government organization, and the development of Treasury control, all contributed to the increased responsibility and authority of the civil servants at the centre. The civil servants, rather than the Ministers, dominated the ministerial organization, as the political ministers in the 1950s discovered.[1] The service was, moreover, strictly hierarchical, authority residing at the top. Within the civil service therefore the group of senior, experienced men in higher places dominated the process of government, and had a pervasive influence throughout. The resulting tradition of civil service dominance within the government machine remained after the transfer of power, even though an African government assumed full control over that machine.

It is time to sum up this institutional legacy. Part of Kenya's political inheritance was the strong sense of localism out of which grew the tradition of decentralized political power. Party institutions were consequently weak in organization. The legal and administrative inheritance was in contrast very different. It left Kenya with a strong centralized hierarchical machine that had over the years provided an effective counter balance to localism, the grid that held the country together. Although power might have been decentralized in the nationalist movement, in the Government it had been highly centralized.

The attainment of independence meant for Kenya, as for all newly independent states, the beginning of a new phase of consciously

[1] Ibid.

building a nation out of the different peoples encompassed within the borders of the new state. To build the nation Kenyan leaders had to unite the racial and tribal groupings, whose differences were intensified by the economic imbalances of a dual economy inherited from the past: imbalances between subsistence and modern sectors, and African and non-African.

After independence Kenya's drive to nation building made it essential to forge an institutional base able to contain and control those centrifugal forces within the country that were part of the colonial inheritance. The institutional base that emerged in the first five years owed much to the legacy of a weak party structure and a strong government machine. When they were in opposition and fighting the colonial régime, KANU leaders questioned the dominant authority of the civil service and demanded the abolition of the Provincial Administration. Once in power, however, they modified their position. During their first year in office they faced a series of difficult situations that they could not resolve through party political channels. Authority in the party was too diffuse and branches too independent, to permit the central government easily to control their own party members, particularly in the Central Province. To centralize the authority structure in the party immediately was difficult in the light not only of the strong local loyalties and the enduring pattern of boss politics, but also of the continued leadership conflicts within the top ranks of the party. Although Kenyatta's position was unchallenged that of his lieutenants was not. Independence did not put an end to the personal rivalries that had always bedevilled KANU; these rivalries delayed any changes in the party structure. The battle for control of the party continued; but while no single leader was sure that he could retain ultimate control, none of them was likely to accept a new centralized party machine that might be used against him. Under these circumstances authority in the party remained dispersed and the formal party institutions unused.

Although the party machinery could not be used to enhance governmental control and ensure acquiescence in the Government's decisions, the existing civil service machinery could. The bureaucracy was well established, and it was responsible to the Executive. In the case of the Provincial Administration, it offered the Government a superb machine that provided a direct chain of command and control from the centre down to the sub-location: it was the centralizing agency that the new Executive needed. Not surprisingly they used it. During 1964, the year of regionalism, the central government's most important asset in their battle against regionalism was the civil service machine. Although constitutionally the Civil Secretary

29

(formerly the Provincial Commissioner) was responsible only to the Regional Authority, he remained in practice the Agent of the Central Government. The full decentralization of the Administration was consequently avoided. When in December 1964 the former unitary state was restored, the Administration was also restored to its former position as the Agent of the Executive now responsible directly to the President.[1] The inherited institution was retained, to perform the functions for which it had formerly been responsible: control and development.

The KANU debate after independence revealed increasingly divergent views on policy, which had remained beneath the surface while the dominant objective had been the achievement of independence. This policy debate, primarily on certain economic issues, was compounded by the continued struggle for power within the party hierarchy beneath Kenyatta. It was carried on not within party institutions but within the National Assembly, where the legacy of vigorous parliamentary debate endured. Although Members were slow to realize it, their debate raised the fundamental issue of the relationship between party and government; and in the process of arguing with their critics and in their efforts to secure party discipline, the KANU Government took significant steps in the process of defining that relationship.

A weak party that left its members a considerable degree of independence had hitherto been able to contain the personal rivalries in KANU, as well as reconcile the strong pluralism of Kenya's society. But such a fluid party situation was after independence a constant source of danger to a government working within the parliamentary system. While the party itself might be kept quiet by the expedient of delaying its meetings, the Members of Parliament could not. The parliamentary record from 1963 onwards showed the KANU Parliamentarians, the only organized group within the party able to challenge and on occasion to defeat their own Executive in the legislature; it also raised the question of the relationship between the Party, the Parliamentary Party and the Government. The upheavals in the party after 1964 and the major constitutional changes since independence are best understood as part of a process of defining that relationship, and so to a large degree the country's institutional base. The timing of the successive stages in the argument, and the manner in which the issue has been resolved, have been closely related to the successive phases in the struggle for power within the party itself – a struggle fought out primarily in Parliament. The

[1] See C. Gertzel, 'The Provincial Administration in Kenya', *Journal of Commonwealth Political Studies*, Vol. IV, No. 3, November 1966.

process has been one of disciplining and subordinating the Party to Government in an attempt to reverse the tradition of decentralized political power that grew with the nationalist movement.

2

The Politics
of Independent
Kenya 1963-6

The major focus of attention in Kenya politics for the first three and a half years after independence was the continuing divisions within the ruling party KANU. These divisions emerged increasingly into the open, leading in April 1966 to the withdrawal of Mr Odinga, then KANU's and Kenya's Vice-President, from government and party, to lead a new Opposition, the Kenya People's Union. This chapter analyses the political developments leading up to the realignments that took place in the middle of 1966.

The most significant factors contributing to the party split were the differences of opinion, within the KANU leadership group, concerning both policy issues and questions of personal position and power. These differences lay at the root of the conflict within the KANU – a conflict which took place in Parliament rather than within the party institutions. As a result the political developments of the period should be considered within the framework of the parliamentary system. The differences revealed in the debate were only marginally ideological in their beginnings. The argument between the leaders indicated a basically pragmatic approach to the contest, the object of which was essentially to define the issues on which the political debate should be based. This in turn presumed that those who could determine the issues would emerge dominant. As the issues were defined, however, both parties to the debate then tended to state them increasingly in ideological terms; and so the debate took a more ideological turn. The party structure was unable during this period to contain the conflict arising out of these policy and personality issues; so they combined to produce the open breach in KANU and the establishment of a new opposition party in April 1966.

The dominant trend in Kenya during this same period was the increasing assertion of central government control over the whole country, and the further consolidation of the powers of the Executive, through the civil service rather than the party. When Kenya became independent in December 1963, it was with a system of government and administration considerably more decentralized than that of the colonial period. The independence constitution had provided for a considerable devolution of power from the centre to the seven new regional authorities that were set up under the new quasi-federal government structure.[1] The KANU Government made no secret, however, of its view that regionalism was a political mistake,[2] so that it is not surprising that during their first year in office they delayed its full implementation.

One important step taken by the Central Government was the retention of a much closer control over the civil service at the regional level, and particularly over the regional (formerly the provincial) administration than the constitution allowed.[3] The Central Government (through the Ministry of Home Affairs with whom responsibility for the Regional Administration then lay) used the Civil Secretaries (formerly the Provincial Commissioners) to maintain a much more direct line of communication with the regions than was provided for in the constitution. The most publicized use of this Central Government control of staff in the regions was the retirement (by the Ministry of Home Affairs) of a large number of chiefs, from all parts of the country, on the grounds of their unsuitability for the job in the new post independence situation.

A second step was to delay the full implementation of the financial provisions laid down in the constitution, and so retain central control of regional finances beyond the date of June 1964 originally set down as the time when the regions would assume full responsibility (within the provisions of the constitution) for their own finances.[4] A third decision delayed the transfer of certain services to be taken over by the regions, which were therefore still in Central Government hands at the end of 1964 when the constitution was amended.

While they procrastinated on implementation the Government also

---

[1] The regional structure was introduced under the internal self-government constitution of April 1963. Certain important modifications in this structure were made by the independence constitution, with reference to the civil service (the original proposal for seven civil services being withdrawn) and the police. Otherwise the independence constitution followed the same pattern. The seventh region, North Eastern, was from December 1963 under a state of emergency, and for this reason the Regional Authority there did not become fully operative.

[2] For KANU's stand on regionalism see C. Sanger and J. Nottingham, op. cit.; Rothchild, op. cit.

[3] Circular 1/1963 of 31 July 1963, and Establishment Circular No. 55 of 22 December 1963, were the most important directives issued in this matter.

[4] Central Government Directive 29 May 1964. See *East African Standard* 30 May 1964.

sought public support for their intended constitutional amendment to abolish regionalism and reintroduce a unitary state with a strong central government. This proposed change was announced to Parliament on 14 August, when the then Prime Minister, Mr Kenyatta, made a statement on the Government's intention to introduce a republic and abolish regionalism.[1] Before that date he and his ministers had toured the country seeking public support for such changes, as well as for the idea of a one-party state. At the same time they wooed KADU Opposition Members of Parliament, who began slowly to cross the floor in a movement that culminated in the voluntary dissolution of that party by its leaders in November, just in time to allow the Senate (then the major stumbling block to the proposed constitutional changes) to pass the first constitutional amendment unanimously. Kenya therefore became a Republic and a *de facto* one-party state in December 1964.[2]

The Republican constitution[3] took Kenya a significant step closer to the strong central government that KANU believed necessary for Kenya. The powers of the regions were abolished and an Executive President, both Head of State and Head of Government, was introduced. The constitution gave the President extremely wide powers (which were to be enlarged substantially eighteen months later in May 1966, when his emergency powers were strengthened)[4] but bound him closely to an elected legislature of which he himself had to be a constituency (i.e. an elected) member. As Head of Government he remained Head of a Cabinet, which he chose himself from elected members of the legislature, and was responsible to that body. The Lower House[5] acquired the right to pass a formal vote of no confidence in the Executive, and the Executive retained the right to dissolve Parliament at any time. Thus the Executive and Legislature continued to be linked closely together in a system of government based essentially on parliament supremacy. The Government argued in October 1964 and later, that this parliamentary supremacy was the

[1] *Official Report*, House of Representatives, Second Session, First Parliament, Vol. III, (Part II), 14 August 1964, cols. 1707–10.

[2] The major public meetings in the series were: March 20–23, Kenyatta toured the Western Region; August 2 Kenyatta visited Nyanza; in September a meeting of Kalenjin in North Baringo supported KANU leaders and a one-party state and urged the Kalenjin KADU Members of Parliament to join KANU. The first amendment to the constitution was passed in the House of Representatives on 3 November; on 6 and 8 November, six KADU Members of Parliament crossed the floor; and on the 11th Mr Ngala announced the dissolution of KADU.

[3] Act No. 28 of 1964, the Constitution of Kenya (Amendment) Act 1964. This is referred to as the first amendment.

[4] See below, Chapter 6.

[5] The bicameral legislature remained in being until December 1966, when a further amendment merged the Senate and House of Representatives to establish a unicameral legislature. See below, Chapter p. 153.

essential check upon the Executive that would prevent the latter assuming dictatorial powers and ignoring the country's elected representatives and thus the people themselves.[1]

While parliamentary control of the Executive remained a major provision of the Republican Constitution, further amendments in 1965 and 1966 undoubtedly enhanced the Executive's powers *vis-à-vis* the legislature. The third amendment, for example, abolished the special provisions for amendment of those entrenched sections of the constitution (relating to the regions and to fundamental rights); consequently amendment of the constitution now required only a two-thirds majority of all members of each House.[2] The fifth amendment, passed in April 1966, required any Member of Parliament who resigned from the party that had supported him at his election to resign his seat in Parliament, thus providing the Executive with additional, if unstated, disciplinary powers over Members.[3] It was as a consequence of this amendment that the little general election took place in June 1966. The enlargement of the President's emergency powers, already mentioned, were provided by the sixth amendment passed in May 1966.[4] Although the KANU Government did not therefore secure the unicameral legislature which it believed essential for strong central government until December 1966, by the middle of that year it had by constitutional changes considerably enhanced the position of the Executive.

This was the constitutional position. At the same time the Government was able in 1965 to reassert full administrative control over the country. It chose to do this through the civil service rather than through the party machine. The division of services that had accompanied regionalism was abandoned and all ministries resumed full control of their activities in the provinces, except for those services such as primary education and certain medical services, which were the responsibility of the Local Authorities. Even there, however, the Ministries tended to assert their authority through their officers, notwithstanding that the latter had in fact been seconded to the County Councils; and the Ministry of Local Government itself resumed full direct control over all local authorities. The conflicts over local government services were once again therefore fought out in a triangular battle between that Ministry (not the Regional Authorities) other central government ministries, and the local authorities.

[1] See for example *Official Report*, House of Representatives, Second Session, Vol. III, Part III, 27 October 1964, cols. 3879–905 for Mboya's speech on the first amendment.
[2] Act No. 14 of 1965.
[3] Act No. 17 of 1966.
[4] Act No. 18 of 1966.

The most important assertion of control was, however, that of the Office of the President, through the Provincial Administration, responsibility for which was transferred in December 1964 to that Office from the Ministry of Home Affairs. The President deliberately restored to the Provincial Administration the dominant role of Agent of the Executive in the field and made it his major organ of control. Provincial and District Commissioners resumed their former position, at provincial and district level respectively, as the senior executive officer and the co-ordinators of all government activities. They also resumed most of those responsibilities that they had lost in June 1963 to the Regional Assemblies or the County Councils. Thus, for example, in 1965 they resumed responsibility for the collection of Graduated Personal Tax on behalf of the Local Authorities, Chairmanship of the Provincial and District Agriculture Committees, Chairmanship of the Divisional Land Boards, and, in a number of districts, became Chairmen of the self-help co-ordinating committees at district and provincial level. When a new development committee structure was proposed by the Ministry of Economic Planning and Development, to assist in the implementation of development projects the Provincial Administration was assigned the major role as Agent of Development.[1] Provincial and District Commissioners became chairmen of the proposed new committees. These Development Committees did not in fact become effective bodies in the period under review; nevertheless the dominant position proposed within them for the Provincial Administration was another indication of the importance attached by Government to the Administration's authority.

The most significant reassertion of the Administration's authority concerned law and order. Provincial Commissioners and District Commissioners once again became chairmen of the Security and Intelligence Committees and thereby ultimately responsible for law and order, ousting the police from that position. This established them (and therefore the Office of the President) in a crucial position so far as the control of the district was concerned, symbolized above all by their responsibility for the licensing and control of public meetings, including meetings held by Members of Parliament.[2]

The Provincial Administration (which had by the beginning of 1965 been fully Africanized) therefore dominated the countryside. It was clearly this group of officers directly responsible to the President, and not the party, who were regarded by the Executive as its major line of communication with the people. This network enabled the

[1] Revised Development Plan 1966–7, Nairobi: Government Printer 1966, para. 24.
[2] See below, Chapter 6.

President to maintain a direct and immediate influence on district affairs; it also ensured the pre-eminence of the Executive within the administrative system as a whole. The functions of the Administration were therefore essentially those of control. Its developmental functions, and its significance as a symbol of national unity that could counter the centrifugal forces still persistent in most areas, were by no means negligible. But these in effect remained subordinate to the primary task – to exercise control.

The Administration was consequently being used in very much the same way that it had been used by colonial governors in the past: to maintain an effective network of control and communication between the centre and the districts. In two important respects, however, the position of the Administration had changed significantly. In the first place, the Administration – particularly the Provincial Commissioners – had less influence in this period upon central government policy than their colonial predecessors had had. They were expected to implement Government policy and to act as the major Government spokesmen of that policy; but they were no longer allowed to make it. On more than one occasion the evidence suggested that the views of Provincial Commissioners had been overruled by a central government more concerned with the political implications of particular issues than with the ideas of administrative officers.

In the second place, the Administration had no powers over the new, directly elected local authorities set up in 1963.[1] On this matter the views of the Administration and of the Office of the President coincided: they would have liked the Administration to enjoy the right to intervene directly in local government matters, especially finance. But the Republican Constitution, although it restored full responsibility for local government to the centre, restored it to the Ministry of Local Government, not the Office of the President; and it was to the Ministry that Local Authority Councillors and Officers had to turn. Administrative Officers became (where they had not previously been) nominated members of the county and other local councils, but without any executive authority in local government affairs.

A majority of the local authorities during the first three years of independence faced considerable difficulties in making the new local

---

[1] The structure of local government laid down by Local Government Regulations of May 1963 provided for two tiers of Local Authorities: first tier, municipal and county councils; second tier urban, area and local councils. In all councils the majority of members were directly elected, but there was provision for a number of members nominated by the Minister for Local Government to represent special interests. See The Local Government Regulations 1963, Kenya *Gazette* Supplement No. 33, 30 April 1963.

government system work. The major problems which County Councils encountered were those of finance and of staff. First, the collection of a completely new form of local government tax (Graduated Personal Tax) imposed a serious burden upon these Councils in 1963 and 1964, and the shortfall in the amount collected indicated their difficulties in setting up suitable collecting machinery. The position improved after the Provincial Administration assumed responsibility for collection in 1965, but not markedly so. Secondly, County Councils had difficulty in recruiting adequate numbers of qualified and experienced staff, at a time when there was a premium on such men, and when the central government could exert an overwhelming pull on those available. Thirdly, elected Councillors, of whom an overwhelming majority had no previous experience in local government, were slow to settle down and accept the limitations as well as the responsibilities of their office. For these and other reasons a large number of the county councils (but not the municipalities) were by 1966 in considerable financial difficulties. This brought them under considerable fire from central government ministries; but they remained a significant source of influence and patronage which party leaders might exploit. Two results followed: firstly the County Councils remained important bodies from which criticisms of central government were made and secondly the district remained an important arena of political activity.

Public criticism of Government policies was however by no means restricted to the county councils. While the Executive demonstrably increased its control over the machinery of government in this period, it did not halt public debate about its activities and policies. In addition to the debate between central government and local authorities, pressure and criticism emanated from non-party movements such as the trade unions, from commercial interests, from the farmers, from districts seeking advancement, and from party spokesmen. The party was, however, for reasons which will emerge below, the least effective organization in articulating these various demands. And in the absence of functioning party institutions the Members of Parliament, who became the most vocal party spokesmen, used the legislature as their major political forum. The first African elected members had used the Legislative Council to advantage in 1957. The new Members elected in the general election of 1963, few of whom had had previous parliamentary experience, also quickly appreciated the value of the National Assembly. The constitutional links between the Executive and Legislature gave them an additional advantage in so far as they made it more difficult for the Executive to dismiss them. And notwithstanding the increasing dominance of the Executive the fact remains that during this period it was either unable or unwilling to silence this legislature.[1]

It was to be expected that in the two-party legislature of 1963 the KADU Opposition would challenge Government policies; as it did. The most vigorous element in the Kenya policy debate was, however, from the outset, not the KADU Opposition, but a group of KANU's own backbenchers. In 1963 and 1964 these KANU backbenchers became vigorous critics of certain of their own Government's policies, which they challenged as departures from the party policy on which they had all been elected. As a result, KANU discipline within the Assembly was on numerous occasions strained.

This backbench criticism was in the first place an indication of backbenchers' frustration at the Cabinet's apparent ability to ignore Parliament and their consequent fears of Cabinet oligarchy. 'It is time we were told whether this is a dictatorship type of government or are we also having some share in forming the Government of the country,' Mr Maisori-Itumbo (KANU, Juria) demanded in August 1964. This sense of frustration was shared by many of his fellow backbenchers, who believed that the Government was ignoring the party and the Parliamentary Group, neither of which was kept informed of what was going on. Since their fears of Cabinet domination were shared by the KADU Opposition in 1963 and 1964, this established the basis for a measure of co-operation between Government backbench and Opposition in an attempt (not altogether unsuccessful) to make the Cabinet aware of its responsibility to Parliament.

The KANU backbenchers insisted that their critical stand was due not simply to any preoccupation with their own position or any parochial interests, but also to their concern for the national interest. In the national interest they asserted their right to act as the 'watchdogs' of the people as a whole. 'We members of KANU, especially the backbenchers,' said Mr Anyieni (KANU, Majogi-Bassi) in October 1964, 'do not mind whether it is KANU or KADU provided it is right for the people of the country.'[2] They did not, they insisted, wish to overthrow their Government; they did want to moderate its actions. They consequently sought to use their pivotal position in the two-party House to influence the Executive to adopt policies that they regarded as closer to the national interests. Mr Wariithi (the chairman of the group) in 1964 put their position in the two-party system clearly, when he said:

[1] As a result, the parliamentary record provides perhaps the most valuable source of information for most of the major events of the period, especially of the emergence of new alignments within KANU.

[2] *Official Report*, House of Representatives, First Parliament, Second Session, Vol III, Part III, 7 October 1964, col. 3253. Cf. below pp. 135–6.

... the Backbenchers' Group has no grudge whatsoever with our Prime Minister. This group supports our Prime Minister and his Government and the planning to overthrow the Government is unfounded. . . . The backbenchers . . . take a different line from that taken by a Minister. They may criticize the Government. They may vote against the Government: we have an opposition, which can never hope to win a motion unless the backbenchers support them, and this should not be underrated. My group, knowing this, will have to be a kind of watchdog or pressure group to our Government . . . (last Thursday) we were only reminding our Government to fulfil and stand by the promises it had given to the voters. . . .[1]

In 1963 KANU backbenchers had established a backbench group separate from the party's Parliamentary Group. This backbench group in 1963 and 1964 achieved a considerable degree of cohesion, which enabled its members to dominate the Parliamentary Group and to press their views upon the Government with some degree of success. The climax of KANU backbench activity in 1964 was reached when they defeated the Government in the House on the issue of East African Federation, on which they joined hands with the KADU Opposition. But throughout the year they regularly criticized Government measures. This criticism increased in the one-party House in 1965, when the considerably enlarged backbench group challenged the Government's alleged dictatorial measures, and asserted the need, in the one-party House, for the backbench to be accorded adequate representation on the various parliamentary committees as well as in debate. In February 1965 they defeated the Government on a purely procedural motion concerning the formation of a new Sessional Committee, on the grounds that it was not sufficiently representative of their group. In February also they threatened to hold up the Supplementary Estimates. In March they challenged the Agricultural (Amendment) Bill, on which the Government finally avoided defeat only after considerable argument and a long adjournment of the debate during which time the Bill was discussed by the Minister and the Members, in private.

Out of this vigorous debate between the Government and its backbench, in the one-party House of early 1965, a pattern of consultation began to emerge by which deadlock between the Executive and the Legislature was avoided. If the criticism on the floor of the House indicated that the Government was unlikely to get the measure through, then the discussion was withdrawn to the privacy of the Parliamentary Group, where argument was usually resolved by the personal intervention of the President. Deadlock between Ministers and back-

[1] Ibid., Second Session, Vol. III, Part III, 23 June 1964, col. 481. See also below, Chapter 5.

benchers was thus avoided primarily as a result of the personal influence of the President rather than compromise by the Cabinet on the points at issue. The Government did not, in fact, make any major policy changes as a result of the debate, but the backbenchers secured recognition of their right to be consulted; and the rearranged parliamentary timetable indicated government acquiescence in principle of full parliamentary debate.[1]

Members of Parliament were in effect seeking to control their party executive from within parliamentary, rather than party, institutions. The result was that the Members became the most vigorous and critical group within the party; and indeed the only group which had a definite forum and opportunity for debate. They therefore as a group assumed a more influential role within the party than was provided for in the party constitution. In this way the parliamentary caucus emerged as the most significant element in KANU.

Divisions rapidly appeared, however, in 1965, within the enlarged backbenchers group that resulted from the dissolution of KADU. Consequently the backbench group's influence was weakened; and the group was subsequently disbanded. The divisions (which arose out of policy disagreements that will be discussed below) first became apparent in the contest within the Parliamentary Group, in March 1965, over the election of a successor to the late Pio Pinto, who had been a specially Elected Member until his murder at the end of February. The defeat of the Parliamentary Group's official candidates by two independents was, under the circumstances, an indication that the backbenchers were no longer as united as they had been.[2] These divisions were further highlighted by the backbench group's elections in June when the then officers were ousted and new leaders installed. In July, a month later, the group was finally disbanded at the President's request, on the grounds, as he said, that there was no need for such a body in a single party Parliament.

By July 1965, as a result of these events, the Government's most vigorous backbench critics had been ousted from any official position. They suffered a similar defeat in the Sessional Committee. This Committee, responsible under Standing Orders for the ordering of the House's business, was chaired by a senior Government Minister, and had a Government majority, although its membership (proposed by the Government at the beginning of each session) included Opposition Members during the days of the two-party House. Mr Odinga was at the time its Chairman. On 24 July Mr Ngala (formerly Leader of the KADU Opposition, then a backbencher) moved a Private Member's

[1] See below, Chapter 5.
[2] *East African Standard*, 25 March 1965 and 3 April 1965.

Motion to change the membership of this Committee so as to exclude certain of its backbench members, on the grounds that a majority of the Parliamentary Group had lost confidence in them. He urged that these changes were necessary in the light of the 'proved political ganging up in the Parliamentary Group and the changes in officials'. The motion was passed.

The effect of these changes was to make it more difficult for the backbench critics to dominate the KANU parliamentary caucus. This was due partly to the abolition of the backbench group itself, from within which, as a small, cohesive group, the most vigorous critics had lobbied effectively among their colleagues. Equally important too was the fact that President Kenyatta's chairmanship of the Parliamentary Group had an inhibiting effect upon arguments within the body, primarily because of the deep sense of loyalty that all Members still felt for him. Backbench criticism did not come to an end, and the debate between back and front benches was as lively as ever. Its leaders were however less effective as a lobby.

At the same time, the demise of the formal backbench group meant that the division between backbench and Government, which had dominated debate in 1964, receded. The real divisions within KANU, which cut right across the party, across both back and front bench, became more apparent. By the middle of 1965, consistent alignments based not on the backbench-Government cleavage but on differences of opinion on policy, emerged as the most significant divisions within Parliament and therefore within KANU. These policy differences consequently moved into the forefront of the debate.

One disagreement clearly concerned the allocation of resources. Most Members of Parliament were understandably anxious to put the case for their own constituencies as strongly and as frequently as possible. Backbenchers, especially those from poorer areas, feared the neglect of their districts, by comparison with those represented by more senior members of the government. Cabinet Ministers were seen as enjoying greater opportunities, compared with ordinary Members, of promoting and satisfying the demands of their own constituencies. The backbenchers therefore challenged anything that implied neglect of their own areas, in terms of allocation of resources, services and development projects, loans to farmers and traders, and posts in the civil service. Their anxiety on this score led KANU backbenchers on more than one occasion in 1964 to support KADU Members who shared the same fears of neglect by the Government of the minority tribes whom they represented. Mr Oduya, for example, KANU Member of Parliament for Teso North, twice supported KADU motions expressing dissatisfaction with the treatment given the

42

Western part of Kenya, from which he came. 'I do not think,' he said on one occasion, 'that this motion is an affair that merely concerns the Opposition because it has been moved by the Hon. Muliro. It is an affair that concerns us all in this House as well as those outside.'[1] This fear of neglect of the backward areas, which continued in 1965, stimulated criticisms of government policy on the grounds that it did not spread development and economic benefits evenly.

Because of the ethnic basis of representation such demands for recognition of district needs and allegations of preferential treatment had explicit tribal overtones. In 1964 KADU leaders regularly alleged that the Kikuyu and Luo were given far too much preference in both appointments to the civil service and the allocation of resources, especially loans to farmers and traders. Thus Mr Muliro (then a KADU Member) in October 1964 challenged the draft republican constitution and the proposed unitary state, on the grounds that the restoration of full control of the Central Government would be used, not in the interests of the nation, but of the 'composite major tribes in the Government'.[2] Such feelings were not restricted to KADU; they were shared by a number of non-Kikuyu KANU backbenchers. In the 1964 Budget debate, for example, strong criticisms of policy allegedly determined by tribal influence were voiced by Anyieni (from Kisii), Mahokha (from Busia), Obok and Agar (both from Nyanza), all KANU backbenchers, as well as from the then KADU Opposition. Such criticisms all followed the same pattern – the underdeveloped areas were neglected because the six-year Development Plan provided for 'most of the money to be spent in already established districts like Kiambu'.[3] Complaints of this nature against the alleged special treatment of the Central Province continued in 1965.

Tribal overtones were moderated by the fact that Central Province backbenchers were themselves critical of much about the Government's allocation of resources and decisions about development. Nyeri and Murang'a Members were particularly critical of the alleged favouritism accorded to Kiambu, in contrast to their own districts, which they believed to be the result of the dominance of Kiambu Ministers in the Cabinet. A 'marginal District' was thus a relative term, and it was not only representatives of the poorer districts who believed their areas to be neglected. The Kikuyu backbenchers tended

[1] *Official Report*, House of Representatives, First Parliament, Second Session, Vol. III, Part II, 10 September 1964, col. 2260. The motion in question expressed dissatisfaction with the Government's statements of policy for the promotion of literacy on backward areas.

[2] Ibid., Second Session, Vol. III, Part III, 28 October 1964, col. 4032. He did, however, subsequently accept it when KADU was dissolved, and with its other leaders he joined KANU.

[3] Ibid., Second Session, Vol. V, 22 June 1965, col. 642.

43

understandably to see the problems in somewhat different terms from their non-Kikuyu colleagues since they did not wish to see development slowed down in their own areas. They were more inclined to argue the case for a national policy that ensured a fair redistribution of the returns of development rather than one which held the richer districts back while the poorer caught up. At the same time they voted and spoke in favour of motions that specifically urged support for the poorer districts, because they feared uneven development in the Central Province as elsewhere.[1]

Nevertheless, although there were influences to counter divisions upon tribal lines during 1965, references in Parliament to the problem of tribalism increased. These references were predominantly to the alleged dominance of the Kikuyu over all other tribes. The Kikuyu appeared to many to be the major beneficiaries of independence, dominating both the bureaucracy and the country's economy. So explicit did this become that one Luo Member of Parliament, speaking at a public luncheon in July 1965, felt it necessary to warn that there was no place 'for establishing one clan or one tribe as a ruling class in African society'.[2] By the end of the year fears of Kikuyu dominance in government and therefore control over policy making were regularly voiced in and out of Parliament; and the debate on the Presidential address at the November State opening of Parliament demonstrated the extent to which Members shared this fear.[3]

Disagreement about the allocation of resources between districts and the consequent emphasis on tribal position was by no means the only source of dispute over policy that could be detected during 1965. There were more fundamental disagreements; and the consistent groupings that emerged among Members during that year were also the outcome of strong disagreements over certain basic assumptions underlying Government policy. This came out most clearly in the debates on land, nationalization and Kenya's foreign policy.

The most significant of these disagreements concerned land. In each successive budget debate in 1963, 1964 and 1965, Members from all parts of the House challenged the Government's land and settlement policies. Much of the criticism was directed at specific aspects of settlement policy: the squatter problem, the future of labourers evicted from former European farms, the organization of the Ministry of Settlement, the behaviour of settlement officers, the loans policy which

---

[1] Ibid., Second Session, Vol. IV, 26 February 1965, cols. 359–60.
[2] *East African Standard*, 15 July 1965. Mr Okelo-Odongo, then Assistant Minister for Finance, was speaking at a United Kenya Club luncheon.
[3] *Official Report*, House of Representatives, Vol. VII, 9 November 1965, col. 212; 10 November, col. 278; 11 November, col. 354; 30 November, col. 576.

required payment of loans from new farmers within what was regarded as too short a period, the size of deposits required from new farmers in the settlement schemes, which many Members insisted were too high for ordinary Africans. Most Members believed that the Government had failed to deal satisfactorily with these practical problems. Most were also doubtful about the economic viability of the settlement schemes policy as a whole, which many insisted had been designed to assist outgoing European farmers rather than new African farmers (a point on which Government subsequently agreed). The settlement schemes could not, the critics argued, solve the problems of landless Africans in Kenya whose landlessness and unemployment constituted a major economic, social and political danger to the state. Some back-benchers challenged the idea that land in the former scheduled (European) areas should have been bought at all. Since the land had belonged to the Africans in the past it ought not to have been bought, but requisitioned as needed; and distributed free, not sold, to Africans. They argued that this land should have been nationalized, and either given to the landless, or worked as state farms.[1] Those who adopted this stand argued that the criterion for settlement should have been the absorption of a maximum number of landless, not the settlement of the problems of European farmers. To spend £26 million to settle 30,000 families was not enough. They insisted that a policy of co-operative farming on the former large-scale farms would much better achieve these ends than settlement of individuals on individual plots.

The major exponent of this view was Mr Kaggia (the Member for Kandara), who made no secret of his opposition to the Government's land and settlement policies, even before he relinquished his post as Assistant Minister for Education. After his departure from office in June 1964 he quickly assumed open leadership of the KANU back-bench group, from which position he vigorously criticized what he believed to be the Government's departure from the party's policy on land. In February 1965 he said:

It is very important for this House and the country as a whole and the world to know the policy on which KANU and other previous parties in this country had struggled for so many years and on which they have fought and won election. Our policy, Mr Speaker, Sir, has been that the land in Kenya belonged to the African people and this land was stolen from us. This is the policy not the slogan as many people tend to make us

---

[1] These views were stated on more than one occasion, but see for example Ibid., House of Representatives, Second Session, Vol. III, Part II, 2 September 1964 and 30 September 1964. For Kenya settlement policy see *inter alia*, H. Ruthenberg, *African Agricultural Production Development Policy in Kenya 1952–1965*: Berlin, 1966.

believe. We have used this for all these years as a policy and in fact it has been the backbone of our political struggle.[1]

Kaggia's attitudes on land led him into public collision with President Kenyatta, who made his view clear on successive occasions, that the policy the former advocated was inconsistent with the principles, also upheld by KANU, of the freedom of the individual and the protection of his several rights, including the right to the ownership of the property, all of which were protected in the constitution.[2] In a sense, however, the two men were debating different things. Kaggia was arguing that social justice demanded the return of African land to the Africans, without any cost to them or to the country. This was the argument of the 1930s, the 1940s and the 1950s. Kenyatta was arguing that social justice demanded recognition of the individual's right to the enjoyment of certain things, including fair treatment and just compensation if his property had to be resumed. Nationalization of property was not therefore possible. This was the argument of the 1960s.

Land had always been a highly emotional issue in Kenya. It had been the major issue in colonial politics. It was also, in the independent state, a vital economic issue since proper land use was fundamental to development. But the context within which the land debate was argued had changed radically since the colonial period. Africans, and the Kikuyu in particular, had fought during the colonial period for the return of the lands in the former Scheduled areas from the Europeans to African ownership. Their victory had been established in 1959 when the Highlands had been opened up to African ownership. A radical change in land policy, so far as racial ownership was concerned, had thus been achieved. At the time the question of what system of land tenure should apply and which Africans should own these lands, had not been in the mainstream of the debate. But once the right of African ownership had been won and the policy of Africanization of the (European) large-scale farm economy of Kenya got under way, this latter question became the major issue.

Africans were settled in the former White Highlands after 1962 in three different ways. First in the settlement schemes, by which land primarily in the mixed farming areas was bought by the Government from European owners and transferred to African ownership, either in high density schemes, in which plots were small, or low density schemes,

---

[1] *Official Report*, House of Representatives, Second Session, Vol. IV, 26 February 1965. Odinga, in *Not yet Uhuru*, pp. 262–9, discusses Kaggia's land policy, and quotes written Memoranda by Kaggia on this subject, and his correspondence with the Prime Minister and Minister for Lands and Settlement.

[2] See, for one statement, *East African Standard*, 26 July 1964.

where larger plots were taken over. Second, in areas of the former Highlands which had never been opened up, the Government emphasized State enterprise, through the African Development Corporation, either independently or in joint ventures with private firms. Third, individual Africans, some sponsored by family groups and by co-operatives, began to buy large holdings, with loans from the Land Bank or other sources.[1]

In 1965, although just over a million acres had been resettled under the settlement schemes, this was predominantly in the mixed farming area; and a large proportion of the lower-potential lands in the former European areas remained in European hands. A large belt of farming land stretching from Nairobi to Mt. Elgon thus remained to be taken over. The question at issue thus became the manner in which this land should be resumed. Whether or not it should be on the basis of individual ownership already laid down; and which Africans should have the right of access. Interest in this question of land ownership was by no means restricted to the Kikuyu; it concerned all Africans, especially those Kalenjin whose tribal lands bordered on the former Highlands and who wished to take them over. Attitudes towards land were still therefore largely determined by tribal considerations. Attitudes concerning right of access and the basis of ownership, however, cut across tribe, and divided leaders as well as people according to whether or not they accepted the established system of transfer which emphasized free access to individuals and individual ownership.

Attitudes towards the ownership of land were also influenced by the changing economic situation in much of the former 'African areas'. At the time of the Emergency the Colonial Government had embarked upon a major new agricultural policy for African farming which had emphasized the development of smallholder agriculture.[2] That policy summed up in the Swynnerton Plan, had been based upon land reform and registration of title as well as cash-crop development in the African areas, the better use of land in pastoral areas, resettlement on unused land, and increased services. The primary focus was the reform of the land tenure system, which proposed consolidation and registration of lands formerly held under customary tenure. The changes introduced were most marked in the Central Province where, by 1960, as a result of this policy, all land was individually owned; but in several other parts of the country also by 1960 the movement for enclosure and consolidation had developed considerably, and with it an increased emphasis on individual ownership. This move to consolidation and

---

[1] In August 1967, 800 farms in the former scheduled areas had been purchased privately by Africans. On the transfer of the scheduled areas to African ownership see Rutenberg, op. cit.

[2] See above, Chapter 1.

individual title, which was by 1965 official Government policy, had also influenced attitudes towards access to and the ownership of land.

The context within which many people in Kenya viewed land issues in 1965 was therefore different from that of 1963. The issue was no longer only the return of the land from European to African owner-ship. The question was now which Africans should own the land and on what terms. And on this question there was disagreement. Members of Parliament were demonstrably involved in this debate. This was made clear by reactions to any suggestion that land should be nationalized or farmed on the basis of state owned co-operatives. Talk of nationalization raised fears in the minds of some Members that this might constitute a threat to African control of their own tribal lands. But a more immediate question in their minds seemed to be the question of property. 'It is my deep conviction that anything to do with the nationalization of land in this country will never work,' said Mr ole Tipis, one of the Masai Members (for Narok East) on one occasion.

The African people are proud, and rightly too, to own and possess property which a man or a woman can call his or her own, and if anybody comes along with some strange ideas, having been indoctrinated some-where with the idea of applying nationalisation then he would be looking for trouble. Nationalisation of the land would never work.[1]

Mr Khasakhala (Emukhaya) said forcefully on another occasion, 'It is most unfortunate that such a Motion should come to this House, because already, Mr Speaker, Sir, in Kenya today, Africans own their own property which they are proud of us to own. You cannot say that you are going to divide the property of someone which belongs only to him as a person.'[2]

Kaggia and his associates opposed uncontrolled individual private purchase of land in the former scheduled areas, outside the settlement schemes. They did so on two grounds. They argued the need to settle those landless Africans who were too poor to buy land for themselves; and warned of the dangers of the emergence of a new class of African large-scale landowners who simply stepped into the former European farmers' shoes. Kaggia suggested that to allow an individual to own large amounts of land while poor Africans were starving was to en-courage capitalism at the expense of the latter. His arguments raised apprehensions among other Members about the future of private ownership.

[1] *Official Report,* House of Representatives, First Parliament, Second Session, Vol. IV, 2 April 1965, col. 1156.
[2] Ibid.

These apprehensions were clearly demonstrated in a debate in March 1965 on a motion seeking to limit individual land purchases in the former scheduled areas. This motion, moved by Mr Anyieni, asked the Government to set up a Committee to recommend the maximum acreage that could be held under private ownership in the former Scheduled Areas.[1] Mr Anyieni's case was straightforward. The independence struggle had been dominated by the determination of the African people to resume control of their lands. Many politicians in those days had told the masses that when independence came the land would belong to them. Since independence, however, it had been a small group of individuals, many of them politicians, who had been buying land and amassing large acreages. Others who would like to buy land would in the future be unable to do so, because very quickly land would have been taken by a few people. More important, many other Africans would be left landless. To avoid this, he urged the Government to set up a committee to investigate methods by which the amount of land any one individual could own could be controlled, and a maximum acreage (economically viable) established for each part of the country.

A majority of Members who spoke rejected this proposal. The Government also rejected the motion, pointing out how much had already been achieved in settling people, and asking Members to give credit where credit was due. Replying for his Ministry the Assistant Minister for Lands and Settlement, Mr Gachago, suggested that Members were confusing Government projects with the open market in land. Land must be acquired in economic units and not necessarily divided up into small plots (which Anyieni denied was the intention of his motion). At the conclusion of the debate, however, Mboya, the Minister for Economic Planning and Development, made a Ministerial statement indicating that he was by no means unaware of the issues involved. He pointed out that the land question would be raised in the revision of the Development Plan then in progress. The Government's rejection of the motion was 'not against the principles outlined but against the unfortunate timing and unfortunate insistence on a vote even after Government assurances of what was being done'. He stated on behalf of the Government that the Government was not satisfied with the existing land policy and intended within a short time to make public its approach to the land problem including if necessary the setting up of a working party to investigate the whole question. The possibility of such an investigation into a ceiling on private ownership of land was referred to in the Sessional Paper No. 10 on

[1] Ibid., House of Representatives, First Parliament, Second Session, Vol. IV, 26 March and April 1965.

African Socialism and its relation to development. The available evidence suggests, however, that no real agreement had been reached within the Cabinet on this issue. No such Committee was set up during 1965 or 1966.

This debate suggested that what divided members was the question of property, which was fundamental to the debate on land. Whether or not all Members consciously recognized the problem at the time, the issue was not simply the ownership of land. It was whether individuals should be free to amass and own as much private property as they wished, or whether there should be a limit set by the state in the interests of the society as a whole on the amount of property of all kinds that the individual might own.[1]

The second policy issue on which Members voiced strongly conflicting views was nationalization – how far Kenya as an African democratic socialist state should nationalize the means of production. The Government rejected any doctrinaire approach of nationalization for its own sake and insisted on a more pragmatic policy, that permitted both state and private enterprise but ensured Government control in the interests of development. In September 1964, Mr Kenyatta told the Nairobi Chamber of Commerce:

We consider that nationalization will not serve to advance the cause of African socialism. . . . There would be a partnership of private enterprise and Government participation. . . . Our aim is to establish a mixed economy. By (this) we mean that we shall work to a situation in which the role of private enterprise and that of Government are complementary to each other. . . . We are determined that the development of African businesses and industries should be carried out without damaging the existing fabric of the economy.[2]

The Sessional Paper No. 10, published and debated in May 1965, followed the same lines.

Nationalization, since it does not always lead to additional resources for the economy as a whole, will be used only where the national security is threatened, higher social benefits can be obtained or productive resources are seriously and clearly being misused, when other means of control are ineffective and financial resources permit, or where a service is vital to the people and must be provided by the Government as part of its responsibility to the nation . . .[3]

This policy failed to satisfy one section of KANU, who demanded, on both economic and moral grounds, that the Government should nationalize public utilities and certain industries, including the East

[1] Mboya was the first to recognize this and to state it in its most fundamental sense, in a speech at University College, Nairobi, 3 November 1966.
[2] *East African Standard*, 30 September 1964.
[3] Paras, 33 to 37.

African Power and Lighting Company, the East African Breweries, and the Nairobi Bus Services. They advanced three arguments in favour of such a policy. First, only nationalization would secure the genuine economic independence of Kenya from other countries, and end 'the colonial tradition of exploiting Kenya to make money for outsiders'; second, this would ensure the transfer of control of the economy to Africans; and third, such nationalization would provide sufficient funds to enable the Government to provide additional free social services, especially free education.

The Government argued in reply that when a country had limited capital resources, as was the case in Kenya, it must use those resources for productive development. It was therefore preferable to use capital to establish and encourage new industry, rather than to buy out existing concerns. Where nationalization was necessary because it was the only means of securing adequate Government control of a particular sector of the economy the necessary steps would be taken. So far as the specific measures proposed by KANU critics were concerned the Government pointed out that these could scarcely provide the funds necessary for the full-scale expansion of social services. Furthermore nationalization raised the question of expropriation and compensation, with its implications for attracting the foreign investment necessary for economic development. The Government did not have the resources to pay compensation on a vast scale. Kenya did not intend to jeopardize her chances of attracting overseas private investment which had been so useful up to date. She therefore would not indiscriminately nationalize or deny private property rights. 'We are not going to rob people of property and then claim that we are carrying out the tenets and the requirements of African socialism', Mr Odero-Jowi had argued as early as July 1963. The debate on nationalization also turned people's minds, therefore, to the question of property.[1]

The third issue on which Members strongly disagreed was foreign policy. The Government took its stand on the principle that Kenya must remain independent and non-aligned but should be prepared to establish such economic and political relations with other States as the country's interests demanded. Such independence was a fundamental commitment of the African socialism that formed the basis of the Government's overall policy. 'We have declared ourselves for African Socialism', Mr Mboya insisted in the foreign affairs debate in September 1964, 'and this means, Sir, we have chosen against Western

[1] See, in particular, the debate on the Foreign Investment Protection Bill, *Official Report*, House of Representatives, First Parliament, Second Session, Vol. III, Part III, 7 October 1964, cols 3242–3260, and the debate on the Electric Power (Amendment) Bill, *Ibid.*, Second Session, Vol. IV, 3 March 1965, cols 461–486.

capitalism and we have also chosen against Eastern Communism.'[1] Sessional Paper No. 10 in 1965 restated this need 'to avoid making development in Kenya dependent on a satellite relationship with any country or group of countries', but pointed out that 'economic non-alignment does not mean a policy of isolation, any more than political non-alignment implies a refusal to participate in world affairs'.[2]

While no one doubted the desirability of political and economic independence, a number of Members questioned whether Kenya was so independent. This challenge ran continuously through the debate in 1964 and 1965. The critics argued that Kenya's existing economic structure and her relationships with Western countries established a commitment to the West which resulted in her domination by the Western World. The country's economic structure was too capitalistic and too dependent on Western companies to allow Kenya to call herself non-aligned. Among those Members who alleged this Western dominance, some suggested that to redress the balance Kenya should 'lean a little more to the East',[3] a proposal rejected not only by the Government but also by many backbenchers who obviously feared a commitment to the Eastern bloc. The backbenchers who sought thus to 'lean a little more to the East' were labelled 'pro-Eastern', a label which drew the retort of 'pro-Western'. The debate on foreign policy therefore divided Members in terms of their alleged preference for the Western or the Eastern countries.

The parliamentary debate throughout 1964 and 1965 therefore demonstrated the existence of certain strong differences of opinion on policy matters among KANU Members. In 1964 the public conflicts arising out of these policy disagreements were primarily between the KANU Government and its own backbench. In 1965 however certain consistent alignments, based on these policy views, emerged within the Parliamentary Group as a whole including the senior members of the party. The argument focused on the modern sector of the economy in which large-scale farming and modern industry had developed, and which was still, in independent Kenya, dominated by Europeans and Asians. The hard-core critics challenged Government policy concerning this sector on three grounds. First it was not Africanizing this sector fast enough. Therefore – and this was the second complaint – foreigners by virtue of their dominant position in the economy, still controlled Kenya; and this control enabled the West in particular to exercise too great an influence over the country's affairs. Third, the proposals for the gradual Africanization of this sector meant simply the replacement

[1] Ibid. Second Session, Vol. II, Part III, 11 September 1964, col. 2298.
[2] Para 23.
[3] *Official Report*, House of Representatives, First Parliament, Second Session, Vol. III, Part III, 11 September 1964, col. 2314.

of the existing white rich class by Africans who would assume the same class position. African economic classes were as a result being created. The critics rejected this legacy of the colonial economy, demanding instead much greater participation by a much larger number of Africans, through state and co-operative enterprise. Only in this way, they asserted, would the wealth of this sector be fairly distributed. What the critics emphasized, therefore, was not necessarily a socialist economy. They insisted upon the desirability of greater nationalization of the public sector of the economy; but this was not their most fundamental point. The crux of their case was their emphasis upon the need to create the kind of egalitarian society in which the full range of economic opportunity would be open to a much larger section of the population than was currently the case, and which precluded sharp economic class distinctions. The introduction of free education, which subsequently became a major issue, symbolized the equality of opportunity demanded.[1] They did not reject the institution of private property. What they rejected was the uncontrolled acquisition of such property by one group at the expense of the rest of the population, because this would destroy equality of opportunity.

Those who rejected the case put by this group of critics did not dispute the desirability of an egalitarian society in which opportunities were open to all. What they disputed were the methods by which the critics wished to achieve such a society. They accepted the legitimacy of individual private ownership on a much larger scale than the other group, and therefore the continued existence of economic inequalities between different sections of the community based on property. These differences would be redressed by Government action to redistribute the total wealth of the country, for example by taxation. This second group laid a greater emphasis on private enterprise and the stimulation of individual effort rather than on public enterprise as the basis for economic development. It was essentially their views which were reflected in Sessional Paper No. 10 of 1965.

It is difficult to find neat labels for these two major groupings among the Members of Parliament which adequately express their attitudes and their objectives. During 1965, they were variously described as Socialists and Kenyans; Communists and American stooges; the National group and the Kenya group. The hard-core critics were frequently labelled communists and scientific (as opposed to African) socialists. Some of them referred to themselves as socialists, and labelled their opponents after March 1965 as the 'Corner Bar Group'. In February 1966 they were referred to as the Socialist or Progressive

---

[1] See Ibid., Third Session, Vol. VII, 3 December 1965, for one debate on the issue of free primary education.

Group, and the Left as opposed to Right. The words socialist, communist and capitalist were generally bandied about a great deal over this period. None of these labels accurately reflects the stand taken by each group. They do indicate, however, that whatever other factors help to account for the groupings of 1965, there was an ideological strand to the debate.[1]

The terms that will be used here to describe the two key groups which were party to the policy debate are Radical and Conservative. These terms are not ideal; but keeping their limitations in mind they will serve to distinguish between the two. The hard-core critics were seeking radically to change the structure of the economy overnight. Those who opposed them were prepared essentially to conserve the existing structure, although they saw the need to modify it.

Ever since its formation there had been such a division between members of KANU on questions of both the economic and the political structure of the independent state. On more than one occasion before independence these divisions had nearly split the party; but Kenyatta's leadership and the common desire to win independence had enabled the leaders to paper over the cracks. In the first year of independence the common front had been maintained out of the desire of all groups in the party to establish the Republic and abolish regionalism, both of which objectives required party unity. For the same reason the economic issues had been, during 1964, to a large degree subordinate to the political. The abolition of regionalism in December 1964 meant however that the debate about the country's political structure for the time being was concluded. The question of the relationship between Party and Government, especially in the *de facto* one-party state, remained unanswered. Nevertheless the debate moved back to economic questions, and the earlier divisions within KANU again came to the fore. As this change occurred the Radical Group of the pre-independence period[2] found itself increasingly weaker in numerical strength. The dissolution of KADU had the effect of enlarging the Conservative element within the KANU Parliamentary Group. It also stimulated increased rivalry for leadership, especially of the backbench group which the Radicals had up to that date dominated. As a result, the Conservative element in KANU combined with the former KADU Members to oust their Radical rivals from official positions first in the Backbenchers Group and then in the Parliamentary Group as a whole. By the middle of 1965, as the policy debate sharpened its focus, the Conservatives had gained the

[1] All these labels were used at various times in the debate in Parliament and discussion in the Press over 1965 and 1966. See especially *Official Report*, House of Representatives, First Parliament, Second Session, for the debate of 15 February 1966.
[2] Bennett and Rosberg, op. cit.

54

dominant position within the parliamentary caucus, as the changes in the Parliamentary Group and the Sessional Committee proclaimed.[1] Disagreement on policy was not however the only factor that determined Members' alignment with either the Radical or the Conservative Group. A second and vital consideration was the position adopted by the individual Member towards the continued rivalry for leadership among KANU's leaders. This rivalry did not touch Kenyatta, whose position remained unchallenged; but it made it increasingly difficult for him to impose unity upon his Ministers. Although ministerial disagreements were kept off the floor of the National Assembly itself during 1964 and 1965, increasingly bitter and personal statements were made outside the Chamber. The consequent frictions within the Cabinet also contributed to the alignments within the KANU parliamentary group, and the party itself. More than one backbencher in Parliament placed the responsibility for continued internal party feuding upon Ministers seeking to exploit existing KANU divisions to their own advantage.

This personal rivalry among KANU leaders was a continuation of the earlier rivalries that had bedevilled Kenya politics before independence. The earlier causes of this rivalry persisted. Two new exacerbating factors now appeared. First, the constitutional amendments proposed in 1964 raised the question of the political succession and focused greater attention on Mr Odinga's position. As Vice-President of KANU, with a demonstrable national stature, Odinga stood second only to Kenyatta himself; but his implicit claim to the succession did not go unchallenged by many of his own Cabinet colleagues, as the constitutional restrictions on the position of Vice-President laid down in the December 1964 Republican arrangements made clear. Second, the enlargement of the KANU leadership group that followed the dissolution of KADU served to intensify the contest for power, within the enlarged Cabinet.

Three main strands were woven into the complex relationships that contributed to the continuing rivalry for the intermediary KANU leadership group. These can be categorized as tribal suspicions, the contest between the older generations of politicians, particularly among the Kikuyu, and younger men who had emerged in the later 1950s, and the old contest between Odinga and Mboya.

Tribal attitudes were increasingly characterized by allegations of Kikuyu domination, and a noticeable weakening of the old alliance between Luo and Kikuyu that had formed the original basis of KANU. In this situation the position adopted by the other major tribal groups, particularly Kamba, Luyia and Kalenjin, became of paramount

[1] See above, p. 41.

55

importance; and the manœuvres among KANU leaders reflected renewed attempts to forge useful alliances that would assure them of the support of these ethnic groups. But notwithstanding increased public discussion of tribal political positions in the period under review it was the third strand in KANU relationships, the old rivalry between Mboya and Odinga, which continued to receive most public emphasis; and as a result other divisions were polarized around these two men. Not the least important factor contributing to this polarization was that these two leaders became increasingly linked with the two major policy stands within KANU: Odinga with that of the Radicals, Mboya with that of the Conservatives. The origins of this identification lay in attitudes attributed to them in the years before independence, when Odinga had publicly shown his preferences for the East, and adopted a more populist stand on domestic policies, and Mboya had been associated in people's minds with the West. It was given much sharper focus in 1964 and 1965 as a result of the public stand each adopted in their renewed public debate.

Odinga's public statements in 1964 and 1965 accorded more with the Radicals rather than the Conservatives in the KANU parliamentary caucus. At a Mombasa rally in July 1964, he suggested that the Government should give undeveloped lands to the poor to farm. In September, at Machakos, he attacked Africans who bought large farms. In February 1965, at another Mombasa rally, he announced that the Government would introduce a limit to the amount of land any one man might buy, and in March suggested that European farms and businesses should be bought by companies and co-operatives, rather than individuals, in order to create a classless society. At an April KANU rally at Kimilili (in Western Province) he supported a resolution on nationalization, and in May, on his home ground at Kisumu, announced that Kenya would become a socialist state as soon as possible. All these views accorded with those of the backbench Radicals, who accompanied him on most of these occasions, as did his Cabinet colleague Achieng Oneko. The Radicals, seeking a national figure as leader, found one in Odinga. Those who supported his claim to the succession were bound to support the Radicals. Odinga's leadership of the Radicals was at first implicitly, then explicitly, acknowledged.

None of Odinga's statements necessarily conflicted with broad outlines of Government policy; but they implied a more radical approach particularly on land, than official policy acknowledged, and they brought him increasingly into public conflict with his Cabinet colleagues. His more provocative statements on land early in 1965 were countered, for example, by Mr Gichuru, Minister for Finance, at a May rally in his constituency, with the remark: 'I own my small plot of land and no one will take it away from me.' But Odinga's challenge was taken up first and foremost by Mboya, whose position as Secretary General of KANU enabled him to arrogate to himself the role of major spokesman on KANU party policy. In this capacity he made, during 1965, a series of public statements that clearly and consistently challenged Odinga and the Radicals on the grounds that they had departed from that policy. Furthermore as a senior Member of the Cabinet, and one of the House's most experienced parliamentarians, he regularly turned the tables on the Radicals when Government policies were attacked in the House of Representatives. And as Minister for Economic Planning he guided the Government's Sessional Paper on African Socialism through the Assembly. For all these reasons he emerged as the leading opponent of the Radicals. It was he who most clearly and vigorously enunciated the official Government policy of African Socialism, based upon a mixed economy and with a strong individualism tempered by state control to ensure the fair distribution of wealth and equality of opportunity that the Government promised. He therefore implicitly assumed the role of leading spokesman of the Conservatives. This alignment of Odinga with the Radicals and Mboya with the Conservatives emerged clearly at the end of May 1965, when Odinga, at a major rally in Kisumu, directly attacked his Cabinet colleague, his alleged associations with the West, and his influence on Kenyan policies. This attack, Mboya's reply, and a call for Odinga's resignation from a number of Members of Parliament including several Ministers, put the contest between Mboya and Odinga publicly on to the centre of the political arena, and linked it directly with the policy dispute between Radicals and Conservatives.[1]

In seeking to strengthen their respective positions within the Cabinet both Odinga and Mboya actively campaigned for the support not only of fellow Cabinet Ministers but also of their fellow parliamentarians. Each privately sought to establish a parliamentary following, which would strengthen his position in the Cabinet and also in the party. This campaigning influenced the alignments within the Parliamentary Group; and it became evident that Members of Parliament were grouping themselves, throughout 1965, not only in terms of common policy attitude, but also in terms of their attitudes towards the struggle between the two leaders at the top.

The dialogue between Radicals and Conservatives was essentially a party debate and a battle for the future leadership of KANU. It was conducted within the National Assembly rather than the party

[1] *East African Standard*, 31 May and 2 June 1965. Odinga gives considerable attention to these months in his autobiography.

executive or annual conference because those bodies did not meet. In July 1965 Mwai Kibaki, then Assistant Minister for Economic Planning and Development, referring to the open disagreement among KANU leaders, attributed it to the absence of party organization. In fact the reverse applied; the party lacked an effective country-wide organization because of the leadership conflict, which had affected that organization since its inception. KANU's national executive institutions had remained weak since 1960 because rival leaders had discouraged a strong national organization. The basis of those leaders' authority had at that time been their district support, and strong district leaders had preferred not to have a strong national machine whose existence might enable one leader to gain full control of the party. KANU had become a 'loosely knit organization vigorously resisting any suggestion that one man could impose his leadership'.[1] Although Kenyatta had after his return imposed his leadership on the party this had not led to any significant improvement in its organization. The party remained decentralized with district bosses left in control of their own areas.

This situation continued after independence. No meeting of the National Executive or the Governing Council was called between 1963 and 1966. The central party machine remained weak. The difficulties of organization were increased by the preoccupation of the national leaders with the responsibilities of office; but more important was their continued predilection not to have a strong party machine while doubts remained as to which leader (in Kenyatta's absence) would control it. As a result the party machine scarcely functioned. KANU headquarters in Nairobi remained empty except for the occasional minor official. The telephone was disconnected because the account was not paid. Party finances were said to be in disarray. At district level branches were equally lacking in formal organization, and membership dues were not collected. This remained the position throughout 1965 notwithstanding denials to the contrary.[2]

The only functioning group within KANU was therefore the Parliamentary Group. The Members of Parliament occupied the most

[1] Bennett and Rosberg, op. cit., p. 42.

[2] See the Secretary-General's Report to the Delegates' Conference held in February 1966 at Limuru, Nairobi, 1966 (mimeo). John Okumu, in Charisma and Politics in Kenya, *East African Journal* February 1968, has argued that KANU's organizational weakness was due to Kenyatta's unique position in Kenya politics. Since 'all activities of the political system converged on the President' the party machine was emasculated. Yet this does not necessarily follow, unless Kenyatta himself deliberately rejected the use of the party as a means of communication. If he did so reject it, this provided an additional obstacle to those who wished to make it a viable organization. If he used it, on the other hand, and established such a machine, he had first to settle the disputes in the intermediary level of leadership. This meant taking sides. Yet his role until February 1966 had always been that of mediator.

significant place in any debate between Party and Government. Thus any member of the Cabinet seeking support either for himself or his views was bound to seek to increase his backing among the Members. Furthermore the constitutional provisions for the election of a President gave the Members further power, since it was in effect they, and not the party or the electorate, who elected him. Thus anyone aspiring to the Presidency had also to seek parliamentary support and the Parliamentary Group was therefore an important source of legitimacy.

At the same time the party itself could not be ignored, for notwithstanding its organizational weaknesses, there was still a considerable popular loyalty, throughout the countryside, to KANU as the national movement that had won independence. KANU was not dead, even if it was unorganized. It was living on its past; but the past had endowed it with the aura and reputation of the nationalist movement that was not quickly lost. Furthermore, continued loyalty to the party was ensured by the leadership of Kenyatta, who stood alone as the 'Father of the Nation', as the man above tribal, party and personal conflicts who had won independence for Kenya. Loyalty to KANU was in fact in the immediate post-independence period, to a large degree loyalty to Kenyatta. There was therefore still a very real degree of support for KANU as a movement. The 1965 Senate by-elections provided evidence of this. At that time, in the *de facto* one-party state, no KANU branch was able to prevent independent candidates from standing for elections; and only three out of twelve official candidates won. On the other hand all the Independents stood as KANU Independents, and campaigned on the basis of KANU's manifesto and the KANU Government's record. The low polls in that election suggested public disinterest in elections as well as the absence of any effective party organization; but the voting established the fact that in 1965, to win, a political leader still had to convince the electorate of his association with KANU. A year later, in June 1966, on the eve of the Little General Election, a public opinion poll in Nairobi indicated that there was still a considerable residual loyalty to the party. The majority of the people interviewed indicated that although they would not vote for the same Member of Parliament again, they would still vote for KANU, notwithstanding the party's disarray.[1]

KANU itself therefore remained a significant source of legitimacy; and whoever wished to retain control of the Government could not ignore the party, even if he did not wish it to participate actively in the political process. The assumption on which the parliamentary battle

[1] Marco Surveys (Nairobi). Public Opinion Poll No. 14, 1966. Question 23, p. 39. Information on the 1965 Senate Elections is based on field work carried out by the writer at that time.

for leadership was based was that the man with majority support in the Parliamentary Group could claim the leadership of the party. But this was in turn based on the assumption that the individual Members of Parliament would themselves control their district branches, and through them the choice of party representatives to any national conference at which leaders would be chosen. These two assumptions underlying the debate between Radicals and Conservatives and the contest for leadership of the Parliamentary caucus, drew the party branches into the conflict, as each group sought to establish its ascendancy within them. A crucial precipitating factor in this was Odinga's own position. As he became estranged from his Cabinet colleagues he sought to enlarge his own support at branch level in order to secure a party base that would check opposition to him within the parliamentary caucus. As a result the ministerial conflict was carried into the districts and played out, at district level, in the successive branch elections that took place between 1964 and 1966.

Early in 1964, having announced the need to re-examine and revive the party machine to meet the requirements of the post-independence situation, Mboya, in his capacity as Secretary General, held a series of reorganization conferences at regional level. But reorganization went no further than holding branch elections. After the dissolution of KADU a second round of elections was held, concentrated this time upon the former KADU-dominated Provinces, to integrate KADU and KANU branches, as the necessary preliminary to the national delegates conferences for which there was by that time considerable demand. These elections were in most cases carried out without incident; but in a number of branches, and particular South Nyanza, Muranga, Kitui, Machakos, Nakuru and Mombasa, they were the source of bitter dissension, intense rivalry, and a considerable degree of confusion resulting from the refusal of one or another group to accept defeat. It was on these contested results that attention focused.

In a large number of KANU branches local control was clearly divided between rival groups, neither of which could oust the other completely from power. Much of this rivalry had existed in the pre-independence situation. After independence, however, additional sources of conflict, not all present in the same branch, emerged. First was the straightforward struggle for leadership between the elected Members of Parliament whose constituencies were in the same district and who were therefore members of the same branch. Second was the contest for local branch control between the elected Members of Parliament and locally-based branch officials, many of whom quickly grew dissatisfied with the former, and began to think in terms of contesting future elections themselves. Third, branch officials were in some cases challenged by newcomers to the political scene who sought position within the party. Fourth, in the former KADU strongholds, former KADU leaders now within KANU sought to preserve their leadership by taking over from the former KANU officials. One or another of these different types of contest for district leadership was at the root of the divisions manifested in 1964 and 1965.

In such situations there was ample opportunity for anyone seeking to establish influence in a particular district to use a local conflict to his own advantage. Not surprisingly, therefore, spokesmen for the various groupings alleged repeatedly during 1965 that national leaders were exploiting local conflicts to establish a dominant position for themselves in a particular branch. The evidence of such interference is largely circumstantial such as visits of national leaders to districts, and known associations between these leaders and particular local groups. It cannot, however, be discounted; nor can the subsequent events and the explicit alignments between particular branch leaders and members of the Cabinet. The pattern that emerged is reasonably clear. The groupings within the Cabinet influenced the groupings within the National Assembly. These in turn were paralleled at local level by groupings within the branch leadership that were determined by the association of branch officials with one or other of the national leadership groups. In South Nyanza the intense conflict within the branch resulted from the conflict among the South Nyanza Members of Parliament for control of that branch; and the groupings among these members were the result of their association with either Mboya or Odinga.[1] In Muranga the openly acknowledged conflict between Mr Kaggia and Dr Kiano, each claiming to be the branch chairman, reflected their conflict at the national level. In both Kitui and Machakos, where two KANU branches existed side by side (known as KANU A and KANU B) the divisions followed the former divisions between KANU and APP, and so were linked with the question of Ngei's leadership of the district, and therefore (because of their association) with Odinga. In the Western Province the conflict for the leadership of the Luyia people was seen to be linked, through the major participants, Otiende and Muliro, with the parliamentary conflict. In Mombasa the leading contestants in a complicated party conflict founded both on ethnic groupings and the old KANU–KADU rivalry, were associated, through the Members of Parliament, with the parliamentary groupings behind Odinga and Mboya. These party divisions at district level, and the resulting contests for control, were

[1] See *Official Report*, House of Representatives, First Parliament, Second Session, Vol. 4, 23 June 1965, cols 714–24 for Adjournment Motion on Party affairs in South Nyanza. Also ibid., Fourth Session, Vol. X, Part I, 7 October 1966, col. 572–5 for Mr Odero-Jowi's statement on Mr Odinga's activities in South Nyanza.

all directly connected with the continued battle of the national leaders for ascendancy at the centre; and therefore with the division within the parliamentary caucus between Radicals and Conservatives.

During this struggle both sides repeatedly alleged that their opponents were buying support, liberally distributing money (acquired from foreign sources) to influence elections. The Radicals were alleged to receive funds from Eastern, Communist sources; the Conservatives from the United States. Allegations of this kind were by no means new. The question of the use of money in Kenya politics had been raised at least as early as the 1961 elections. In 1965, as in 1961, it was still extremely difficult to prove or disprove such allegations, except with purely circumstantial evidence. Certain other features of this branch conflict can be established. Firstly, the outcome of branch elections for office was not necessarily an indication of popular attitudes within the district, for few of the groups involved in the leadership conflict had very much of an organized mass following at that level. The absence of any effective party machine at branch or lower level was also a serious obstacle to popular participation in such elections. It made it relatively simple, on the other hand, for a small group to monopolize the branch and branch elections.

Secondly, the concept of the district boss still played an important part in district politics, even where individual district bosses were themselves being challenged. In the Rift Valley, therefore, Arap Moi's influence, and on the Coast Ngala's, remained a significant factor in determining local/central alignments, notwithstanding the local challenge to their leadership that each of them faced. Conversely, the absence of one single, undisputed leader of the Luyia people of Western Province, made it extremely difficult for any one national leader to dominate that area.

Thirdly, as a result of this leadership contest, something of a new and perhaps more genuinely nation-wide organizational network was being set up. Branches lost some of their earlier independence of action as a result both of their association with one or other of the national leaders, and also of the direct intervention into branches outside their own home district by the key national political figures. Whether or not they were setting up factions rather than party followings, Mboya and Odinga were both laying the foundations of country-wide organizations which were none the less important because they were in effect personal rather than party machines.

Fourthly, there was a group of branch officials who were prepared to challenge the Government and Government policies independently of the Members of Parliament and the parliamentary caucus. This group wanted a more active role for the party and a clearer definition of the relationship between party and Government in the *de facto* one-party state than anyone had hitherto given. They also wanted more extensive nationalization and greater immediate participation by Africans in the modern economy. It might perhaps have been expected that young branch leaders would be more radical than those in power so far as their ideas of development were concerned. They were closer to the ordinary people than a majority of Members of Parliament or Government officers, and therefore more responsive perhaps to local grievances and the need for more radical immediate solutions. On the other hand, the available evidence suggests that these branch officials were influenced not so much by an awareness of local grievances as by their associations with Odinga and the more radical element in KANU, as well as visits, in some cases, to Eastern countries. Some of them appeared to stand further to the left in their thinking than the Radicals. Nevertheless, they constituted a natural ally for that Radical element within Parliament and so provided non-parliamentary support that could be used by the Radicals in their attempts to gain control of the party.

In 1964 this group of branch Radicals had no organization within which they could successfully present a common front to influence Government or party. While the central party institutions remained inactive, their scope for action at the national level was limited; and for this, among other reasons, they vigorously demanded a party revival. Early in 1965, however, their position changed, when they found themselves brought together at the Lumumba Institute for a course in party management and organization for officials from all KANU branches.

The Lumumba Institute was opened by the President without any prior publicity, at the Republic celebrations in December 1964. Intended primarily as an institute for training party officers, its founders were Kenyatta and Odinga, and the Chairman of the Board of Management, Mr Kaggia. Financed largely with Russian funds, and with two much-discussed Russian lecturers on its staff, the Institute appeared to be heavily biased in favour of the Radical group in KANU, who dominated the Board of Management and the general course activities. Mboya was noticeably not involved in it at all.[1]

The first (and in the event the only) course ran from March to June 1965. During this period, not only was the Lumumba Institute used as a platform by Radical Members of Parliament to publicize their views; but a section of the students also set themselves up as a pressure group demanding from Government both radical policy changes and party reforms. The highlights of this student activity included their press announcement that they intended to use their prerogative under

[1] See *East African Standard*, 14 December 1964, and 23 March 1965.

the party constitution to call a national delegates conference;[1] their rejection of Sessional Paper No. 10 because it did not fully accord with 'scientific socialism',[2] and, in July, an abortive attempt to take over KANU headquarters in Nairobi and put their own nominees into national office.[3] Long before this last event, however, the Conservative group had raised the question of the Lumumba Institute and its activities in Parliament; and a private member's motion at the end of April urging the Government to take over the Institute, although tactfully amended by the Minister for Education, had been passed.[4] The Institute subsequently ceased to function.

The critics of the Institute drew attention to its allegedly one-sided interpretation of policy and events, and insisted that it was a source of friction between the party and the Government. The President's original intentions for an institute to train party workers were, it was claimed, being distorted, and the students trained to feel that they were 'a class apart', a special group within the party. A number of Members of Parliament were obviously frightened by the presence of Russians, and the possibility of their influence leading to increased left-wing tendencies within the party. Whatever the ideological basis of the instruction the students received, the root of the Conservative fears expressed about the Institute lay in their awareness of the extent to which it offered the students an opportunity to establish a united front, and the potential advantage it therefore offered the Radical group in the party and Parliament.

The debate on the Lumumba Institute was not the first occasion on which fears of communism and communist subversion had been expressed by Members of Parliament. Much of the debate between the Radicals and the Conservatives had from the outset been couched in ideological slogans. During the debate on the Foreign Investment Protection Bill in October, 1964, (which protected and thus explicitly accepted foreign investment) Dr Kiano, then Minister for Commerce and Industry, had complained, 'Whenever a Member stood to support the Bill he was called a capitalist, and he who opposed it is a socialist. I would like to remove the debate away from these two phrases socialism and capitalism because all these words have done is to create bad feeling about individual Members.' While Mr Kaggia could allege 'We are not socialist because we are dominated by Western capitalist investors', Mr Odero-Jowi could answer 'what is the opposite of Capitalists? Communists. Maybe these people who are shouting

[1] *East African Standard*, 22 June 1965.
[2] *Daily Nation*, 30 April 1965.
[3] *East African Standard*, 8 July 1965.
[4] *Official Report*, House of Representatives, First Parliament, Second Session, Vol. IV, 30 April 1965, cols. 1725–60.

are also advocating the interests of Communists. We are talking of our people and not for the capitalists and definitely not for the Communists.'[1]

Such use of ideological slogans continued, both in and out of Parliament, in the eighteen months that followed. In the debate between Conservatives and Radicals, Odinga and his Radical supporters were labelled as communists, and implicitly therefore disloyal to the state. They, in turn, labelled their opponents capitalists. Much of this exchange was part of the tactics used by each side to discredit the other. In view of their known past associations it was not difficult for their respective critics to attack Mboya as a 'capitalist' and 'pro-West', or Odinga as 'communist' and 'pro-East'.[2] Odinga's statements about communism throughout this period were moreover essentially provocative. On the other hand, the debate suggested such an intense preoccupation with the idea of communist subversion in Kenya, unparalleled for example in Kenya's neighbours, that it is necessary to ask whether it was anything more than tactics. The evidence suggests that the tactical use of communism to discredit the Radicals reflected certain genuine fears of communism and an ideological side to the debate none the less genuine though it was based on a considerable confusion of ideas. The debate on the merits of capitalism and socialism confused the economic, political and social issues at stake; but at the same time it revealed that the fears expressed about communism were by no means entirely insincere.

Talk of communism was no new element in Kenyan politics. After the Second World War there had been lively talk among certain sectors of the European community, both official and unofficial, of the possibility of communist interference in domestic politics.[3] The subject had been raised twice in the Legislative Council in the 1950s, and implicitly in many European eyes the African political leadership that had emerged at that time had been associated with communist as opposed to Western ideas.[4]

[1] Ibid., Second Session, Vol. IV, Part III, 7 October 1964 and 21 October 1964, for the full debate.

[2] See Rosberg and Bennett, op. cit., p. 129, for a discussion of this. Also *Manchester Guardian*, 12 June 1961. In 1961 conflict between Mboya and Odinga had at one stage taken exactly this form, when each had used against the other an incident concerning certain allegedly forged telegrams concerning the stockpiling by Britain of nuclear weapons near Nairobi. Odinga had implicitly alleged Mboya's duplicity with Gichuru, in a plot with the British to keep himself and Kenyatta out of office. Mboya in turn had implied Odinga's involvement in communist intrigue.

[3] Sir Philip Mitchell, when Governor, had conceived of his agrarian and other economic reforms largely as a means of establishing a stable class that would act as a counter-balance to any communist infiltration.

[4] Report of the Proceedings of the Legislative Council, Vol. LXVII, Tenth Council, Fifth Session, Second and Third meetings, 6 March 1956, col. 394 and Vol. LXIX.

The influence after independence of a large European community in the country, many of them disposed still to think in the same way, cannot be dismissed lightly as the possible explanation of Governmental fears of subversion. The Radicals charged with communist leanings certainly attributed the charges to European, Western influence, brought home through Western diplomats in true neo-colonialist style.[1] Kaggia put it very bluntly:

There was a story among Europeans; they used to call us all Communists, those who were fighting for the wishes of the people. I used to be termed one of them, our President used to be called one. We would like to know, to see who these Communists are in this country. If it means those who are fighting for the wishes of the people then I would like to be told.[2]

'Communist' he insisted was merely a label for a 'true nationalist', who was fighting for the people, and who thus in 1965 was bound to challenge Government policy if it did not accord with the interests of the people as opposed to those of a particular group. Outside Parliament a leading Trade Unionist, Dennis Akumu, then General Secretary of the Dock-workers' Union, took the same line when he challenged the 'wild allegations' about communism as a bogy to scare workers from demanding the nationalization of large firms and a more equitable distribution of wealth.

Other factors also have to be taken into account. To understand the emphasis placed on the danger of communism (as opposed to any other ideology) it is necessary to consider not only the influence of foreigners, but the attitudes and ideas of a section of the African population concerning property.

Over the previous fifteen years, the agrarian revolution described earlier in this chapter had greatly strengthened the idea of individual ownership of land, not only in the Central Province, but in other areas (notably certain Kalenjin groups) where there had been extensive enclosure or consolidation of land. This had strengthened the concept of private property and reinforced existing attitudes towards the ownership of land. The entry of a growing number of Africans into the commercial sector of the economy was likely to reinforce such views. In the minds of many Members of Parliament and other articulate sections of the political community, there was clearly a crude equation between communism (or socialism) and nationalization and

[1] An allegation that to many seemed to come home to roost when the former American Ambassador to Kenya, William Attwood, published his book, *The Reds and the Blacks*.
[2] This argument came out very strongly during the Budget debate in June 1965, which was probably the peak of the political crisis period, when allegations and counter allegations were at their strongest. See *Official Report*, House of Representatives, First Parliament, Second Session, Vol. V, June 1965, *passim*.

the state ownership of property. Communism was therefore a challenge to their interests. Any defence of nationalization was interpreted by this group as a defence of communism, and therefore a challenge to the ownership of property. It is not insignificant that whereas the debate on communism in 1958 had emphasized the dangers of the totalitarian organization of communist society, the debate in 1965 focused primarily on communist economic policies and the rejection of private ownership. Property raised the question of land; and land was still the fundamental political question in Kenya. The fears of a communist danger could not have been unrelated to fears of loss of land stimulated in this way.

For some, if not all, of the Conservative group the fear of communism was influenced not only by ideas on ownership, but also by its association with the forcible overthrow of government and the acceptance of the legitimacy of the use of force. Two factors help to explain the noticeable preoccupation with the possibility of subversion and violence in 1964 and 1965. First, Kenyan politics has a tradition of violence that has not been forgotten. Second, a succession of events after independence emphasized the fragility of the new state.

The Army Mutiny of January 1964 was quickly overcome but not quickly forgotten. The border dispute in the North Eastern Province after independence rapidly became a running sore. In Central Province serious difficulties were encountered before the last of the freedom fighters and their leaders were forced out of the forest. Rumours of oathing and of a new secret society in the Province added to the sense of a security risk. The threat of violence was highlighted in another way in February 1965, when a Specially Elected Member of Parliament, Pio Pinto, who had long been associated with the nationalist movement, and was identified with the Radical Wing of KANU, was murdered in Nairobi.[1]

Politics were as a result conducted during 1964 and 1965 in an atmosphere of apparent political crisis engendered by these and other events. This encouraged the suspicion that there existed in the country a group of people prepared to use force to overthrow the Government. The association of these suspicions with fears of communist interference was due not least to a succession of events and rumours which specifically implied communist backing for such a group. An anonymous letter circulated to Members of Parliament at the time of Pinto's death alleged communist complicity in the murder. Members immediately took fright. In April the magazine *Revolution in Africa*

[1] *East African Standard*, 15 February 1965 and 2 March 1965. Also *Official Report*, House of Representatives, First Parliament, Second Session, Vol. IV, 2 March 1965, cols. 423–8.

appeared in Nairobi, prophesying revolution. The Government promptly banned the publication. In June Mr Chou En Lai, visiting Dar es Salaam, remarked in a speech that Africa was ripe for revolution, a statement to which the Kenya Government took strong exception. Earlier, in March, over the Easter weekend, Nairobi had been alive with rumours of an impending *coup*, and of the existence of a cache of arms in a Government office that were allegedly to be used for that purpose. So strong were these rumours that the Minister for Defence felt compelled to hold a press conference to assert that the Government was in no danger; but the subsequent events surrounding a mysterious shipload of arms from Russia convinced many people that such a danger had existed. The discovery in late May of a consignment of arms at Kisii was further proof for many people that a subversive group existed in the country. These arms were in fact the property of the Uganda Government which had been re-routed through Kenya, without the Kenya Government's prior knowledge. The local reaction was nevertheless one of intense suspicion that they had been intended for the subversion of Kenya.[1]

Whatever the truth behind this sequence of unexplained events, they undoubtedly helped at the time to create the atmosphere of crisis that permeated Kenya politics for several months in 1965, and prompted many leaders to see a communist danger in Kenya. Odinga's known associations with Eastern countries readily explained the ease with which many associated him with these events.

Denying these charges of communism the Radicals asserted, both in Parliament and at public rallies, that their views on land and nationalization represented the true KANU policy. They claimed, therefore, to be the true nationalists, a claim carried on to the floor of the House in March 1965 when Anyieni, a leading Radical backbencher, defended Mr Odinga by saying:

Those members who spoke at Kisumu spoke the truth, the true policy of the party. But, Mr Speaker, sir, what has been difficult is that Government has been unable to fulfil some of these promises. . . . We would like to say here again that those people who are trying to accumulate a lot of wealth and are going around the country shouting out 'Communism', 'Communism', must know that we are not interested in any isms; what we are interested in is the set up which will be for the interests of the majority of the people of this country.[2]

This was a strong weapon with which to attack Government policies at a time when many people in the countryside were beginning to ask

[1] *East African Standard*, 1 April 1965.
[2] *Official Report*, House of Representatives, First Parliament, Second Session, Vol. IV, 5 March 1965.

what benefits independence had brought them. In its attempt to prevent the Radicals exploiting this claim further, the Government produced a new statement of policy to which the former could not object, but which explicitly rejected their more radical demands. This statement, Sessional Paper No. 10 of 1965, defined African socialism in terms to which the Radicals could not logically take exception, although it explicitly rejected expropriation of property and full nationalization of the means of production.[1] The party and Government view was therefore explicitly aligned with the more moderate policies of the Conservatives in Parliament. Having achieved acquiescence in this definition, the Government was able subsequently to label those KANU members who continued to adopt a more radical stand on land and nationalization as dissenting from the party view.

The Conservatives at the same time set out to establish in the minds of the public the notion that the ideas of the Radicals were a denial of party policy, and would endanger the right of the individual to the possession and use of land. The accusation of communism was used, in an attempt to turn the strong attachment of Africans to the land against their Radical rivals. These tactics were first used in the 1965 Senate by-elections, which were essentially a contest between Radical and Conservative wings in KANU for popular support. During these by-elections several candidates sought to associate communism in the public mind with a challenge to property and so to arouse fears of their opponents who belonged to the Radical group. The Kitui official KANU candidate's manifesto, for example, read 'Reject he who brings Communism to Kenya, Communism means shambas and all possessions belong to the Government. Wives are communal, the Government takes the children after birth.' His opponent ignored the challenge, based his campaign on the KANU Manifesto, called himself the KANU Independent, and won the election, primarily because he was the more popular man. In the Embu campaign attempts to discredit one of the candidates by publicizing his association with Eastern countries, especially China, equally failed to arouse any response; the candidate won, primarily because his organization was better than that of either of his two opponents. In 1965, therefore, it seemed that a majority of the people in the countryside were not greatly concerned by the threat of communism as such. The threat of communism and the fear of subversion in Kenya was felt, at that time, primarily by the political leaders and not their followers.

In the early months of 1965 the Radicals in Parliament had a number of successes to their credit. In the country at large Odinga and his

[1] Sessional Paper No. 10, *African Socialism and its Application to Planning in Kenya*, May 1965. Nairobi: Government Printer.

associates had held a series of successful meetings publicizing their views, and they interpreted the Senate by-election results as a sign of popular backing for themselves. By that date, recurrent crises and the attempted nomination by the Radicals of two of Odinga's known associates to fill the murdered Pio Pinto's seat in Parliament and the Central Legislative Assembly, provoked the Conservatives into action; their backbenchers organized to secure the election of their own nominees to office. This marked the beginning of the rising dominance of the Conservatives first in the backbenches, then in the Parliamentary Group, and then in the House. Changes in the composition of the Sessional Committee made in July, and changes of the Whips, marked their victory.[1] Whether or not they organized in the 'Corner Bar',[2] those who opposed the Radicals were from that date referred to in these terms. But the whereabouts of their meeting place was irrelevant. Membership was clearly determined by opposition to the more radical policies then expounded about land and nationalization combined with opposition to Odinga's leadership. The Radicals' failure in November to regain control of the Sessional Committee demonstrated their weaker parliamentary position.[3] Nevertheless they had not been defeated in all party branches, as the continued dissension in Nyanza and Machakos indicated. And they began publicly to press home allegations of the emergence of a new propertied class which, having established itself in power, did not intend to benefit the ordinary man.

Up to the end of 1965 the Cabinet had remained intact. Subsequent events suggested that by the end of the year a decision had been made to force the Radicals to retreat or withdraw from the party. An open Cabinet split was finally precipitated by a Government motion moved in the House by Mboya in February 1966 which, reiterating confidence in Mr Kenyatta and his Government, specifically asserted and deplored the existence of groupings among Members of Parliament. Insisting that he had no prior knowledge of it, and that it could not therefore be a Government motion, Odinga left the House in protest. The conflict between the Ministers was thus brought on to the floor of the House. The wording of the motion had the effect, moreover, of

---

[1] See above, p. 41.

[2] The 'Corner Bar Group' was the label attached to those who opposed Odinga and the Radicals; the group was said to have first begun to organize from that particular bar in Nairobi. *East African Standard*, 1 April 1965.

In March 1965 a cyclostyled document purporting to be a record of the first such Corner Bar meeting was circulated to Members of Parliament. It is printed in Odinga, *Not Yet Uhuru*, p. 289. Since its authenticity cannot be established it is of doubtful value as evidence, although it is an indicator.

[3] *Official Report*, House of Representatives, First Parliament, Third Session, Vol. VII, 4 November 1965, cols. 88 to 132.

turning the issue into one of confidence in the President personally; and although it was passed unanimously (after a rowdy, intense, heated debate in which seven Members were removed from the Chamber for misconduct) the policy and personal conflicts that it highlighted could subsequently be interpreted in terms of loyalty to President Kenyatta. The debate between Radicals and Conservatives had been given an added dimension.[1]

The Radicals expressed their confidence in the President and evaded the challenge to resign. Nevertheless, Mr Odinga's withdrawal from the debate, the Radicals' unsuccessful bid to amend the motion, and the clashes that took place between several Ministers, combined with the substance of the motion passed, manœuvred them on to the defensive and established beyond doubt that the Conservatives were in control in Parliament.

The debate proved to be a dress rehearsal for a full scale KANU conference, at which the Conservatives established their ascendancy in the party hierarchy as well. Up to the beginning of 1966 branch elections were still being contested in certain key branches, including Nyanza, Muranga and Machakos. Nevertheless, on 27 February Mboya announced that a KANU Delegates' Conference would be held on 12 and 13 March at which President Kenyatta would outline new plans for the party and introduce a new constitution.[2] This proposal was strongly opposed by Trade Unionist and Parliamentary Radicals, as well as others known to be associated with them and with Odinga, on the grounds that it was unconstitutional (the requisite number of days' notice not having been given) and that the proposed amendments were nothing more than a move by Mr Mboya to evict Mr Odinga from the party. Mr Odinga's attitude was made clear in a Press conference held on the 9th when he alleged 'rough treatment' at the hands of his Cabinet colleagues. Notwithstanding a petition to the President against the conference from fifty-two Members of Parliament (which suggested that the Radicals had considerable potential support) a majority of the Parliamentary Group approved the conference. This was regarded by Party leaders as a sufficient sanction for the delegates' meeting to take place. The delegates met at Limuru on 12 and 13 March, adopted the new constitution and elected new office bearers.

The major changes effected by the new constitution were of political rather than administrative significance. First, the post of National Vice-President was abolished, and eight provincial Vice-Presidents, one for each Province and one for Nairobi, established instead. These

---

[1] Ibid., Third Session, Vol. VIII, 15 February 1966, cols. 913–1020.
[2] *East African Standard*, 28 February 1968.

Vice-Presidents, while elected by the party conference, were to be responsible directly to the President. They thus provided a new, direct link between the centre and the districts. Second, it was agreed that the national party posts need no longer be filled by full-time appointees. In future the national office bearers, elected by the party conference, would be part-time, assisted by full-time party employees, to be appointed by the National Executive Committee.

The changes in the party leadership were crucial. Odinga, whose former position as national Vice-President was abolished, was not elected to any other party office. All those known or thought to be associated with him and the Radical group also failed to win re-election. All the new party officials were known to be associated with the opposition to Mr Odinga. The Conservatives thus captured the Party organization as they had the Parliamentary Group. In the process Kenyatta himself tacitly entered the arena on the side of the Conservatives, by his decision to hold the Convention.

3

The Little
General Election
1966

The Limuru conference not only gave the Conservatives control of
KANU; it led directly to the end of the *de facto* one-party state. A
month after the conference Odinga resigned from both the Government and KANU and, taking a small core of supporters with him,
crossed the floor. Constitutional changes made immediately after his
resignation from the party forced him and those Members of Parliament who went with him to resign from Parliament and seek re-election.
Thirty House of Representative and Senate constituencies were, as a
result, involved in a 'little general election' in the middle of 1966. Thus
the intra-party debate that had divided KANU for the previous
eighteen months was deliberately referred to the wider arena of the
electorate. This chapter considers the manner in which that debate
took place in this wider setting.

Odinga's resignation on 14 April[1] led directly to the re-establishment
of a parliamentary opposition. Thirty other Members, including two
Ministers (Achieng Oneko, Minister for Information, Broadcasting
and Tourism and Okelo Odongo, Assistant Minister for Finance)
followed him. Under his leadership, with Kaggia as his deputy, on
22 April they requested recognition from the Speaker as the Official
Opposition. (Though before Parliament was recalled on the 28th a
number defected back to KANU, so that the group recognized as the
Parliamentary Opposition that afternoon was only thirteen strong.[2]
At the same time Odinga was invited to assume the leadership of a
recently formed, but as yet unregistered political party, the Kenya

[1] *East African Standard*, 15 April 1966.
[2] These resignations were spread over a period of ten days. One other Assistant
Minister, Dr Waiyaki, who had been Assistant Minister in the Vice-President's Office,
also resigned from the Government in protest at the conduct of the Limuru Conference
but did not leave KANU. He remained in the House of Representatives as a KANU
backbencher. Of those who resigned ten were Senators. The Kenya Press carried full
reports of events over this period. See especially the *East African Standard* of 18 and
20 April for resignation statements and KANU replies.

People's Union (KPU). When he accepted that office the parliamentary opposition group acquired a party and the Kenya People's Union became the formal parliamentary Opposition. The two-party system was thus restored.[1]

In the process of the establishment of the new party it was acknowledged explicitly to be the outcome of the long struggle for power within KANU. The new party brought together all the threads of the internal party debate of the previous months. There was first the personal element. Odinga's resignation statement appealed to the public for support against the treatment he had received at the hands of his Cabinet colleagues, and interpreted the events of the past eighteen months as a neo-colonialist-inspired conspiracy to force him out of the Government because of his views on policy. He had resigned, he stated, because he no longer believed that he could correct the situation from inside the Government, controlled as it was by the foreign press and 'underground masters'. He was joined in these criticisms by those who had originally formed the KPU; and by old associates in the Trade Unions as well as the Members of Parliament who had supported his resignation. Clearly the new party was, so far as its personnel was concerned, a demonstration of support for Odinga.

At the same time those who resigned with Odinga emphasized the influence upon their decision of their long-standing disagreements with KANU colleagues over policy. The Government had, they alleged, as a result of foreign influence over the party, the Cabinet and the economy moved increasingly away from the people. This, they said, was demonstrated by its deviation from the promises of the 1963 KANU manifesto. Free education had not been introduced. Employment opportunities had not expanded. Land was being bought by the rich instead of given to the poor. Kenya had as a consequence remained a capitalist country in which the promise to build a society free from economic exploitation and characterized by social equality had become meaningless. The Limuru Conference, in precipitating their resignation at that particular moment, had in fact only brought to a head a situation that had existed for some time.[2]

The parliamentary and party record suggested that there were three

---

[1] *Official Report*, House of Representatives, first Parliament, Third Session, Vol. VIII, 28 April 1966, col. 1994. The Kenya People's Union had applied for registration immediately after the Limuru Conference; and although at that date no Members of Parliament were openly associated with it, it was undoubtedly the Radicals' immediate reaction to the results of that conference, and their first counter move to their removal from KANU office. The party was registered on 20 May. See *East African Standard*, 16 March and 27 April 1966.

[2] None of the thirty Members who resigned referred directly to Odinga in their statements, but laid the emphasis upon their disagreement with the direction of Government policy.

74

groupings within the new Opposition party. First there were those whose critical attitudes towards the Government had been dictated primarily by local or personal factors and who left KANU out of a sense of grievance and perhaps a desire to be on what might be the winning side. (It was this group who attempted to return to KANU.) They all represented economically backward areas and were strongly influenced by the slow development of their districts. The deep sense of embitterment that Mr Khalif (Wajir North) felt at the treatment of the people in the North Eastern Province, must have been an important influence, for example, leading to his decision to cross the floor. This group had no strong personal loyalty to Odinga and, it appeared, no deep ideological convictions. Second were those Luo Members from Central Nyanza who for personal and ethnic considerations had to move with Odinga as the dominant leader in Nyanza.[1]

Third, there were those who had always been identified with the more radical wing in KANU and who had since independence consistently voted against the Government on issues of economic and foreign policy. This third group included men of the older generation like Oneko, Kaggia and Kali, who had learned their politics in KAU and in detention.[2] It also included some of the next generation of younger politicians, such as Anyieni, Gichoya, and Okelo-Odingo all of whom had studied abroad before entering politics in the early sixties. All of them had been associated before independence with the 'ginger group' in KANU, which had represented 'a collection of uncompromising nationalists who refused to accept any necessity for moderation'.[3] They all therefore stood in the radical tradition that had existed within KANU since its formation. The charges that they brought against the Government at this date echoed that tradition. Some of this group, particularly the Luo members, had always been close to Odinga; some of them, seeking a leader who voiced their radicalism, became so. Their past record of radical dissent was as much a reason for the new party as personal loyalty to him.

Their resignation from KANU indicated one fundamental change in the position of the third group. This was on the question of leadership. In the past their loyalty to Kenyatta had been enough to prevent their departure from KANU. During the debates of 1965 their objective had been to change the party's intermediary leadership, not to

[1] Not all the Central Nyanza Members resigned with Odinga. Jamal (Kisumu Town), Argwings-Kodhek (Gem) and Oselu-Nyalick (Winam) remained in KANU. All three had previously been associated with Odinga, Argwings-Kodhek closely. Their decision to remain with the Government meant they now joined the Nyanza opposition to Odinga, which is discussed below in Chapter 4.

[2] Rosberg and Nottingham, op. cit., *passim* and Bennett and Rosberg, op. cit., *passim*.

[3] Ibid., p. 129. *Official Report*, House of Representatives, First Parliament, Third Session, Vol. VIII, 15 February 1966, cols. 974–84.

unseat Kenyatta himself. In resigning they still avoided criticism of Kenyatta. They did not place the responsibility for events upon him, but upon those around him. They attacked his advisers, particularly Mboya, as the architect of the Limuru conference. They were dismayed that they now had to oppose the man whom they regarded as the founder of Kenyan nationalism, and with whom some of them had spent years in detention. Their departure from KANU was a clear indication that personal loyalty to him was no longer a sufficiently binding force to keep them in the party. They now accepted an alternative political leadership for the country.

The new Opposition, recognized on 28 April, was allowed to occupy that position for only one day. On the same afternoon that they took their seats on the Opposition benches the Government introduced a new constitutional amendment as a result of which they were forced to resign and seek re-election.[1] This amendment laid down that any Member of Parliament who resigned from the party that had supported him at his election, but which had not subsequently been dissolved, must also resign his parliamentary seat and (if he wished to retain it) fight a by-election. It was justified in the debate that took place on 28 April in terms of the concept of representation in the democratic state and of parliamentary supremacy. Mboya, as the major spokesman for the Government, argued that the amendment was an essential protection for the people in the exercise of their democratic right to vote. The Member of Parliament was a representative, not a delegate, and therefore should both lead his people and, in certain situations, initiate policy. At the same time, if Parliament was to be the mouthpiece and the instrument of the people, the Member must reflect the views of his constituents. The Government was required constitutionally to have a majority in the House of Representatives, on the assumption that if they enjoyed such a majority they also enjoyed the confidence of a majority in the country. By the same token the individual Member of Parliament must have the support of the people. Mboya argued that this support was given to the individual Member on the basis of his party affiliation. It therefore followed, in his opinion, that resignation from the party that had elected him must be interpreted as a departure from a Member's original position and implied the withdrawal of constituency support. He was no longer a representative. In other democratic countries, he argued, a Member of

[1] Act No. 17 of 1966, Constitution of Kenya (Amendment) (No. 2) Act 1966. The debate on the amendment is in *Official Report*, House of Representatives, First Parliament, Third Session, Vol. VIII, 28 April 1966, cols. 1994–2122. The Act required that the Member must resign at the end of the parliamentary session then in progress. Parliament was in fact adjourned the following day, 29 April, see ibid., 29 April 1966, cols. 2137–68.

Parliament would under such circumstances consult his constituency committee and, if his actions did not meet with their approval, resign. The KPU Members had failed to recognize an established convention on which parliamentary democracy depended. The Government therefore had to force them to respect such practices in order to allow the people to make the decision and to 'declare their verdict on current events and the current confusion can be cleared up. Only in this way moreover, could the contract between voter and Member established through an election be honoured.

The Opposition challenged this on principle. They argued that the amendment protected not the voters but one section of the Government, by removing Opposition Members from office. It was an intimidating measure designed to prevent further resignations that might endanger the Government itself. They also rejected it on the grounds that it infringed, rather than protected, the individual's fundamental right of choice because it dismissed elected Members without reference to their electorate. Kaggia did not fail to point out that the President had refused to dismiss him a year before when one faction in Murang'a had sought his removal. They agreed that an election established a contract between the Member of Parliament and his constituents, but insisted that the mandate thus given to a Member was given to the individual and not to the party. They also agreed that broken pledges constituted a break in the mandate, but argued that it was KANU, not they, who had retreated from the pledges of 1963; therefore it was for KANU to resign. They did not reject the concept of the Member of Parliament as the link between people and Government. They rejected the claim that the party was the necessary basis of representation, on the grounds that the electorate voted for the individual rather than the party.

The men who argued this case were those who had in the past been the strongest advocates of the party as the link between the Government and the governed.[1] One of the complaints that Kaggia and the other Radicals had made consistently since independence was that the KANU Executive had emasculated KANU, and refused to accord the party its proper place in the political system. Their apparent change of emphasis at this time was not necessarily surprising for the debate was now not about representation but about party discipline. It arose logically out of the importance Parliament had assumed as the KANU party forum. Just as in 1964 and 1965 the Radicals in KANU had tried to use the Parliamentary Group to control the Government, so in 1966 the Government in turn used Parliament to control the party critics. The KPU's argument that the amendment was an act to intimidate

[1] See, for example, *Not Yet Uhuru*, pp. 269–72.

KANU Members who would otherwise have joined them ignored the fact that it had been introduced only after their resignations had been given and accepted. On the other hand it could be argued that all fifty-two Members who had petitioned the President to postpone the Limuru conference[1] might have been expected, in the event of renewed conflict within KANU, to resign. This assumed greater significance in the light of existing constitutional provisions for a vote of no confidence in the Government. Under these circumstances the constitutional amendment might be interpreted as a potential disciplinary measure which increased the control of the Executive over its party supporters in the legislature. It introduced a formal sanction against recalcitrant party members that had not hitherto existed, by amending not the party but the parliamentary rules of the game. In this way the Government dealt with what was essentially an internal party problem by defining more precisely the constitutional relationship between legislature and executive.

The amendment, passed after a vigorous and heated debate, immediately affected not KANU Members but the new KPU Opposition, all of whom were as a consequence required to resign. The little general election followed in June 1966.

Thirty Members crossed the floor (one a Specially Elected Member); but it was not immediately clear whether all of them would have to contest an election. When thirteen defected back to KANU there was some doubt as to whether the Government would insist upon their resignations from Parliament. After some initial hesitation KANU rejected their appeal to be taken back and they had to resign and seek election, which they did on a KPU ticket. Of the others, four, although they subsequently joined KANU, had been elected in 1963 as Independents; and the technicalities of the law initially raised doubts as to whether they could be forced to resign. In the event they were. Twenty-nine Members therefore had to seek re-election in a campaign that involved eighteen districts.[2]

The delays arising out of these doubts as to whether all the KPU Members would have to seek re-election meant that not all the House constituencies went to the polls on the same day. In addition the Senate poll was held a week after that for the Lower House. The whole election was as a result spread over a period of five weeks. Nomination

[1] See above, p. 71. It is important to remember in this context that not all the Radicals left KANU. See an interview with Dr Waiyaki, *Sunday Nation*, 23 May 1965.

[2] *House seats:* Nairobi East; Gichugu; Kandara; Majogi-Bassi; West Pokot; Nakuru Town; Nandi South; Baringo South; Elgon West; Elgon South West; Machakos East; Rendille; Wajir North; Isiolo; Ugenya; Alego; Bondo; Kisumu Rural; Nyando. *Senate seats:* Uasin; Gishu; Lamu; Nanyuki; Turkana; Nakuru; Baringo; Machakos; Central Nyanza; Tana River; West Pokot.

days were on 21 May and 4 June; polling for sixteen of the House constituencies on 11 and 12 June; for the Senate on the 18 and 19 June; and finally for the the three northern constituencies of Wajir, Isiolo and Rendille on 25 and 26 June. Although the parties continued to campaign sporadically until the final voting, the major election activity took place during the three weeks from the first nomination day on 21 May until voting on 11 and 12 June. After that date a period of anti-climax ensued while everyone awaited first the Senate polls and then the voting for the northern seats. Counting was delayed until the latter polls had taken place, two weeks after the first voting.

The election did not draw any significant new element into the national political leadership. KPU automatically sponsored all those Members who had resigned, so that for them the question of bringing new men into the centre could not arise. Eleven of KANU's candidates had unsuccessfully contested national elections in the past, either in 1963 or 1965. Most of the KANU candidates were drawn from among party branch officials; several were County Councillors; two had been Members of the East African Legislative Assembly. Despite this they did not represent an influential element from the district level, nor did the election provide the occasion for KANU branches to assert their influence within the party as a whole.

The style and tactics employed by each party were dictated largely by their different circumstances and resources. Most of the advantages in the campaign lay with KANU. First, as the ruling party they had all the authority and prestige of the Government behind them. This was most obviously demonstrated by the tacit association of the Provincial Administration with the KANU campaign. Since civil service etiquette, if nothing more, required Administrative Officers to attend upon Ministers when in their Province or district, they were present at a considerable number of KANU meetings, where their presence symbolized the association of KANU with Government, and so with governmental power and authority. Second, KANU leaders could and did combine their party campaign with normal ministerial activities and tours. The party's informal campaign began with Kenyatta's May Day speech in Nairobi, when he launched a strong attack upon the new Opposition. Ministerial visits to the districts were used in the following three weeks for preliminary campaigning, particularly in Kandara, where at a large rally on 14 May party leaders launched their attack on Kaggia. The Opposition was at that stage at a considerable disadvantage, since the delay in the registration of the new party (not announced until 21 May, nomination day) meant they could neither hold public meetings, nor build up their national organization. Odinga and other interim party officials held a number of press conferences to reply to KANU allegations; and on 20 May Odinga launched the first part of the new party's manifesto. But since seven days' advance notice was required for all meetings their campaign proper could not be set in motion until a week after nomination day.

Third, KANU had the advantage of the Government-controlled radio, which reported KANU affairs in full but gave no information about KPU candidates, meetings or statements except in so far as KANU statements referred to them. The KANU campaign also received considerably more press publicity than the KPU's.[1] This was not necessarily an indication of press reluctance to give publicity to the Opposition's activities. The KPU campaign was more difficult to cover since the party held fewer large rallies than KANU, and their small meetings in the rural areas were much less easily reported. All their press conferences held in Nairobi were reported in full. Nevertheless, KANU held the advantage so far as national publicity was concerned.

The Ministers dominated the KANU campaign. KANU Headquarters in Nairobi was not noticeably more active during the election period than it had been before. It remained difficult to find a party official or to obtain information there. President Kenyatta chose the party headquarters to announce the KANU candidates and to open the official campaign on the eve of nomination day, and press statements were issued from that office. But the centre of election organization was not there but in the Ministers' offices[2] and at State House. Local constituency campaigning was supported in each district in turn by ministerial visits organized from the centre. In addition, individual Ministers, particularly those whose districts were directly involved in the election, devoted most of their attention to their home districts, in several instances for the full three weeks of the Lower House campaign. In Kisii District, for example, the Minister for Local Government, Mr Sagini, and the Minister for State in the President's Office, Mr Nyamweya, spent much time campaigning for the KANU candidate for Majogi-Bassi. In Busia District Mr Khasakhala, the recently-elected Vice-President for Western Province and Assistant Minister for Agriculture, similarly devoted himself to the two constituencies Elgon West and Elgon South West, contested in his Province. In the latter constituency all KANU public meetings were licensed in his name.

Such ministerial support to KANU candidates was doubtless all the more important in view of the fact that the party was not prepared at

[1] The *East African Standard* carried reports of twenty-two KANU rallies compared with six KPU.

[2] Particularly, it appeared, the Ministry of Economic Planning and Development, not least because of Mboya's role of Secretary General of the party.

branch level for an election campaign. District organization was virtually non-existent, so that no constituency candidate found a party machine that could be swung into action behind him. The candidates were in this respect on their own, left to organize their campaigns for themselves. This had, of course, been the case in 1963; but on that occasion a good team in headquarters had overcome the major organizational deficiencies. In 1966 this teamwork was much less in evidence. In most cases each branch was provided with a vehicle from headquarters, but no sustained organizational support.[1] As a result most of the individual constituency campaigns were conducted on a markedly *ad hoc* basis. Branch organization counted for less than candidates' own personal activity, assisted by individual local or ministerial support.

The Opposition was equally limited in the support its headquarters could offer the candidates, not least because they had barely set up their organization before the campaign began. Although their Nairobi office was full of supporters during the campaign period, there was little to indicate that headquarters officials were co-ordinating party activities into a national campaign. The men in the Central Office provided the press statements, held a series of press conferences and addressed some meetings (including the party's opening rally in Nairobi); but they were only marginally involved in campaigning outside the capital. In Central Nyanza and Machakos, where KANU had formerly had a well-established district machine and where the branch was taken over by KPU, the Opposition acquired a viable and successful organization, as well as experienced district campaigners. In these two districts the Opposition organization was markedly superior to that of KANU. Elsewhere, however, they lacked a strong party machine; and KPU campaigns were therefore left to the individual candidates to organize, on an *ad hoc* basis, with their own agents and a minimum of assistance from party headquarters.

Odinga himself, it should be added, did not openly participate extensively in his party's campaign. He spoke at party rallies only in Nairobi, Machakos and Nakuru; and at one or two smaller meetings in Nyanza and Busia. He held a series of press conferences in Nairobi. Otherwise he restricted his activities to informal communication, particularly in the rural areas in Nyanza.

KANU appeared generally to place a greater emphasis on large rallies, attended by groups of Ministers, whereas KPU emphasized smaller meetings and house-to-house campaigning, particularly in Central Nyanza and Machakos where the organizational advantages lay with them. KPU's national leaders did not range as widely over the

[1] The extent of financial support can only be a matter of conjecture.

81

country as the KANU Ministers, and complained of official restrictions upon their freedom of movement and right to hold meetings.[1] One result was that the two parties appeared to be operating at different levels – KANU at the national, KPU at the local level.

At the beginning of the campaign fears were expressed that violence might become widespread; particularly after KANU's first Nairobi rally, at which the police moved in with tear gas to disperse hecklers at the end of the meeting.[2] There was marked tension throughout the campaign in several constituencies, particularly in Central Nyanza, the Nakuru area and Kandara, where KANU Youth Wingers were prominent. But as had been the case in the 1963 general election, there was less violence than might have been expected. The most serious reported incidents occurred in the Rift Valley area and in Central Province. In Nakuru Town the KPU candidate, Achieng Oneko's first public meeting was brought to a standstill after five minutes by KANU Youth Wingers and police moved in to prevent further rioting.[3] His second meeting was as a result cancelled by the police. Other KPU rallies in the Nakuru area were reported to have been stopped by KANU Youth Wingers. Arap Moi, Minister for Home Affairs, speaking at a KANU rally at Eldama Ravine, warned KANU Youth Wingers not to take the law into their own hands.[4] In Kandara, Kaggia's constituency, KPU followers and Kaggia himself were reported to have been attacked by KANU supporters; but few details reached the press.[5] One of the KANU Ministers, Ngala Mwendwa, was involved in an incident between KPU and KANU supporters in Machakos.[6] All eight KPU candidates who presented petitions against the election results alleged as one of their grounds that intimidation and threats of violence had deterred voters from supporting them. How far intimidation was an element in the campaign was difficult to substantiate. Such pressure could take many forms, including an appeal to loyalty.[7]

The election resulted in an overwhelming victory for KANU, who

[1] Alleged refusal by the Administration, without reasonable cause, to permit him to hold more than three public meetings was one of the grounds given by the KPU candidate in Nandi South for his appeal against the election results. See Election Petition of 1966, in the High Court of Kenya, Simeon Kiptum arap Choge, against P. J. Kimwele (the District Commissioner) and John Kipruto Cheruiyot (the KANU candidate). KPU candidates made several Press statements on this point. See, for example, *Daily Nation*, 6 June 1966.

[2] *Daily Nation*, 24 May 1966.

[3] *East African Standard*, 31 May 1966; 16 June 1966.

[4] Ibid., 31 May 1966.

[5] *East African Standard*, 31 May 1966.

[6] Ibid., 10 August 1966.

[7] Intimidation is always difficult to su˙ıstantiate. There were other reported incidents, such as the arrest of Sijeyo, the KPU candidate for the Nakuru Senate seat, for entering Baringo District without a permit.

won eight of the ten Senate and twelve of the nineteen House seats. KPU was left with only nine Members of Parliament (seven in the House, two in the Senate), six of them from Central Nyanza, two from Machakos and one from Busia district. KPU, on the other hand, polled a majority of the votes. Whether either party could claim an outstanding popular victory was however problematical since the poll, averaging 33 per cent, was low. The highest polls were in Kandara, where KANU's candidate soundly defeated Kaggia, and in Bondo, where Odinga had an overwhelming victory. Elsewhere, including Central Nyanza and Central Province, which were the main foci of attention in the election, the polls indicated that only a limited section of the electorate took the trouble to vote. Only in five seats could there be said to have been a close contest.[1]

This was the first major election since the general election of 1963 had put the KANU Government into power. There had been several by-elections in the intervening three years, occasioned by the death or resignation of Members and by the Senate by-elections of 1965. None of those elections had, however, been the occasion of a major confrontation between Kenyan leaders such as now took place; nor had they been the occasion of serious policy debate. When the KANU Government actively campaigned in 1964 for public support for their decision to establish a Republic and abolish the regional structure of government there had been some debate between the two parties, but the issue had in effect already been decided by the vast majority that KANU had previously won in the 1963 election. Although both major groupings within KANU had during 1965 appealed for public support against their rivals that appeal had been for the most part, but with certain notable exceptions, covert. The 1966 election was therefore the first occasion when the issues that had divided KANU were specifically referred to the electorate.

The election therefore constituted a significant occasion in the political debate in Kenya. In the rest of this chapter I wish to examine the nature of the choice presented to the electorate. The absence of firm survey material on voters' attitudes makes it difficult to do more than speculate broadly about the public interpretation of the contest, and what the election results meant in terms of party support.[2] Something more concrete can, however, be said of the choice with which the public

---

[1] For the results see the *East African Standard* and *Daily Nation*, 28 June 1966.

[2] The writer spent the period of the campaign in Nyanza, which is dealt with in the next chapter. Information on other constituencies came not only from the press and interviews in Nairobi, but also from colleagues who visited those constituencies, whose information will, in some cases, be published separately. I am particularly grateful to Lionel Cliffe, Eliud Maluki and Goran Hyden, who discussed their work in Central Province, Machakos and West Pokot and Nandi with me.

was presented by candidates and parties, and the way in which Government and Opposition interpreted the contest.

The issues that had divided KANU provided a starting-point for a debate about the kind of society into which Kenya should develop. In the course of the campaign both parties attempted to move beyond the broad nationalist demands of the pre-independence period to define more precisely the conditions under which those demands could be achieved in the independent state. Whereas KPU emphasized the need for communal activity and a socialist economy, KANU stressed the need for hard work and individual effort. They were therefore offering specific alternative courses of action.

The policy issues debated during the election campaign were not surprisingly those that had dominated the parliamentary debate of the past two years. Allegations of tribal preferences in the Government allocation of resources were again made. The policies on land, nationalization and social services as well as foreign policy and foreign alignments were still the main sources of disagreement. These issues were debated in much the same terms as before, although with a stronger ideological emphasis by both parties. One new issue was raised at the outset by the Opposition, when they challenged the legality of the constitutional amendment and argued that the constitution had been manipulated by the Government for its own advantage. The constitutional issue was, however, submerged in the broader policy debate, primarily as a result of KANU's counter accusation that the Opposition itself had in its policy proposals disregarded the guarantees of individual ownership provided by the constitution. It was on those policies, rather than constitutional matters, that the inter-party debate focused.

The starting-point in this phase of the policy debate was the KPU Interim Manifesto published on the eve of nomination day.[1] This embodied the Radicals' demands of the past two years, to which were added new demands for the guarantee of the rights of individual freedom and of political association contained in the constitution. Strongly populist in its appeal, it dealt with socialism, African tradition, land, agriculture, employment policies, the civil service, corruption, and education. The party condemned the Government's capitalist policies which were creating a small class of rich people while the masses lived in poverty. It promised, if it formed a Government, to introduce genuine socialist policies. To extend national control over the means of production and break the foreigners' grip on the economy. To distribute free land to the neediest, either by expropriation or through land consolidation, as well as restricting land ownership to

[1] Nairobi (Pan African Press Ltd), May 1966.

84

Kenyan citizens. It also promised a reduction in the permitted size of farms to a 'size consistent with democracy and socialism'. Once this had been achieved maximum assistance would be given to individual owners for the development of their holdings. The manifesto, recognizing the central place of agriculture in the Kenyan economy, promised increased agricultural services and marketing facilities. It stated that unemployment would be relieved by the provision of more jobs in industry. Finally, the manifesto promised the introduction of free primary education immediately after the party had formed the government, as well as increased technical education and improved conditions for teachers. On the major issues of land, nationalization and education the party thus committed itself to a definite line of action which constituted a radical change from Government policy. It appealed to those who were dissatisfied with their position and promised more socialist policies as a step towards a more egalitarian society.

There were two significant weaknesses in the KPU position. The first was a failure to consider the economy as a whole. The second was a failure to indicate how these policies would be financed. During the campaign, however, party spokesmen attempted to overcome these weaknesses by a more detailed discussion of some of the broad statements of policy. This was particularly true of land and agriculture, which policies were under strongest attack. Here the party was arguing on three different issues: first their rejection of the Government's settlement policy, based upon the purchase of lands in the former European Highlands; second the need to prevent the emergence of a new class of African large-scale landowners in that area; and third the need to approach agricultural development in a different way, to place a greater emphasis upon co-operative and communal farming. Challenged to explain how their policies would not balkanize agriculture and so threaten the economy Denis Akumu, the party's administrative secretary, defined their objectives as a combination of State farming for difficult agricultural land that had to be worked on a large scale, and a co-operative system which would ensure that individual farmers retained their individual title and received individual remuneration while voluntarily pooling their land. This, he pointed out, presupposed the existence of legal private ownership of land, not its abolition. Reminding his readers that Mau Mau had been the outcome of landlessness he argued that the capitalist system of farming on which Kenyan agriculture was based required enclosure of land and a high degree of mechanization. Such a system would increase social problems and create a new landless and unemployed class. The KPU was not, he insisted, advocating a communist system of agriculture. Its policy was based upon a system of agricultural holdings which would

D

respect Kenya's social and political requirements and at the same time meet her economic needs.[1]

KANU's reply to KPU's policies relied upon the three documents which had come to represent its ideological and policy stand: the 1963 manifesto, the Republican constitution, and Sessional Paper No. 10 of 1965 on African Socialism. The revised Development Plan published at the beginning of May[2] was used as a further elucidation of the Government's plans and objectives and an outline of the methods by which they would be achieved.

With these documents to support them the Government rejected the charges of neglect by listing the development record of the period since independence.[3] In education there had been a large expansion in schools and intake of pupils; in health the introduction of free out-patients' services; in labour the Tripartite Agreement of 1964 and other efforts to reduce unemployment; in land the resettlement of 35,000 landless families, and the transformation of the former White High-lands into an African farming area. A Special Commissioner had been appointed to deal with squatters. Steps had been taken to introduce more Africans into the commercial sector as, for example, the transfer of all sugar agencies from Asians to Africans and the establishment of the National Trading Corporation. They denied any loss of Govern-ment contact with the people, which on the contrary was sustained by the President's regular tours and the Administration's *barazas* (meet-ings) by the representative nature of all Local Authorities and the Africanization of statutory boards and other government agencies. They also denied the growth of a class of rich Africans at the expense of the rest of the country, and insisted that the Sessional Paper's pro-visions for a just tax system would ensure the equitable distribution of wealth.

The party and the Government rejected KPU policies on land, education and nationalization. Free education could be achieved, they insisted, in due course, but only on the basis of careful planning for the steady expansion of facilities over a period of time; and they chal-lenged the Opposition to explain how they would finance its immediate introduction. Nationalization was not, they argued, the solution to the country's social and economic problems arising out of the continued domination of the economy by non-Africans. This difficulty would be resolved more effectively by giving Africans the opportunity to develop their own industries and commerce. They therefore emphasized the benefits of individual entrepreneurship. Finally, land was not free. The

---

[1] *Kenya Weekly News*, 10 June 1966.
[2] The Revised Development Plan, Nairobi Government Printer, 1966.
[3] *East African Standard*, 2 and 10 June 1966.

idea that land could be distributed free to the poorest section of the community constituted a demand for 'free things', which implied a wholesale expropriation of property and therefore a disregard for the individual rights of ownership, guaranteed in the constitution and accepted as one of the fundamental tenets of African socialism.

Both Government and Opposition accused each other of foreign alignments that constituted a denial of Kenya's independence, and a betrayal of African nationalism. On the one hand KPU accused the Government of having abandoned the nationalist struggle to liberate Africa: by refusing to take any action in Rhodesia;[1] by betraying the movement for East African federation; and by its alleged subordination to the Western Powers. On the other, KANU accused the Opposition of subordination to the Communist powers; but felt compelled to issue a long and detailed account of their record in foreign affairs in terms of the objectives of the 1963 manifesto.

A close analysis of the two parties' policy statements suggests that there was not a great deal of fundamental difference between them. The two issues on which they clearly differed were land and nationalization. In other policy matters, however, their differences were more a question of degree related to the more egalitarian attitudes of the Radicals. There was a more explicit contrast in the more definite statements of ideology that emanated from each party. KPU rejected the official policy of African socialism as 'a cloak for capitalism', and offered instead their own socialist stand which expressed the demands of the nationalist movement. 'If anything,' Denis Akumu wrote, 'the difference between our party and the KANU Government is that the latter is now basically conservative and right wing, our party is interested in transforming socialism to suit African conditions without distorting the universal tenet of socialism. . . . KANU puts the emphasis on the private sector and no attempt is made to bring into the public sector the basic essentials for production and distribution . . .[2] On the other hand KANU condemned KPU and its manifesto as communist and alien to the African way of life, and pointed to the KPU's policies on economic and foreign issues as proof of their acquiescence in a foreign ideology, and therefore of their disloyalty to Kenya. Thus the ideological interchanges followed the pattern of the debate of 1965, when the Conservatives had attempted to label the Radicals as communist and the latter had argued that they stood as

---

[1] One of the events that precipitated the final clash between Radicals and Conservatives had been a statement by Mr Gichuru, Minister for Finance, when in Lagos in February 1966, in which he allegedly said Rhodesian Africans were not yet ready for independence. Radicals in KANU had seized upon this to attack their opponents in the Cabinet, on the grounds that they had compromised the nationalist cause.

[2] *Kenya Weekly News*, 10 June 1966.

the true nationalists. In these exchanges KANU explicitly emphasized the questions of property and property rights that had earlier been raised by the Conservatives. Kenyatta summed up the KANU position in his Madaraka Day speech when he said:

There are some individuals who claim that I should give everything free to the people. This kind of slogan is a cowardly way of trying to win popularity. Whether in Kiambu or Kakamega, in Kilifi or Kisumu, in Kapsabet or Kirinyaga, all things belong to someone. . . . Those who speak about getting everything for nothing must mean that I should call out the Army and the police to seize by force a lot of land or buildings or livestock, or equipment which belongs to some of you. . . . We believe we must safeguard the personal and property rights of all our people as a vital element of our hard won freedom.[1]

Statements issued by the party argued that since the KPU Manifesto was communist it accepted the possible confiscation of all private property by the State, such as occurred in Russia or China. KPU would provide 'so called free things' by the complete removal of all rights and freedoms cherished by the people. The same accusations were made at public rallies. In Nanyuki Mboya told an audience that if KPU wished to achieve its nationalization plans it would be forced to take over all land as state property and make people work in forced labour.[2] In Kisii on another occasion the Minister for Local Government condemned collective farming and state ownership of land as communist and unsuited to Africa.[3]

KPU might be regarded as the first party of the left to have emerged in Kenya. Its leadership was associated with the more extreme nationalist wing of the pre-independence years. Its socialism was in the first place the loosely defined socialism of the nationalist movement summed up in their appeal to the 'dissatisfied'. In their attack upon the Opposition KANU however emphasized other associations which might destroy its claim to legitimacy, particularly with the Eastern bloc, and the totalitarian aspects of communism. Underneath the recourse to slogans it was possible to detect the beginnings of a debate about the shape of the future Kenya society. Each party approached this question from a different starting-point. KPU from the need for equality, KANU from the need to protect the rights of the individual to acquire and own property.

These questions constituted only one element in the appeal to the electorate. The fundamental issue was not a question of policy but of legitimacy. The KPU claimed, as the Radical backbenchers had done earlier, that they, not the Government or KANU, represented the

---

[1] *East African Standard*, 2 June 1966.
[2] Ibid.
[3] Ibid., 19 May 1966

national interest.[1] The early justification for this claim was on the grounds of policy. But the argument took both parties beyond policy to questions of leadership, of ethnic loyalty and of governmental power, which together constituted the broad base of the appeal now made by the parties and their candidates.

The rivalry within the national leadership had not, in the one-party state, presented any threat to Kenyatta. While the contest had been for the intermediary leadership, the contestants had regularly reaffirmed their loyalty to the President. The formation of the KPU was, however, a direct challenge to Kenyatta himself. The Party offered Kenyans an alternative government with an alternative leader. Odinga's challenge was now explicitly to the President. It was not therefore surprising that KANU portrayed the election, from the outset, in this sense. A party statement issued at the beginning of the campaign made this clear and appealed for loyalty to Kenyatta as the leader of the nationalist movement.

The issues are clear in the little general election which is about to start. On the one hand the voters have the Government of Mzee Kenyatta which has led the country since independence and which is implementing KANU's policies. On the other side is Mr Odinga who wishes to usurp the powers of Mzee . . .[2]

At the same time KANU launched a strong personal attack upon Odinga himself, whom they accused of establishing a personality cult to promote his own position and power. Of thirty KANU statements issued over the campaign eight included a direct personal attack upon him, questioned his record as a nationalist, and denounced him for his challenge to Kenyatta. KPU was portrayed as no more than a clique which owed its existence to Odinga and thus could have no national legitimacy. This presentation to the voters of a choice not between candidates or between parties, but between Kenyatta and Odinga,[3] constituted the major line of KANU's assault upon the Opposition. This enabled KANU to exploit to the full Kenyatta's unique position in Kenyan politics. He was the major asset in KANU's campaign as the personification of Kenyan nationalism, the father-figure of the nation, the one man who had been able to establish unity. Kenyatta, not KANU, was therefore used to legitimize the KANU candidates. His own active participation in the campaign at four major rallies, in

[1] See above, Chapter 2. Odinga had repeated this claim in the debate on the constitutional amendment on 28 April, and again in his resignation statement.

[2] *East African Standard*, 21 May 1966.

[3] For example, Ibid., 16 May, 29 May and 30 May 1966 for reports of meetings at which KANU leaders explicitly presented the choice as one between Odinga and Kenyatta.

Nairobi, Nakuru and Kandara, emphasized not only his symbolic leadership of the nation but also his continued active engagement in politics as the leader of KANU.

The portrayal of the election as a choice of leadership carried with it, however, strong ethnic overtones, for both Kenyatta and Odinga symbolized an ethnic identity as well as a political stand. Kenyatta embodied not only Kenyan nationalism but the spirit and identity of Kikuyu nationalism with all that this implied after the long years of Kikuyu political conflict. He stood above the rivalries that divided the Kikuyu, unchallenged in his leadership of his people. Odinga was, on his side, more personally involved in the struggles that divided the Luo people. Nevertheless he symbolized the identity of the Luo for the greater part of the Luo community; a position highlighted and reinforced by the events that had preceded his resignation, and emphasized by the subsequent attacks upon him and his party as an isolated Luo group separated from the rest of the country.[1] The choice before the voters was thus not only between Kenyatta and Odinga, but also in part between Kikuyu and Luo. This notwithstanding the fact that several Luo Ministers remained in the Government. While both parties denounced any appeal to tribalism, neither could entirely avoid this ethnic identification.

The outcome of the election in Central Province and Nyanza suggested that in those areas the ethnic identification with party and leader was the most significant element in the party appeal. KPU's appeal to the dissatisfied was essentially an appeal to economic interest, specifically to the interests of the poorer section of the community in each district. They were seeking to establish themselves as a party cutting across the old ethnic alignments. There were internal district divisions based upon economic position within Central Province, and in Nyanza, to which the party could direct itself. Kaggia's appeal on land, for instance, was primarily to the poorer and the landless in Central Province. But KPU's claim was weakened by Odinga's own position as an ethnic leader, which in Nyanza and Central Province emerged as a significant issue. The campaign in Nyanza will be considered in detail in the next chapter. Here a brief note may be given about the outcome of the campaign in Kandara, where Kaggia was overwhelmingly defeated by a man who had himself, a year before, failed to retain his seat in the Senate.

As a former KAU leader closely identified since the 1940s with the Kikuyu political movement, and the Emergency, and detained for several years, Kaggia's place in Kenyan politics was assured. In Kikuyu politics he probably stood second only to Kenyatta. The failure of his

[1] See Chapter 4 below.

opponents over the previous two years to destroy his influence within the Muranga branch of KANU had demonstrated that he did not lack support in the district. At the Limuru Conference he had won the first nomination for post of Vice-President of Central Province, but had been defeated in a second ballot. He therefore constituted a challenge to Kenyatta among the Kikuyu. At the beginning of the campaign his position appeared to be strong. In the event, however, he polled only 10 per cent of the votes in what was the highest poll in the election.

Kaggia's appeal was to the poorer section of the population in a constituency where there were visible signs that growing material prosperity was leaving some people behind. There was also a sense of grievance at Muranga's slower development, compared with the other Kikuyu districts, and a feeling of central government neglect. KANU's appeal was explicitly for loyalty to Kenyatta. KANU leaders from the outset portrayed the election as a challenge to Kenyatta and all he symbolized for Kikuyu leadership from Kaggia who had allied himself with Odinga and he Luo.[1] This choice was brought home dramatically by Kenyatta's eve of polling day rally at Kandara. They also made a strong appeal to the omnipotence of the Government, which could not fail to influence people who had felt the full force of governmental power during the Emergency. The combination was too strong for any sense of economic discontent to prevail.

Outside Central and Nyanza Provinces the questions of ethnic association and ethnic loyalties were more complicated. In a number of constituencies there were local grievances and situations that influenced attitudes towards each party. In the Elgon South West constituency, bordering Central Nyanza district, there was a history of border disputes between Luo and Luyia which worked to KANU's advantage. In the second constituency in that western area, Elgon West, the KPU candidate, on the other hand, identified the area's economic backwardness with Kikuyu dominance in government. Generally in the Kalenjin constituencies ethnic culturalism, and particularly the custom of circumcision, could be used to support a closer association of Kalenjin with Kikuyu than with Luo. In Nandi South there was a tradition of conflict between Luo and Nandi over cattle and land and a history of poor relations between Nandi and Luo working on the tea estates. As in the past, therefore, there were local social and economic issues that could be translated into ethnic terms; and in turn cultural identity reinforced attitudes determined by those issues.

Kalenjin support for KANU cannot however, be explained simply

[1] *East African Standard*, 16 May 1966.

in terms of ethnic association, for economic issues might well have been seen in the Rift Valley as a reason for opposition to a party associated with the Kikuyu. Economic issues, particularly the land question, had in the past made the area a KADU stronghold against both Luo and Kikuyu. The Kalenjin remained concerned about the future of land in the Rift Valley and especially the areas that remained in the hands of European farmers. In the past the Kikuyu had been seen as the major threat to their expansion into these areas. In 1965 Kalenjin back-benchers had been among those who voiced strong fears of Kikuyu domination. On the other hand they had also been among the strongest opponents to the Radicals' land policies, and now in 1966 their opposition to KPU was influenced by that party's land policies. Thus economic interests still led to ethnic alignments, although this time of Kalenjin with the Kikuyu against the Luo.

Two additional features of the campaign which must also be considered are the presentation of the concept of Government, and the continued influence of district leaders. One of the strongest and most explicit themes in the election debate was the idea of the omnipotence and power of Government. KANU presented the voters not only with a choice between Kenyatta and Odinga, but also between Government and Opposition, where Government was portrayed as strong and legitimate and Opposition as illegitimate and weak. A vote against Kenyatta was a vote against the Government. Nor did KANU spokesmen hesitate to point out that it was the Government which controlled the country's resources and through which all development took place. Any Opposition was left outside the Government, and since KPU, no matter how many seats they won in this election, would remain in Opposition, they would have no impact upon the development of Kenya. Moreover no one could expect to support the Opposition and still obtain Government assistance for development since the Opposition was the enemy of the Government, and no one helped his enemy. Any district in opposition would thus be isolated from Government and the rest of the country and must expect to be left behind.

At the same time KANU emphasized the power and strength of Government. 'Those who tried to play with the Government would be trampled on like mud,' Kenyatta thundered at his May Day rally. Drawing on the political past to illustrate the point KANU leaders stressed the party's strength. They had defeated KADU and Ngala, and APP and Ngei, they would defeat KPU and Odinga, who were too weak to survive.

Finally KANU challenged the concept of Opposition itself. On more than one occasion since independence the Government had rejected the idea of a *de jure* one-party state, and emphasized both the value of the voluntary basis of the existing *de facto* one party system and the need to permit an opposition party to function if in the future one should emerge. In the election of 1966, however, they emphasized the need for unity and denied the legitimacy of Opposition, and of KPU, which had destroyed the unity necessary for development.

The Opposition did not, at any point in the campaign, specifically advocate either a two-party state, or the devolution of power from the centre. The centralization of power was not at issue. The issue was who should control the central government. KPU acknowledged that they could not expect immediately to form the government; but they argued that a vote for them at this date meant they would be returned to power in the general election of 1968. In the future they would therefore control the Government machine; for the present they accepted the possibility of suffering.

For Kalenjin voters in particular, who had already experienced a time in Opposition, this may have appeared no alternative. KANU and the Government presumably offered them the more favourable safeguards for their interests in the changed situation that followed the formation of KPU, not least because the Government controlled the resources available.

The little general election also demonstrated the continued influence of the district boss in determining a constituency's political choice. This was most dramatically shown in Nyanza and Central Provinces, where Odinga and Kenyatta each stood as the dominant district boss. It was equally significant elsewhere, in the Rift Valley. The Kalenjin leaders who had dissolved KADU in 1964 and taken that party into KANU had established the Kalenjin-Kikuyu alliance from the top. Their influence at home secured the acceptance of that alliance at the lower levels. Daniel arap Moi, the senior and still the most influential of the Kalenjin leaders, and now Minister for Home Affairs, symbolized the association of Kalenjin with the Government and with the power of the Government. His influence in the Rift Valley constituencies had been recognized by his election as KANU Vice-President for the province at the Limuru Conference. He used this influence vigorously in his active campaigning over all the Rift Valley constituencies, and played a crucial part in the campaign. Similarly the influence of Daniel Moss was important in West Pokot. Moss had been leader of the West Kalenjin Congress to which the West Pokot had earlier given their support, and had taken them into KADU when the Congress became one of the constituent elements of that party. As Member of Parliament for Mt Elgon since 1963, he was still the dominant political figure in the area. Such campaigning as was carried

93

on by KANU in West Pokot constituency was in his hands.[1] In Elgon West, on the other hand, Oduya Oprong, the KPU candidate was the only political leader the Iteso had thrown up and his success indicated his continued influence in the district.

Where there existed a single leader who had formerly been acknowledged as the district leader, his influence was still a crucial factor in determining the area's alignment. In the little general election both parties sought to challenge the influence of such leaders where they belonged to the opposite party. Both failed. The characteristic pattern of Kenyan politics based upon the existence of such district leaders was preserved.

Consequently the pattern of local central relations based upon national alliances between such leaders was also preserved. But in 1966 the basis of these alliances was an alignment not between Kikuyu and Luo but between Kikuyu and Kalenjin. This was the alternative offered to the electorate. The attempt to move the party divisions on to a basis other than that of territorial interests had had only a limited success.

[1] I am grateful to Dr Goran Hyden for information on West Pokot. Moss was also, of course, associated with the Government as an Assistant Minister, and so represented Government strength.

4

The Little
General Election
in Central Nyanza 1966

WITH JOHN OKUMU

This chapter examines the little general election in Central Nyanza.[1]
The results showed that in 1966 this district was a KPU stronghold. All
KPU candidates were returned with overwhelming victories, and all
save one of the KANU candidates lost their deposits. The Nyanza
election thus raised in an acute form the question as to how far district
alignments were still determined, as the election as a whole suggested,
by the influence of a district boss. Since this was Odinga's home territory it was to be expected that his leadership would be a significant
factor in the election, as proved to be the case. The campaign demonstrated the close interconnections between personal and ethnic
loyalties. It suggested that the question of Odinga's leadership involved more than his personal position, and that leadership was
intimately associated with the identity of the Luo as a group; also that
the quests for individual and ethnic position were closely interwoven.
They were moreover closely linked with the contest for governmental
power at the centre, and therefore control over the country's policy-
making institutions. The support given to Odinga was fundamentally
support for his claims to national leadership and the policies he stood
for. The Central Nyanza campaign on the other hand, demonstrated
another facet of Kenya politics – the underlying continuity in much of
the political conflict at the district level. For this reason it is necessary,

[1] This chapter is based on field work carried out by both authors in Central Nyanza
during the period of the little general election in May and June 1966. One of us is
Luo-speaking; the other had an interpreter throughout the period. We are grateful to
all those members of both parties, particularly the candidates, who were willing, in the
midst of a busy campaign, to stop and discuss the issues with us. Background material
has also been drawn from earlier research undertaken by each of us separately, into the
political and administrative development of the district. Dr Okumu has subsequently
used some of this material in an article, The by-election in Gem: An Assessment, *East
Africa Journal*, June 1969.

before turning to the election itself, to look first at earlier developments in Central Nyanza since the Second World War.

The Background

Central Nyanza is a large district with considerable variation in physical conditions, from the lakeshore savannah to the highland plateau country in the eastern part of the district in Nyando Division, to the undulating country of the western and north-western divisions of Alego and Ugenya. With a total population of around a million it is one of the most densely populated parts of Kenya. Pressures upon the land, however, vary considerably. They are much greater in the northern part of the district, in Alego and Ugenya than in the south and around the lake shore where (as in Bondo) there are large un-cultivated areas.

The district economy is predominantly agricultural; but natural agricultural potential is limited. The lakeshore savannah country, although fertile, is difficult to drain and to work; rainfall is irregular, and parts of this area, as well as some of the higher country in the north-west, are infested with tsetse. Conditions in the plateau country are more favourable but the population density is much higher. Natural conditions therefore offer less attractive opportunities for profitable cash farming than elsewhere in Kenya. Certain high-priced crops like tea and pyrethrum cannot be grown at all and conditions for grade cattle are not ideal. It is not altogether surprising therefore that agri-cultural developments have lagged behind other parts of the country. As much as 90 per cent of agricultural output was still in 1964 grown for subsistence. The pressure of population and traditional methods of land use have resulted in considerable land fragmentation and, in some parts of the district, extremely small holdings. Agricultural practice was still generally backward in the mid-1960s, not least because of the long period of strong political opposition to Government efforts to introduce improved methods of husbandry, which reached its peak in 1957–8.[1]

Economic development in the district has also been influenced by the extent to which able-bodied Luo men, faced with the need to obtain cash for the payment of tax, school fees and other requirements, have gone into wage employment outside the district rather than to more intensive agriculture at home. At any one time a large proportion of the male population has been absent from home, working in the towns and cities of East Africa, on the railways and harbours and in other government services. In the mid-fifties it was estimated that up to

[1] For an excellent study of Central Nyanza agriculture see John C. de Wilde, *et al. Agricultural Development in Tropical Africa*, Johns Hopkins Press (1967), Vol. II, Chapter 4.

45,000 men might be working outside the district in any one year.[1] The 1962 census showed that at any one time an average 27 per cent of men were absent from the district as a whole; though this ranged from 40 to 50 per cent in some areas, to as little as 19 per cent in others. This migrant labour has brought a considerable amount of cash into the district, so that the population is not as poor as the state of agriculture would suggest. Nevertheless the absence of so many able-bodied men from the area has adversely affected agriculture because it has resulted in inadequate labour being available in the district itself. It has also had significant social and political repercussions, for it has preserved the dominant influence of the older and more conservative elements in the community.

Political developments in Central Nyanza after the Second World War were characterized by a strong sense of popular suspicion and distrust of Government and authority in general. This mistrust, which had existed before the war, was aggravated after 1945 by unpopular government measures such as compulsory labour for bench terracing, and by the presence in the area of a more educated and increasingly vocal group of younger men influenced by the new ideas of African nationalism. Economic grievances arising out of the higher prices of consumer goods and increased taxation after the war aroused further discontent. Later the arrest and detention of some Luo leaders in the early stages of the Emergency increased the sense of bitterness against the Government.[2]

In the rural areas this suspicion of the Government was demonstrated by a sustained reluctance to co-operate on a variety of agricultural measures which, although intended for the development of the district, were nevertheless viewed with deep suspicion. Government attempts to promote better farming methods, including soil conservation, were resisted. The strongest opposition was, however, against the Government's land consolidation programmes begun in 1955, which took on something of the character of an agrarian resistance movement.[3]

This movement was led and co-ordinated by the traditional

---

[1] *Annual Report*, Central Nyanza District, 1954. Also de Wilde, op. cit. Originally forced upon the Luo by colonial labour policies, migrant labour and wage employment subsequently came to be preferred by many to agricultural work inside the district as a means of avoiding the restrictions imposed on the individual by tribe and family. See M. Whisson, *Change and Challenge*, Nairobi: 1964.

[2] J. M. Lonsdale, op. cit. B. A. Ogot, 'Central Nyanza 1900–1960' in *Journal of African History*, Vol. 3, No. 2, 1963. W. Sytek. 'A History of Land Consolidation in Central Nyanza 1956–1962', *East African Institute of Social Research Conference Paper, January 1966*.

[3] On this see especially Lonsdale, op. cit. We are grateful to Dr Lonsdale for many discussions on this subject.

leadership group, the *Jodong Gweng*, or elders of the locality. The position and authority of this group had for some years past been challenged by the system of chieftaincy introduced by the colonial administration, which made the chief the significant authority in the location and the primary link between rural population and Government. Specifically the traditional authority of the *Jodong Gweng* in land matters had suffered as a result of the opportunities that the new chiefs enjoyed for the acquisition of land rights not subject to regulation by the elders. Until the fifties there had been no overt conflict between the two groups. The move towards land consolidation, however, and the introduction of individual land rights, provoked the *Jodong Gweng* to open opposition, largely because these changes seemed likely further to entrench the chiefs as a new landed class and to increase their advantages over the rest of the community. This opposition was supported by a large section of the peasantry, who also feared the possible disadvantages of the new policy.[1] The *Jodong Gweng* also forged close links with most other groups in the community, especially the teachers and traders. As a result they established themselves in a powerful political position as the leaders of a large section of the rural community. Their opposition to the Government's consolidation efforts was highly successful. Between 1956 and 1962 the Government programme to introduce land consolidation into the district was a failure, notwithstanding a total expenditure of £76,000. Up to the end of 1962 no land had been registered.[2]

Jodong Gweng and the people objected to the land consolidation proposals on two grounds. In the first place they believed that these proposals offered the chiefs the opportunity to accumulate more land and therefore more wealth at their expense. In the second place they objected to the political authority of the chief, which endangered the traditional political structure. In their role as traditional arbitrators they were seeking to re-establish a local clan autonomy that would give the clan a direct contact with the colonial administration independently of the chief. They hoped thereby to gain two important advantages. First that the people would be able to manage their own affairs through the traditional structure which they understood. Second that direct communication between the clan and the Administration would ensure that the clan and not the individual received

---

[1] Traditional Luo land use was based upon two categories of landholder: members of the original lineage or clan who had inalienable rights of usage, and tenants from other clans who were allowed the right of cultivation in return to specified services. The first feared that consolidation would enable the tenants to secure equality with them; the second that title deeds would relegate them to a position of perpetual legal inferiority.

[2] Sytek, op. cit.

government assistance. The movement against land consolidation in the fifties thus emphasized the traditional and the communal qualities of Luo culture. It also contained the roots of a possible economic struggle between a primarily conservative rural subsistence population and a new class of government employees already associated with the modern sector of the economy.[1]

In fact the resistance to agricultural reform had adverse effects upon the district's economy and so contributed to the economic backwardness in the late 1950s which made Central Nyanza compare unfavourably with other districts, particularly those of Central Province.[2] There were consequently fewer benefits to distribute. This increased the popular sense of grievance and discontent as well as antagonism towards the Government. But the most important political consequence for Central Nyanza was the enhancement of the authority of the *Jodong Gweng* within the local community. This meant a strengthening of the more conservative forces in the district at the time the Luo were being drawn into the growing nationalist movement in Kenya.

The Luo had not been unaffected by the demands for political reform that developed after the war, and the growing nationalist movement of the 1950s; but no political party had established a firm foothold in the district. Although the economic and social grievances that aroused suspicion and distrust of Government had also stimulated demands from younger Luo leaders for political change at the national level, the branch of the Kenya African Union started in Central Nyanza in the late 1940s had not become the main vehicle for the expression of those demands. That party had failed to attract any great local support and its officers had been unable to establish an effective district organization. Kenyatta visited Kisumu twice, once in 1950 and again in 1952 just before his arrest, but those visits were not followed by any notable expansion of KAU activities.[3] Several factors contributed to this failure. There were the continued difficulties of communication in the district, fears of some Luo of what appeared to be a Kikuyu-dominated organization, and official opposition.[4] When the prohibition of African political organizations in 1953 called a halt to any further

---

[1] Lonsdale, op. cit.

[2] See, for example, *East African Standard,* 13 October 1956, for an editorial, 'Choice for Luo' on this question. See also above, Chapter 1.

[3] Odinga, op. cit., discusses the early days of KAU in Nyanza, see for example pp. 98–100.

[4] This accorded with official policy to promote a moderate African middle class. A meeting in Kisumu in December 1952, which urged Walter Odede to resign from the position of national chairman of KAU that he had taken up after Kenyatta's arrest, consisted predominantly of African government officials. Kenya Government Archives, Nyanza Province, unpublished material.

99

attempts at party activity the party had only a limited following in the district.

The organizations which had gained most popular support in the post-war period and which raised what were essentially political issues were the numerous welfare associations and the growing number of independent churches that had sprung up in those years. Ex-servicemen's associations, clan and sub-clan organizations and welfare bodies such as the Ramogi Welfare Association and the Luo Union were the bodies that the Luo supported and to which they submitted their grievances.

Of these associations the most important was the Luo Union, which was formed in the mid-forties as a welfare organization to assist Luo in difficulties and generally to promote the welfare of the Luo people.[1] Its headquarters, originally in Nairobi, were after considerable argument moved to Kisumu in 1946. Branches were set up in many parts of the district and elsewhere in Kenya and East Africa where Luo were working. In 1953 the Union was reconstituted on an East African basis as the Luo Union (East Africa) with Oginga Odinga as President or *Ker*. He and other officers subsequently travelled throughout East Africa setting up new branches and expanding the Union's activities. In parts of Nyanza itself they were able to utilize the existing clan structure as the basis of the Union's organization within which the older men therefore played a vital role. By August 1955 the Union had sixty branches and a membership of 3,557.[2]

Although primarily a welfare organization the Union had not hesitated to take up political issues. In 1946, for example, the Kisumu officials had asked permission to hold a public meeting to discuss not only commercial matters in the province but also the Union's views on Parliamentary Paper No. 191 on inter-territorial organization in East Africa.[3] In 1951 the Union presented a memorandum on the need for constitutional reform to the then Secretary of State for the Colonies on his visit to Kenya. In the Emergency years, in the absence of alternative political organizations, the Luo Union drew the various elements in the community together and 'organized the Luo into a force to be reckoned with'.[4]

The Luo Union provided Oginga Odinga, who had by 1955 emerged as the leader of the younger radical element in Nyanza, with the means

[1] Ogot, op. cit. Odinga, op. cit., p. 87.
[2] *Nyanza Province Archives*, unpublished material. See also Richard Onungu-Adero, *The Luo Union and Political Education* (B.A. dissertation, University College, Dar es Salaam, February 1967).
[3] *Nyanza Province Archives*, unpublished material.
[4] Odinga in *Not Yet Uhuru* traces these years in some detail. Ogot, op. cit., approaches them from a different point of view.

of securing a mass base and established him as the dominant political leader in the district as a whole. Odinga had first become known in the rural areas for his activities within the Luo Thrift and Trading Corporation which he had founded in the mid-1940s to assist the Luo to engage in business. He was also in the 1940s an active member of the African Native Council for Central Nyanza within which he consistently challenged the Government on local issues and won his reputation as a firm opponent of the colonial authorities. His assumption of the Presidency of the Luo Union increased his contacts with the rural population and also with the clan leaders who played such an important role in local affairs. He learned to articulate not only the aspirations for development of the peasantry but also their strong attachment to their traditional way of life. Of his work in the Luo Thrift and Trading Corporation he wrote later

My years spent at the feet of the elders, learning the Luo idiom helped me to speak to the people in examples they understood. Visiting one village after another I made untold numbers of speeches stressing the message of co-operation, unity and economic independence by our own effort. . . .[1]

He adopted the same approach in the Luo Union. In 1954, for example, his proposals put forward to the Union for local development emphasized ideas such as co-operative farming and trade ventures which were attuned to the attitudes of a peasantry among whom the sense of community was still strong. Thus he emerged as the dominant political figure in the eyes of the rural population, as well as the symbol of the Luo themselves and 'all they cherished and desired'. When he stood for election to the Legislative Council in 1957 he campaigned on essentially local issues, and promised that if elected he would deal with grievances such as communal labour, the treatment of lakeside fishermen, and land issues, all of which affected the rural population. When he was subsequently instrumental in obtaining the abolition of communal labour his mass base was as a result even more firmly established. His district leadership was confirmed by his election to the Legislative Council as the first directly elected African Member in 1957.[2]

Odinga did not achieve this position unchallenged. His assumption of the leadership of the rural population brought him into conflict with certain elements in the district, who queried some of his attitudes and demands. His political stand in this period was that of the radical

---

[1] Odinga, op. cit., p. 86.
[2] For the 1957 election see G. F. Engholm, African Elections in Kenya, March 1957, in Mackenzie and Robinson, *Five Elections in Africa* (Oxford, 1960.)

nationalist, as his opposition to the principle of multi-racial government in Kenya symbolized.[1] This radical stand, and his support for the rural opposition to government agricultural reforms, antagonized what could be called the more moderate element in the district, including officials of the African District Council, nominated Councillors and African Government officials. For example, his opposition to ADC by-laws on agricultural improvement and compulsory labour for agricultural purposes brought him into conflict with this group. In the process he also challenged their position within the district. In the past it had been this group of African officials and chiefs who had provided the political leadership in Nyanza. In the inter-war years the best chiefs had been articulate opponents of the colonial authority. But social and economic changes had altered the position and in the post-war years they had become more specifically civil servants subordinate to the colonial administration. They had been absorbed into the official class.[2] While the Provincial Administration still viewed chiefs and ADC officials as the district's leaders, they were no longer so viewed by the people. Odinga's opinion of this group was that 'the old Nyanza generation of political leaders had been tamed or absorbed into the missions, chieftainship or administration; the times needed new leaders, men who did not depend on the colonial administration for their livelihood or survival'.[3] As expected they disagreed with him; and his rise to political prominence brought him into collision with them.

The clash between Odinga and African officials had a second dimension. These men formed the new class of progressive African farmers, what John Lonsdale has called the 'able, energetic or rich Africans' who had accepted government-sponsored agrarian reforms including land consolidation as the means to progress. The rural resistance to agrarian reform, which the *Jodong Gweng* led in the fifties, was against the further acquisition of power and wealth by this group. In challenging the methods adopted by the Colonial Government to achieve agricultural development Odinga was in turn challenging the economic position of this group. His emphasis upon the need to win the prior support of the peasantry before introducing agricultural reform was not only a challenge to the colonial authorities, but also to this emerging class of individual landowners.

Odinga's rural base dictated his style in this period. The tactics and

---

[1] See above, Chapter 1.
[2] Lonsdale, op. cit., takes up the question of internal leadership in detail. See also for example *East African Standard*, 9 March 1955, for an account of a meeting of Luo in Nakuru at which Joel Omino, Secretary of Central Nyanza African District Council, and Paul Mboya, Secretary of South Nyanza Council, were introduced by the Administration as 'outstanding leaders among the Luo'.
[3] Op. cit., p. 98.

attitudes thus imposed upon him were subsequently questioned by a second group of younger men, who began in the late fifties to seek entry into Nyanza politics. These younger men, some of whom had been working outside the district, hoped with the formation of KANU to find a place within Nyanza. Able and politically conscious, they were disturbed by the dominant influence of the traditional and conservative elements in the community and the tactics that this imposed upon Odinga. Some of them were also unhappy at the manner in which the business of the Luo Thrift and Trading Corporation had been conducted, believing that Odinga was using it to enhance his own political position rather than to advance the district. In 1961 they disagreed with the choice of KANU candidates for the national elections, with the result that certain of them stood as KANU Independents. Their opposition did not weaken Odinga's majority support, but it created a potential source of conflict in Nyanza, focused in the first place upon the district leadership and Odinga's dominant position. When Mboya – whose rivalry with Odinga originated in Nairobi not Kisumu[1] – attempted to establish his own base in Kisumu, through a district affiliate of his Nairobi People's Convention Party he became involved in this conflict.[2] Mboya's proposed district party gained the support of some of the older Luo leaders whom Odinga had displaced as well as those younger men who identified his position with the opposition to Odinga. The divisions within Nyanza thus gradually polarized around Odinga and Mboya, notwithstanding the fact that Mboya himself did not openly enter into Central Nyanza politics until much later.[3]

KANU opened its Central Nyanza branch in October 1960, with one of Odinga's key lieutenants as its chairman.[4] Organizationally it owed a great deal to Odinga's Luo Thrift and Trading Corporation. Branches were established at location and sub-location level, parallel to the administrative structure, and closely connected with the structure of the Luo Union. This created links with the clan authority with which the Union was itself connected. In each location the party organization was based upon an executive committee of seven led by a chairman, secretary and treasurer. The primary function of this committee was to co-ordinate and supervise the activities of the sub-location committees known as the committees of fifty, which formed the primary unit of party organization. These committees of fifty were responsible for the

---

[1] See above Chapter 1.

[2] Bennett and Rosberg, op. cit., p. 34.

[3] *East African Standard*, 28 April 1960.

[4] The late D. Makasembo, formerly Chairman of the African District Association (Central Nyanza). For the links between KANU and the Luo Thrift and Trading Corporation see J. M. Lonsdale, 'Some Origins of Nationalism in East Africa', *Journal of African History*, IX, 1 (1968), pp. 119–46.

recruitment of members on a door-to-door basis, for the distribution of party literature and the dissemination of party propaganda. Clan heads, who played an important role within them, thus had a vital influence on party organization at the grass roots level. Most of the members of the committees of seven were, on the other hand, young men with some education, business experience or urban experience. The conflict that might have arisen between these two leadership groups was avoided by allowing the leaders of the committees of fifty a fair degree of autonomy in the management of the local affairs of the party.[1] This organization, which offered an effective means of communication for party politicians down to the grass roots level of the district, was used in both the general elections of 1961 and 1963 to secure KANU's overwhelming victories. It was kept alive after the second election by locational branch chairmen who hoped to use it subsequently to win election themselves to the County Council.

The earlier rifts within the district leadership were not, however, overcome by this organization; and Central Nyanza therefore became not only a 'one-party district' but also one in which KANU Independents, prepared to challenge their own party in elections, became a characteristic institution. These KANU Independents were identified by their association with the earlier opposition to Odinga's leadership.[2] Their participation in the 1961 and 1963 elections indicated that this opposition had not disappeared; as did the emergence of the short-lived Luo United Movement (LUM) in 1962. Odinga believed that the sole objective of this movement was to destroy his support among the Nyanza people. One of its founders, on the other hand, insisted that its object was to bring together the two factions within Nyanza. Its leadership, nevertheless, identified it with, and so sustained, the earlier disagreement.[3] Up to independence, therefore, while mass support in Central Nyanza was undoubtedly behind Odinga's leadership, that leadership was still challenged by a group within the community. This challenge reflected a disagreement within the Luo community about the way in which progress was to be achieved, and the direction that progress should take.

[1] Although considerable publicity was given to the 'Uhuru chiefs' who operated in Central Nyanza the fact that they were appointed in only a small number of locations suggests they could not have dominated the organization. Where they were appointed they were important as a rival to the official chief whose position they hoped in due course to take over.

[2] Bennett and Rosberg, op. cit., and Sanger and Nottingham, op. cit. One of these Independents was Walter Odede, an early post-1945 leader in Nyanza and a former Member of Legislative Council, detained in 1953, who found himself in conflict with Odinga for local leadership after his return from detention in 1961. Their personal misunderstandings dated from then.

[3] *East African Standard*, 20 and 22 August and 6 September 1962; 5 February 1963. Odinga, op. cit., pp. 236–7.

District rivalries acquired a sharper focus after independence as a result of the rivalries within KANU at the national level. As Odinga's position in the central government came under more open attack so his opponents in Central Nyanza intensified their challenge to his position at home. The local rifts were demonstrated afresh, if not admitted, in the Senate election in August 1965, when the official KANU candidate, selected under Odinga's aegis, was unsuccessfully opposed by a KANU Independent known to be associated with Odinga's opponents. Odinga himself, as his national position was challenged, turned to strengthen his own popular support in the countryside beyond Central Nyanza, not least in South Nyanza. This emphasized the ethnic nature of his original base, sharpened his conflict with Mboya (himself active in that district), and highlighted their personal rivalry for Nyanza support.

This also drew the rural Luo community more closely into the national debate. Local concern among the Luo was increased by incidents such as Odinga's withdrawal from the Kenya Commonwealth delegation in 1965, and his removal from the position of Vice-Chairman of the Parliamentary Group in Nairobi.[1] Odinga's position, and the rift between him and other Cabinet Members, became a major topic of discussion within the Luo community. Elders of the Luo Union debated the dangers of the situation for the Luo as a group. At the same time many Luo, particularly in the rural areas, had begun to question the apparent discrimination against the Luo as a tribe. There was talk of discrimination in civil service appointments (provoked not least by the appointment of a Kikuyu to the post of Commissioner of Police leaving a Luo officer as his deputy); of the Luo being forgotten in economic development; of being left behind in the allocation of resources such as agricultural credit. Delays in the commencement of one of the major development projects proposed for Nyanza, the Kano Irrigation Scheme, were interpreted as further evidence of this discrimination and neglect. Such suspicions were reflected in many of the questions raised by Nyanza Members of Parliament, and in the debate on the President's Statement of Policy in November 1965.[2] In fact, Central Nyanza had not been ignored in terms of development proposals. But much of the development proposed, designed as it was to overcome those major physical obstacles that had in the past hindered agricultural progress, was of a long-term nature and could not produce an immediate and visible return to the ordinary peasant. The Kano Irrigation Project or the reclamation of the Yala Swamp,

---

[1] See Chapter 2 above.
[2] *Official Report*, House of Representatives, First Parliament, Third Session, Vol. VII, 9 to 30 November 1965.

for example, would both in due course be of great benefit to the agricultural development of the district; but the rewards would not become available for some time. The old conservative attitudes towards agricultural change were still, moreover, an obstacle to rapid development. Farmers in 1965 were also feeling the effects of lower prices for agricultural produce and receiving less for their crops. To the people in the rural areas therefore their situation did not appear to have improved markedly since independence. By the middle of 1965, the Luo community was engaged in intense discussion on two issues – the position of the Luo in the national community, and Odinga's position as leader of the Luo. The two issues merged into one.

Within the Luo Union there was intense disagreement as to what action the Luo could take to assure themselves of a proper place in the nation. One section, identified primarily with Central Nyanza, urged that they should follow the example of the Luyia, who had recently appointed a 'tribal leader'.[1] They argued that just as Kenyatta had built up a strong Kikuyu group, so the Luo must do the same to assure themselves of a proper position within the country; they fell back on the tribe as the basis upon which national unity could be built. This proposal, which echoed old demands for a paramount chief, made by Kikuyu, Luo and Luyia in the 1930s, provoked intense debate at successive meetings of the Luo Union in Kisumu and Nairobi, between those who argued in favour of recognition of Odinga as such a leader and those concerned at the risks of isolating the Luo from the rest of the country inherent in such an approach. This argument, at first carried on behind closed doors, emerged into the open when the Nairobi branch of the Union announced that it had elected Odinga as 'the political leader of the Luo in East Africa'.[2] This provoked spirited public interchanges on the question of leadership, and the dangers of tribalism and tribal politics, into which both Odinga and Mboya were drawn.[3]

The idea of a tribal leader for the Luo soon receded from public although not from private debate. Nevertheless the exchanges had served to emphasize the sense of community that existed among a large section of the Luo and the growing sense of need for some recognition of their identity as a group. This was a new element in the national political debate. At the same time the exchanges had highlighted Odinga's own special position among the Luo. Local leaders of the Luo Union carried this debate back to the rural areas in Nyanza; and so provided the perspective against which the rural population inter-

[1] *East African Standard*, 21 June 1965.
[2] Ibid., 2 and 23 August 1965.
[3] Ibid., 3 September 1965. *Daily Nation*, 11 and 15 September 1965.

preted the conflict between Odinga and his Cabinet colleagues in the latter months of 1965 and the beginning of the New Year. The events leading up to the Limuru conference and Odinga's eclipse in KANU, his subsequent resignation and the establishment of the new party were consequently identified in the rural areas as a challenge not only to Odinga but also to the Luo people. In the weeks between his resignation and the passage of the constitutional amendment, loyalty to his leadership in the district – which he had established over the previous ten years – remained strong.

This loyalty determined reactions to the conflict over a broad spectrum of the rural community, and meant that Odinga retained the support of the most influential groups within the district. The clan leaders who had provided him with support in the past remained behind him, and with their support went that of the older section of the community. The women whose support he had won in the fifties with his successful opposition to communal labour also for the most part continued to identify with him; this was of particular importance since in some constituencies they outnumbered male voters by almost two to one. The religious movement, Legio Maria, which at its inception had made Odinga their Patron Saint,[1] also remained loyal. Before the election campaign began Legio Maria leaders visited State House to reaffirm their loyalty to President Kenyatta. This did not, however, alter their relationship to Odinga, for they were able to separate matters of state from those of religion and so maintain their loyalty to Odinga and his significant position in the everyday life of their movement. 'We shall go where everybody is going' one of the leaders put it in an interview with one of the writers. 'That will guide our action.'

In addition Odinga had the support of many of the younger members of the community who also responded to him as to the leader who personified the Luo as a group. For the first time there was a feeling among young as well as older elements in the community that the Luo were under attack and their identity questioned. In this situation Odinga's symbolic position became all the more important, and young men who might otherwise have been less sympathetic to him interpreted the attack upon him as an attack upon themselves.

It was in this state of mind that a majority of the people in Central Nyanza approached the little general election. It was the first occasion in these constituencies on which two political parties had contested an election, for although there had on previous occasions been independent candidates they had all insisted upon their allegiance to KANU. In this situation people wanted to know why this contest had arisen; at almost all KPU meetings in Alego, for example, old men sat around in

[1] *East African Reporter*, June 1964.

small groups and attempted to recall whether such events had occurred before in the history of the Alego people. In asking the KPU candidate to explain, they were asking someone close to Odinga who symbolized the earlier security they now felt had been challenged. For these groups and for most others the election was about Odinga's position, and therefore the position of the Luo themselves.

Odinga's own public statements demonstrated that he also saw the election in this light: as a means of reaffirming his own legitimacy and position not only as distinctive leader of the Luo but also as a national leader in Kenya. His press statements issued prior to the campaign made this clear. In March he had openly challenged his Cabinet colleagues to go to the country at any time to test their position with the people. In April he repeated that challenge in his resignation statement. He summed up his position in a speech at Ahero during the campaign when he told his audience that he wished to adhere to the principles that had guided him throughout his political life but which Kenyatta had now left behind. He therefore had to fight Kenyatta; and the Luo people must stand firm behind him. In his mind questions of national policy, of national leadership and of the position of the Luo as a tribe were interwoven with the question of his own personal position. Not surprisingly the Nyanza campaign returned time and again to this theme.

The Candidates[1]

Odinga and the five Central Nyanza representatives who resigned with him automatically became the new party's candidates in the election, each standing in his former constituency. It is unnecessary to say more about Odinga himself. Of the others, one, the former Senator Ondiek Chilo, had scarcely had an opportunity to establish a parliamentary reputation for himself, since he had been elected only the previous April. He had formerly been on the African District Council, and was a Member of the Provincial Assembly. Only the former Member for Kisumu Rural, T. Okelo Odongo, who had been Assistant Minister for Finance, had been prominent on the national scene. He had, on several occasions, explicitly doubted the wisdom of certain of the Government's economic policies, and expressed specific concern at the uneven development of rural and urban areas that seemed to result from those policies. As an Assistant Minister he had refrained from

---

[1] The constituencies and candidates were: Bondo (Oginga Odinga, KPU, Walter Odede, KANU); Kisumu Rural (Okelo-Odongo, KPU, Yuko Otange, KANU); Nyando (Okuta Bala, KPU, Yusto N. Okal, KANU, Owalla Owino, Independent); Alego (Luke Obok, KPU, Collins Omondi, KANU, J. Olola, Independent); Ugenya (Odero Sar, KPU, D. Owino, KANU); Senate (Ondiek Chilo, KPU, Obuya Odundo, KANU).

voting against the Government and from entering into open conflict with the front bench within the House itself. Outside Parliament, however, his statements had placed him quite clearly in the Radicals' camp, notably a speech at the Lumumba Institute in June 1965 in which he had criticized the Kenya economy as being too much aligned with the Western bloc, and suggested that Kenya would have to 'lean a little more to the East' if she were to achieve the true economic non-alignment that African socialism required. This had provoked a strong reply from Mboya, and a newspaper battle between them.[1] Okelo Odongo was the only one of these Members who could claim any personal following in Central Nyanza independent of the support accorded him as one of Odinga's followers.

Luke Obok, as Member for Alego, had been consistently radical on those few occasions when he had spoken in Parliament. Neither of the other two members who resigned, Okuta Bala and Odero Sar, had emerged as significant figures either in Parliament or on the national political scene. They had usually supported the backbench group in its criticisms of the Cabinet (voting against the Government, for example, in the East African Federation motion and the Agriculture Amendment Bill adjournment),[2] and had therefore been generally associated with the more radical element in the KANU Parliamentary Group. Before they entered Parliament Okelo Odongo had been educated at universities in India, the United States and Britain, Obok had been a journalist, Ondiek Chilo a teacher, Bala a business man and Odero Sar a farmer. But their most important asset in this campaign was neither education nor past experience, but their known association with Odinga. All five of them had intimate links with him and were known in Nairobi and Nyanza as his supporters.

KANU had a formidable task in finding candidates, since in the face of the overwhelming expressions of popular support for Odinga there was considerable hesitation among his opponents about standing. In Bondo only Walter Odede was prepared to stand against Odinga himself; in Ugenya nine men applied for the nomination but only four appeared at the selection meeting. There was a similar reluctance to come forward in the other constituencies. Two results followed. First it was not difficult for an individual prepared to take the initiative to obtain the nomination, as Collins Omondi, recently returned to the district, did in Alego. Second, those who came forward were all men who had in the past been associated with Odinga's rivals. Omondi, although he had not recently been engaged in party politics, had been the first national Executive Officer of KANU in 1960 and closely

[1] *East African Standard*, 9 and 10 April 1965.
[2] See Chapter 2 above, and Chapter 5 below.

associated then with Mboya in Nairobi. He had been prepared to stand as an independent candidate in Nyanza in 1963 against the official KANU nominee, standing down only at the last minute. Yuko, who had been the First Secretary of Central Nyanza KANU branch, had resigned in 1961 after quarrelling with Odinga. Nyamolo Okal, also in KANU since its inception, had earlier been associated with Mboya's PCP. as well as LUM. He had stood as a KANU independent candidate first in 1963 (when he polled 11,572 votes against Okuta Bala's 14,537), and more recently in the Senate by-election the previous April. Odede had the longest record of public disagreement with Odinga since he had unsuccessfully contested the party nomination in 1961.[1] Daniel Owino, the Ugenya candidate, as a former Provincial Commissioner, was in a somewhat different category. Yet he had in recent months been under attack in the Nyanza Times, the *Dholo* paper which was essentially Odinga's vehicle.[2] The KANU candidates generally, therefore, represented that minority group within the district who had for some years challenged Odinga's leadership; and it was in this light that KPU candidates represented them to the public.

These men (with the exception of the candidate for the Senate) were generally better educated than their opponents. Owino had a Makerere diploma and an American degree. Omondi was a practising lawyer. Odede had a veterinary diploma and had attended Liverpool University. Yuko was a trained teacher and Okal a business man. Under different circumstances they might have won more support as alternative representatives for there had over the previous year been some signs of popular dissatisfaction with the former Members of Parliament who were regarded by a section of the population as responsible for the apparent neglect of the district. The low poll in the 1965 Senate election had been in part a demonstration of that dissatisfaction. During 1965 the Central Nyanza Members of Parliament had also found themselves challenged by their own local branch officials, who had begun to articulate local demands more strongly.[3] KANU leaders did their best to exploit this dissatisfaction; but the circumstances of May 1966 ensured that loyalty to Odinga was sufficient to counter any earlier dissatisfaction with the KPU candidates.

KANU candidates were at a further serious disadvantage in so far as

[1] He was also now Mboya's father-in-law. Most of the new KANU Branch Officials as well as several other applicants for the nominations were men who had also for some years been in conflict with Odinga: e.g. Joel Omino, formerly Chairman of the ADC, B. A. Ohanga, former Legislative Councillor for Nyanza, Gerard Olola, who, having failed to obtain the KANU Ugenya nomination, stood as an Independent, had stood as an Independent against official KANU candidates in 1963 and 1965, and, successfully, for a Regional Assembly seat in 1964.

[2] *Nyanza Times*, March–May 1966.

[3] See Chapter 2 above, also *Daily Nation*, 25 and 30 June 1965.

they could be characterized as outsiders in their own community at a time when the sense of community among the Luo was strong. Omondi had only recently returned to establish a legal practice in Kisumu and had had no recent close attachment to his home area. Yuko had been teaching in other districts for some years. Nyamolo Okal, although he had a branch of his bookshop business in Kisumu and family land in Nyakach, was living in Nairobi. Owino had been outside the district for some years until his posting as Provincial Commissioner in Kisumu in January 1965; and his office further separated him from his people, both because of the style of life assumed and the policies that he had to implement. Walter Odede, although resident in his home location, was frequently away from the district either at his farm at Songhor or in Nairobi. All of them had therefore suffered some degree of alienation from the community.

The situation in Ugenya typified the dilemma with which this faced them. Ugenya is a predominantly agrarian community of small farmers in which the apparent absence of serious economic inequalities contributes to its considerable agrarian stability. People in Ugenya feel a general sense of social and economic equality which is strengthened by their cultural unity. This sense of equality created a deep feeling for uniformity and a willingness to support a person who recognized and identified himself with the social and economic conditions of that community. The continued influence and power of clan and sub clan heads hindered individual initiative. There were, for instance, several shopkeepers, better farmers and others in the area who felt themselves forced by community pressure to operate their enterprises at half capacity for fear of being ostracized if they showed signs of greater prosperity. Against this social background Odero Sar was secure because he had nothing to show that he was economically superior to most members of the community. He was regarded in the area as a good family man with a stable home. Equally important, he had been associated with Odinga (who had built him up in the 1963 elections) for many years and with the Luo Thrift and Trading Corporation and the Luo Union. Owino, on the other hand, had lived outside the district, had no strong local ties, and his way of life and the requirements of his office as Provincial Commissioner had emphasized the differences between himself and the local community. Odero Sar was without difficulty therefore presented as the more suitable person to represent the community, notwithstanding Owino's education and overseas experience.[1] The particular circumstances of each KANU candidate

[1] There was also a strong feeling that Owino, as one of the two Luo Provincial Commissioners, could better have served the Luo community in that capacity. This criticism was also levelled against Omondi: that as a Luo he would serve them better as a practising lawyer, of whom they had too few.

and each constituency varied. They were not all in such a difficult position as Owino. In Nyakach, for example, the KANU candidate, although he lived in Nairobi, had close clan associations that were of considerable assistance in identifying him with at least part of the constituency. Nevertheless Ugenya highlighted the problems they all faced in some degree, of separation from the rural voters whom they wished to represent.

The Campaign

The KPU candidates enjoyed a second significant advantage over their opponents when it came to party organization. KPU had taken over virtually the whole of the existing KANU party machine in the district together with its experienced personnel. In this way they acquired an established communication network; and their campaign was mounted by men and women who had already acquired considerable experience in electioneering in 1961 and 1963.[1] The KANU candidates on the other hand faced all the difficulties of creating a new party organization in what might have been described as alien territory. They had first to prove that the party existed in the district, and then to establish a party presence.

Immediately after the breakup of the former branch a small group of those who remained with KANU held a meeting in Kisumu at which they constituted themselves as an interim committee with Oselu Nyalick (Member for Winam) as Chairman and Paul Adeno, a Kisumu shopkeeper and businessman, as Secretary. These two toured the district to establish new committees and to hold nomination meetings. They did this with some difficulty; but the fact that they were able to do so at all suggested they were not in completely alien territory. In those constituencies involved in the election, each location was asked to send representatives to a meeting to select the candidates from the applications received. The names selected were then forwarded to Kisumu and on to Nairobi. Only in one constituency was the local choice quite clearly overruled by Nairobi.[2] Though they carried out the selections with little difficulty the new party officials in Kisumu were less successful in providing support to the candidates during the campaign. They had had limited campaign experience themselves, and little time to set up any branch organization before the election was

---

[1] Although the local situation in 1965 suggested that the KANU branch had slackened its activities, late in 1965 and early in 1966 the officials had begun to revive it, perhaps anticipating difficulties, as the conflict between the Radicals and Conservatives became more intense.

[2] In Ugenya last minute instructions were received from Nairobi that the constituency choice, a school-teacher, should stand down for a new candidate, Daniel Owino, who had up to that time been Provincial Commissioner for Nyanza Province.

upon them. Consequently there was little team work or co-ordination and the candidates were for the most part left to organize their own campaigns, each finding his own assistants, although in one or two instances agents were drafted in from Nairobi.

KPU candidates conducted a busy campaign until the first polling days when the House candidates went to the polls. They organized a series of large rallies which they arranged for non-market days to avoid interrupting normal economic activity. (KANU in contrast sought to exploit the regular market-day crowds.) The number of such meetings varied considerably between constituencies. Luke Obok organized only six large rallies in Alego, whereas Okuta Bala held approximately twenty in his Nyando constituency. The most significant feature of KPU's campaign organization was, however, as was pointed out in the last chapter, the importance attached to small meetings as opposed to large rallies. Among the reasons for this preference for small meetings was the regulation that no licence was required for a meeting of less than fifty people; whereas all others required permission from the District Commissioner and seven days' notice. At large public rallies moreover the police were always standing by, whereas they were not present at small meetings. A second reason was that the existing committee structure and clan connections provided a solution to the problems of campaigning in a large rural area in which homesteads rather than large centres of population were the dominant settlement pattern. At the same time their control of this structure enabled KPU in most areas effectively to prevent KANU from gaining access to the rural population.

Each candidate utilized the structure in his own particular way. In Ugenya, for example, the sub-location committees organized small meetings, usually held in the homes of clan heads and other local notables who were expected to maintain the cohesion of the clan and to mobilize its support behind the party. Odero Sar did not himself attend many of these meetings, leaving them to his agents and supporters, except in the most populous North Ugenya location. In Kisumu Rural, on the other hand, Okelo Odongo left the clan leaders to take the initiative in approaching him and his agents to request a meeting. But he responded readily to such requests and attended a large number of such meetings with clan and sub-clan groups during the campaign. Organization in this constituency was, as elsewhere, based on the committees of fifty and seven; and once a clan leader had put out an invitation the responsibility for the actual arrangements was shared with Okelo Odongo's location agents.

Much the same ground was covered at these small meetings as at larger rallies, but in a more intimate setting where closer relationships could be established between candidate and people. In addition they provided opportunities to refute matters raised at KANU meetings and to deal with questions raised by KPU policies. But perhaps the most significant feature of these meetings was that they took the candidate deep into the countryside and provided him with much closer association with the ordinary people than was otherwise possible. They emphasized the party's grass roots contacts and its claim, symbolized in its party slogan and symbol, to be 'of the people'.

Odinga's role in the Central Nyanza campaign must be especially noted. He carried out very little public campaigning, either in his own constituency of Bondo or elsewhere, and addressed only a few large meetings. Instead of formal campaigning at the beginning of the election period, he spent some time walking in the market-places on market days, talking informally with people and cracking jokes that had a calculated political meaning. At Rangala market, in Ugenya, for example, on one such occasion, he reminded the people that they now lived in a strange world. 'You see,' he said, 'I built KANU and Kenyatta himself all in good faith. At that time I refused to believe in the saying *"chiero wang' mithiedho emagawi"*, (it is the person you have saved who turns against you) but now I do.' This was powerful imagery, conveying a serious warning to people to be on their guard against a government run by 'aliens' in which their own trusted leadership had no part, and at the same time reminding them of his own position.

This imagery typified KPU spokesmen's skilful exploitation of Luo idiom and symbolism to establish their common identity with the people. At a time when the Luo sense of cultural identity was particularly strong KPU leaders' greater ability in drawing on local idiom gave them a vital advantage. This was particularly noticeable in their presentation to the people of their new party symbol and slogan. At the beginning of the campaign KPU leaders were unsure whether they would be able to transfer people's allegiance from their old KANU symbol of the cock which had served them well over the past seven years to the new KPU symbol of the bull. The cock occupied a special place in Luo custom which they themselves had in the past exploited to the full.[1] Moreover, in the 1963 elections, when several of the Independent candidates had used the cow as their symbol they, as KANU, had destroyed any legitimacy it might have enjoyed. For this reason the Central Nyanza members of KPU had been hesitant, initially, about the party symbol, and insisted that if the cattle symbol were to be used it must be a bull rather than a cow. Despite these

[1] In 1957 the cock had been Odinga's symbol in Central Nyanza and Mboya's in Nairobi. See *East African Standard*, 13 March 1957.

problems however they encountered no difficulty in educating people to the association of the bull with KPU, Odinga and themselves. By drawing deeply upon Luo custom they rapidly evoked a favourable response to their new party symbol. In the past cattle had played a vital role in the Luo domestic economy. They had been the ladder to social status which most men sought to climb. They were required for bride price (and used for making shrewd marriage alliances) as well as for ritual occasions. Many Luo ceremonies and dances featured the bull, which was the symbol of prestige and status, as evidenced in the saying *a chi ruath* (I am the wife of the bull). Although cattle have become less important in the economy in recent years, they still retain considerable cultural significance and remain associated in people's minds with Luo custom and tradition. KPU speakers exploited this association to the full, particularly to justify the actual change of symbol. Just as in Luo custom the cockerel, which signifies the beginning of a new home, gives way to cattle when that home has been properly established, so they interpreted their own change. KANU and the cock had launched Kenya into independence; but having secured that independence it was time to replace that party with KPU and the bull. This argument proved effective. 'We have heard the cock is gone,' a group of women in a Sakwa market said to one of the writers early in the campaign, 'now it is the bull'; and this typified the general public acceptance of the change.

Instead of countering symbolism with symbolism KANU attempted to win public support by associating the cock in people's minds with Government and so with power and authority. Under the circumstances this was, however, an ineffective weapon since 'Government' was regarded more as the source of neglect and of Nyanza's troubles than of assistance.

KANU leaders fully appreciated the importance of effective communication with the rural population and clan groups, but their organization was for the most part unable to meet the needs of the occasion. Only in Nyando, where the candidate had built up a group of agents during his two previous election attempts, was there a viable constituency organization; but this covered only the western half of his constituency. In Bondo Odede failed to establish any working party machine, notwithstanding the assistance he received from a former agent recalled from Mombasa for the occasion. In Kisumu Rural the KANU candidate restricted himself to his own clan area, rejecting the advice of agents drafted in to assist him to establish contacts over as much of the constituency as possible. In Ugenya Owino was too inexperienced to establish a local organization that could successfully challenge KPU's hold on the area. Like the other candidates he took on any young men willing with time to spare; but they also were unskilled in the techniques of party organization and recruitment, and the rural areas where the KPU committees reigned supreme remained closed to them. Lack of time, transport, personnel and experience defeated their efforts to copy the KPU committee system. Although they set up KANU offices at every market centre the young KANU activists spent most of their day discussing the distribution of youth-wing dresses and party shirts and arguing about the allocation of party funds. This seriously inhibited KANU. In their efforts to establish contact with clan leaders they were generally out-manœuvred by the superior expertise and longer-established connections of their opponents. Each of the candidates, particularly Okal in Nyando, benefited to some extent from his own direct clan associations within his home area; but otherwise they were unable to break through KPU's close clan associations.[1]

KANU attempted to compensate for their weakness at location level by holding full-scale rallies throughout the district as a means of communicating their stand and Government views on the contest. The peak of this rally activity was the full-scale ministerial tour organized by Mboya, who visited each constituency in the district and provided the major KANU attack upon the Opposition. With two other Luo Ministers, Ayodo (Minister for Tourism and Wildlife), and Odero Jowi (Assistant Minister for Finance), and joined at different times by others, Mboya toured the district intensively, campaigning in each constituency in turn and addressing twelve meetings in three days.[2] Accompanied by a police escort and by Administrative Officers (who were bound by the rules of civil service protocol to accompany any ministerial visitors in their areas), their tour symbolized the association of Government and party against the Opposition. But in the perspective of Nyanza politics as well as the developments on the national scene the ministerial visit had a second and more significant purpose, for it carried Mboya's battle with Odinga deep into the latter's home territory. Despite the considerable speculation in Kisumu as to whether he would appear in the district and the expressed concern at a possible attack upon him, and ignoring the strong opposition to him personally, he struck deep into the countryside to challenge Odinga in his own base.

[1] The Nyando constituency raises an important question for which the evidence does not, however, provide any conclusive answer. Okal had a following in the western part of the constituency, his own clan area, as the voting indicated. The Nyakach area is also, however, one in which land consolidation had gone further at an earlier date than in most parts of the district. It is possible that progress in consolidation, having weakened the clan organization, had thus weakened Odinga's own base.

[2] They were joined for part of the campaign, at different points in the programme, by other Ministers, including Jeremiah Nyagah (Minister for Education) and Ronald Ngala (Minister for Co-operatives and Social Services).

The impact upon KANU's fortunes from this visit was difficult to gauge. Few of Mboya's audiences were either large or receptive. KPU had from the outset portrayed him as the source of Odinga's difficulties and emphasized his challenge (contrary to Luo custom) to an older man, and his willingness to join the Kikuyu against his own people. Clan elders described his actions in terms of the tribal past when a jealous man within the tribe had joined forces with the enemy against his own people. Any success Mboya might have had in exposing the weakness of KPU's position and policies was minimized by the Opposition's successful exploitation of Luo tradition to portray him as an enemy of the tribe.

The Issues

The inter-party debate in Central Nyanza ranged over all those events which had led up to the election, including the constitutional amendment which KPU rejected as a matter of principle. It emphasized each party's position on the resignations, rural development, tribalism, the nature of government in the independent state and above all Odinga's own position.

Throughout the campaign the KPU candidates took considerable pains to explain that their resignation from KANU had been forced upon them by the Government's failure to honour the promises made in the 1963 KANU Manifesto. They appealed for support from the people – whom they now represented – against a Government that benefited only the few. They explained in detail why they believed the Government had failed to implement those promises; but their emphasis was upon those issues which touched directly upon the rural community, particularly land, education, health services, and agricultural credit. They generally approached these issues in terms of governmental neglect. Their strongest criticism was of the Government's failure to fulfil the KANU promise of a minimum of seven years' free education for every child. This was argued against the background of the existing educational difficulties in Central Nyanza. Primary schools in the district were generally in a poor condition, although the number of children of primary school age was in 1966 among the highest in the country. A large proportion of primary school teachers was untrained. There had been a considerable migration of teachers from the district to Rift Valley and Central Provinces, creating additional difficulties for secondary schools. Fees, moreover, had increased since independence (as they had over the whole country). All this gave point to KPU's charges of governmental neglect of the area.

The Opposition similarly explained Central Nyanza's other difficulties in terms of the Government's failure to implement its

E

promises to the people. The paucity of medical facilities in the district was compared with the 1963 promise to increase health services. Attention was drawn to the general backwardness of agriculture and the deteriorating condition of much of the land, which were explained by reference not to the agrarian resistance of the fifties, but to present government neglect. The earlier opposition to land consolidation had by this time been superseded by considerable local enthusiasm for registration as a foundation for development; and KPU now criticized the delays in setting up registration units for the district as the source of many of the agricultural problems. They presented the Government's failure to provide agricultural loans for farmers in Nyanza as the reason for their slow development. It was not difficult to build up a picture of neglect arising out of Government failure to implement popularly accepted policies; nor to add an ethnic dimension to the charge by insisting that this failure was directly the result of Kikuyu domination over the Government. The present situation existed, they argued, because of the Kikuyu domination in the Cabinet and the civil service which gave them control of policy.

KPU also challenged Government policies in terms of class formation and the dangers that this posed for the country. They criticized the recent decision to introduce free education in the two senior forms of secondary school as a concession that benefited only a small section of the population who did not in fact need that assistance, but who would as a consequence be entrenched in power. The failure to introduce free primary education would in their view perpetuate and increase the economic divisions in the society. Only the rich could at present afford to educate their children; but these were the civil servants, the present ruling class. They would in turn therefore be succeeded by their children, and the ruling class would be perpetuated. They demanded the provision of equal opportunities for all children, through free education, as the only means of preventing such developments. The party recognized that such a policy had to be financed; but argued that the necessary resources could be found by nationalizing certain industries, such as the East African Breweries and Power and Lighting Company. (During his three-day tour Mboya cogently challenged the economics of this case, but there was otherwise no one to argue against it.)

KPU's appeal therefore carried strong egalitarian overtones, and suggested an incipient class conflict reminiscent of that which had divided the *Jodong Gweng* and peasants from chiefs and others of a potential middle class ten years before. The association of the richer element in the district with KANU enabled KPU to portray that party as 'the rich' in conflict with 'the poor'. Ideas of class were, however,

118

generally less significant than the appeal to traditional Luo ideas of equality and to the strong attachment to community characteristic of Luo social organization.

This could be detected in their approach to questions of economic development. While they denied the charge that they offered a policy of 'free things' as a basis for development, KPU nevertheless insisted that equal development was impossible unless some special assistance was given initially to the truly needy in society. Only such assistance could enable the man with no assets at all to compete with the more fortunate members of society; and it was the function of government to provide that assistance. Okelo Odongo, for example, defined the legitimate end of government activity as the prevention of extreme poverty through the creation of institutions to protect the individual from exploitation. Reminding people of the security that had characterized the traditional family unit, he insisted that proper government planning could revive it. In so doing he rejected the individualism explicit in recent Kenyan development policy as the only basis for development. He was asking for the adaptation of policy to the social and economic circumstances of any particular group of people, in this case to the communal basis of Luo society. Ondiek Chilo argued a similar case when he advocated a greater emphasis upon communal farming.

KPU criticisms of Government land policy similarly drew upon traditional Luo attitudes, and the deep attachment to land that existed among the rural population. The question of the return of the 'Delamere acres' was not of intense concern to people who had not themselves suffered directly the loss of land to European settlers; and the Opposition could not make this a major issue in the Nyanza campaign. There was, on the other hand, a strong association between land and security, and a deep attachment to a man's own locality. This explained for example the deep reluctance that existed among the people in the northern parts of the district, such as Alego, to contemplate moving elsewhere in spite of the overcrowding in the location. Many people felt that since they could still produce enough for subsistence, which was their major concern, they were secure. 'We grow enough and cannot starve,' was the way in which some of the Ugenya people put it. 'The only calamity that may beset us is in famine or warfare. Only the Kikuyu who have land hunger can go hungry.' Odinga and his party exploited this deep association of security with the land to provoke opposition to KANU's land policy and the idea of land as an economic asset that could only be bought and sold. 'Did you ever have to buy land?' Odinga asked an audience at Ahero. 'You inherit it and you have the land and you work it and get crops from it. It is free to work on the land.'

Although certain of the KPU candidates attempted to separate the question of ethnic rivalry from their differences with Kikuyu Members of the Government on policy, the two issues became intricately intertwined. In this respect cultural symbolism again contributed a vital element to the debate, for KPU exploited Luo tradition and history strongly to highlight the differences between Kikuyu and Luo and to attack the idea of Kikuyu leadership over the Luo. In interpreting Mboya's position and rejecting his policies the emphasis was upon his youth and the challenge to an older man, which emphasized a tribal issue rather than the differences over policies. The election was as a result portrayed implicitly as a contest between Luo and Kikuyu. The Kikuyu, led by Kenyatta, having been assisted to power by the Luo (through Odinga) sought to exclude the Luo from the fruits of independence. The fundamental question of central power was expressed in ethnic terms.

This was not the first occasion on which there had been talk of Kikuyu domination over the Luo. Mention has already been made of the allegations of a Kikuyu bias over KAU, when a local group in Nyanza in 1952 had urged Odede and Awori to leave that party. The spokesman of the Luo United Movement had raised the same question in 1962. Neither of those groups had, however, enjoyed any mass support; and there was nothing to suggest that their views reflected fears held by the majority of Luo in the district. In 1966, however, the KPU leaders who raised the question of Kikuyu domination were in closer communication with the rural population; and they interpreted the Kikuyu challenge as a challenge to Odinga. The ethnic appeal was thus in 1966 of vital consequence, for it took the issue back to that of Odinga's leadership.

The initiative in the Central Nyanza debate lay with KPU, whose emphasis on rural discontent put KANU at a real disadvantage, since in the face of existing conditions it could not deny the slow expansion of services. Instead KANU officials ensured that local difficulties were raised at the meetings attended by the Ministers, and extracted promises of assistance. Thus when the ministerial party toured Ugenya they promised to open a new boys' secondary school at Rangala, gave money for the improvement of Simenya nursery and primary schools, and promised to find some means of aiding the new Harambee secondary school being developed at Sigomere. They hoped thus to win support for the Government, but they found their promises used by KPU to prove the value of an Opposition. Only now, when the Opposition had pushed the Government, the KPU argued, did any benefits come to the district. In Nyando constituency Government leaders were able during the campaign to announce two specific decisions for the area: the commencement of the Kano Irrigation Pilot Project, and the division of Central Nyanza into two districts. But neither aroused unanimous local support. There were local fears about the question of land ownership in the new scheme, and only the western part of the constituency whole-heartedly supported the administrative changes, which had been a local political issue for some time.

KANU spokesmen threw the responsibility for Nyanza's slow development upon the KPU leaders themselves. They recalled the opposition to agrarian reform in the 1950s, and Odinga's part in it. His detractors argued that since independence the Central Nyanza Members of Parliament had failed to take any interest in local development or taken time to explain Government plans and policies to their people, but had engaged only in political activity for their own benefit. Most of all they charged Odinga with the responsibility for Nyanza's situation. His past activities in the Luo Thrift and Trading Corporation, the Luo Union, and business ventures such as the Lolwe Bus Company were interpreted not as benefits to the community but as his way of exploiting the public for his own advantage. The past rifts within the district and between South and Central Nyanza were recalled, to build up a picture of a man concerned only with his own personal position and power. They maintained that it was 'Odingaism' that was at the root of Nyanza's backwardness, for his past behaviour had held up district development for his own ends. Now, they alleged, he wished to plunge the district into further difficulties because of his own vested interests. He had not resigned out of concern for his people but simply because he had lost his office. The issue was not one of ethnic domination but personal ambition. No one had chased him away; he had left KANU because of his desire for power. His resignation itself, his enemies alleged, had done the Luo community a great disservice, for he had lost to them the second most important office in the country.

KANU therefore made a direct attack upon Odinga's legitimacy in his own territory, a challenge symbolized by Mboya's ministerial visit. With the other Luo Ministers beside him on the platform Mboya could deny that the Luo had been ejected from the Government or that Luo participation in the national institutions of the country had come to an end. At this stage, the opposition that had long existed to Odinga's dominant position among the Luo community was brought out on to the centre of the stage.

The question of personal power was closely linked, however, with the contest for power in the central government. In attacking Odinga KANU also challenged the legitimacy of the Opposition. While KANU leaders denied that all Luo had given their support to Odinga, they also warned the district of the risks that that faced if they followed

KPU. If the Luo supported KPU they would be isolated from the rest of Kenya at a time when they needed to work together with the other tribes for their mutual benefit. While KANU denied responsibility for the district's economic backwardness, at the same time they pointed out that if the Luo now supported KPU and opposed the Government which controlled and distributed all the resources available for development they could not at the same time expect assistance. If Nyanza supported the Opposition they would be the enemy of the Government and could not therefore expect development.

They contrasted the weakness of the Opposition with the strength of the Government, and exploited past political and administrative history to demonstrate the impossibility of successfully opposing the Government. KANU had defeated the APP and Ngei and KADU and Ngala; in the same way they would defeat KPU and Odinga. The strength of the Government was visibly demonstrated by the removal from office of a number of chiefs throughout the district early in the campaign. Since all immediately joined KPU point was given to the allegation that they had been removed for political reasons.[1] A subsequent warning to teachers against political activity sharpened the point.[2] Nor did the KANU spokesman fail to draw on events elsewhere in Africa to impress upon their audiences the idea of the omnipotence of governmental power. Direct reference was made to events in the Congo (where four Ministers who had opposed Colonel Mobutu had recently been executed in public) and in Buganda (where the Kabaka had not long since fled after open confrontation with Prime Minister Obote and the Uganda forces).[3]

Odinga's influence in Nyanza was sufficient to withstand this attack on the sterility of the Opposition. But perhaps the concept of an omnipotent government was also less influential in Nyanza than in Central Province, because the Luo had not been defeated in open battle by the colonial Government as the Kikuyu had in the Emergency. The Opposition did not question the need for strong government. They argued pointedly that the Opposition could push a Government to take action – as when new schools were promised during the campaign. But at no time during the election did KPU candidates argue the desirability of a two-party state as such. The sense of Luo identity did not provoke any separatist feelings, comparable for example to those of Buganda. The contest was for power at the centre, not the periphery.

The idea of the omnipotence of government clearly worried some people in Nyanza. It was raised in at least one of Okelo Odongo's

[1] *East African Standard*, 10 and 18 June 1966.
[2] *Daily Nation*, 7 June 1966 and 12 July 1966. KNUT, Central Nyanza Branch, Circular Letter 14/160. 'Teachers and Politics in Central Nyanza District'.
[3] Reported from Asembo, 6 June 1966.

committee meetings, when he was asked whether it was true that a Member of Parliament who belonged to the Opposition had no access to the Government and could, as Mboya had said, do nothing for his people. Okelo Odongo, denying this, pointed out that the people had in fact been able to present Mboya with a petition during his tour, although they did not all belong to KANU.

KPU took considerable pains to explain how a Member of Parliament was a representative with the right to present his constituents' views in Parliament and to the Government whatever his party. At the same time they acknowledged the fact that if they were elected at this stage they still could not form a government and implement their promises immediately. They insisted that a vote for their party at this stage meant victory for that party in the general elections that would follow in 1968. They accepted the possibility that they would suffer in the immediate future; but called upon Luo history to explain the necessity of such suffering, as Luo had in the past suffered in their southward marches before they eventually settled in their present home. Finally, and most important, they challenged the claim to government omnipotence with a broad social appeal. Government was not, they argued, a small group of men in Nairobi; it was the people themselves. The power lay ultimately with the people; and if the people supported KPU it was they, not the Government, who had the backing of the majority. The concept of governmental authority was neutralized by a powerful appeal to the community itself.

Conclusions

There were specific local issues raised in each constituency during the election campaign such as the extension of the municipal boundary into Kisumu Rural or the division of the district in Nyando. But the election in Central Nyanza was essentially concerned with national issues. These were given greater weight perhaps because they were translated into the local idiom. Nevertheless the local idiom could not disguise the fact that the election was primarily about local-central relations and the manner in which the district should share governmental power with the centre. The relative backwardness of Central Nyanza's economy added to the significance of this question, for local neglect or advancement was seen to be directly associated with power at the centre. Although KPU insisted upon the legitimacy of Opposition they sought, not to weaken the power of the central government, but to control it. The debate was about who should control the central government. This raised questions of leadership at a time when Odinga, the dominant leader in the district with a powerful popular base, was under fire. The question of power at the centre was therefore intricately associated with leadership at the district level. The emphasis upon leadership in turn reinforced the importance of the group, because the two issues of personality and of ethnic identity and pride were so closely bound together. A survey by one of the writers in Alego and Ugenya suggested that a vote for KPU was a vote for Odinga. Impressionistic evidence gathered in the remaining constituencies supported this view. Whether or not people were voting for Odinga as a person or as a symbol of Luo identity is difficult, in the absence of more detailed voters' surveys, to assess. What can be said is that the whole campaign, as it was conducted by both parties, emphasized this ethnic role with Odinga at the centre of the stage.

5

Parliament
in Kenya

The December 1963 Independence Constitution provided Kenya with a parliamentary form of government. Executive authority was vested in the Queen, exercised on her behalf by the Governor General, who was advised by his Prime Minister and Cabinet with whom political power lay. The Cabinet was responsible to the National Assembly which was a bicameral legislature. The House of Representatives, the Lower House consisted of 117 directly elected members, elected for a five-year term of office to represent single member constituencies, twelve Specially Elected Members elected by the House sitting as an Electoral College, the Attorney General, *ex officio* and the Speaker. The Senate, the Upper House, consisted of forty-one Senators elected to represent the forty-one districts into which the country is divided, and holding office for six years (one-third retiring in rotation every second year), and the Speaker. Parliament consisted of Her Majesty and the National Assembly.[1]

The first amendment to the Constitution,[2] which established the Republic, radically altered the position of the executive by providing for a President who became both the Head of State and Head of Government. Executive authority in the Republic of Kenya was now vested in the President. The bicameral legislature was, however, retained without any change. Furthermore, the constitution retained many of the checks upon the executive by the legislature which are characteristic of a parliamentary system of government and which link Executive and Legislature closely together. First, the President had himself to be an elected Member of the House of Representatives. He therefore sat in the National Assembly as a member in his own right. Second, the constitution provided for a Cabinet, which consisted

[1] The Kenya Independence Order in Council, 1963, Schedule 2, The Constitution of Kenya, Chapter IV.
[2] The Constitution of Kenya (Amendment) Act, 1964. Act. No. 28 of 1964. First Schedule, ss. 33, 72, 76.

of the President, the Vice-President and such other Ministers as the President might choose. All Cabinet Ministers had to be elected members of one or other of the two Houses of the Assembly. The President, therefore, also sat in the House of Representatives in his capacity as Head of the Cabinet, which was collectively responsible to the two Houses of the National Assembly. Third, the House of Representatives (but not the Senate) could move a vote of no confidence in the Government, on a motion for which seven days' notice was required. If such a vote of no confidence were passed the President had within three days either to resign or dissolve Parliament. Fourth, all legislation, after being passed by both Houses, was to be passed to the President for his assent; but no provision was laid down for a presidential veto. Finally, the President had sole power to dissolve Parliament at any time. If he did, however, he himself also had to resign.

The House of Representatives was directly involved in the election of the President. The President held office for five years, his term of office running simultaneously with that of the House of Representatives, and his election taking place at the same time as the general election. On the occasion of a general election all candidates for the House of Representatives had to signify their support for one of the presidential candidates; and that presidential candidate who, having been elected as a constituency member, had a majority of the votes of the successful candidates, was elected as President.[1] Where an election of a President was necessary other than at the time of a general election (if the President dies in office, or resigns, or is declared unable to discharge the functions of office) it was to be carried out by the House of Representatives acting as an electoral college, under a procedure laid down in the constitution.

It was on these several provisions that Mr Mboya (then Minister for Justice and Constitutional Affairs), when introducing the second reading of the first bill to amend the constitution and to establish the Republic, based his argument that although Kenya would have an executive President the supremacy of Parliament remained secure. This parliamentary supremacy was retained as the vital protection against any abuse of the strong executive power now vested in the President, because it ensured that executive and legislature could not drift apart.[2]

[1] This procedure ensured that, although the presidential election is indirect, the electorate is directly involved, in so far as a vote for a particular candidate for the House of Representatives involves also a vote for a particular candidate for the presidency. Act 28 of 1964 provided that the first President should be the person who, immediately before 12 December 1964, held the office of Prime Minister, under the constitution.

[2] *Official Report*, House of Representatives, Vol. III, Second Session, 23 October 1964, cols. 3879–905.

The first National Assembly was elected in May 1963, when Mr Kenyatta's Kenya African National Union (KANU) won an overwhelming victory against the Kenya African Democratic Union (KADU), its major opponent, the African People's Party (APP) (a break away group from KANU who rejoined the party soon after in August 1963), and a number of Independents, all of whom subsequently declared their support for KANU in the National Assembly. Mr Kenyatta and his Cabinet, who took over in May 1963, when internal self-government was granted, were thus first responsible to a two-party legislature in which they held a very comfortable majority in the Lower House, and a reasonable majority in the Senate.[1] But in November 1964 KADU voluntarily dissolved itself, all but one of its members joining KANU, and the National Assembly became overnight a one-party legislature.[2] The Cabinet that Mr Kenyatta appointed in December 1964, when the Republic was established, was essentially the same Cabinet as before, although several Ministers were moved to different ministries and one former KADU and one additional KANU M.P., were given ministerial posts.

There were at that time including the Speaker, three Europeans (one of whom was a Minister) and three Asians among the Members of Parliament. The Speaker of the Lower House was a European, Mr Slade, elected unanimously in June 1963; the Speaker of the Upper House was an African, Mr Chokwe. The legislature was therefore essentially an African legislature. And in 1963 it was a very new legislature. Few of the members had had any previous experience of the working of parliamentary government: of the 173 members of both Houses elected in 1963 only twenty-nine had been in the previous parliament and only twelve in the former Legislative Council.

Certain modifications in the regulation of parliamentary debate were necessary at the end of 1964 to meet the changed constitutional and political situation when Kenya became a Republic and a one-party state; but the legislature still followed what were essentially the parliamentary practices of Westminster. Both Houses sat each afternoon from Tuesday to Thursday, and then on Friday morning. The Senate started one week later than the House. In January 1965 a programme of fortnightly meetings of both Houses throughout the year, with the exception of a long recess during August and September,

---

[1] Membership, June 1963: *Senate:* Government (KANU group) 21; Opposition (KADU/A.P.P. group) 17. *House of Representatives:* Government (KANU group) 86; Opposition (KADU/A.P.P.) 36. 2 Somalis seats were vacant at that date.

Membership, June 1964. *Senate:* Government (KANU group) 27; Opposition (KADU group) 14. *House of Representatives:* Government 104; Opposition 23. 4 vacancies.

[2] On the dissolution of Kadu see *East African Standard,* 10 November 1964.

was followed. At the beginning of 1966 this arrangement was changed, and the new timetable provided for a long sitting from January to March, a recess of eight weeks, followed by the Budget sitting, of ten weeks, a long recess in August and September, and a short meeting of two weeks in October, the new session beginning in November. Parliament was then sitting for an average of ninety days each year.[1]

The Lower House was the stronger of the two Houses of the National Assembly, and up to 1966 it was this House that influenced the Executive, rather than the Assembly as a whole. The control of money bills, which was secured to the House of Representatives, ensured the House's dominant position in the legislative process; and this position was strengthened by the fact that it was the House, not the Senate, that had the power to move a vote of no confidence in the Executive. The Senate could not, however, be dismissed as unimportant or powerless. It had a continuing life, which the House did not. Its consent to all legislation was necessary, including any legislation that amended the constitution itself. It had the right to propose amendments to legislation initiated in the Lower House, and its use of this right to amend led in several instances in 1965 to disagreements between the two Houses, which, although eventually resolved, held up certain parts of the Government's programme for some time.

The Senate could amend any bill, except a money bill, sent up to it after passage through the House of Representatives; and if it did so, the bill was returned to the Lower House with a notice of these amendments. The House might accept the amendments without opposition and the amended legislation then proceeded easily: it was passed through the House and returned to the Senate. If however the House rejected the Senate's amendments, it could follow one of several courses of action. It could refuse to consider amendments, and move that they be considered this day six months – in other words it could kill the bill for the Session. On the other hand it might consider the amendments immediately, disagree with them, and send the bill back to the Senate for reconsideration. If, however, the Senators insisted on their amendments, the House could either postpone the bill for six months (as above) or order the withdrawal of the bill, or move that the bill be committed to a Joint Committee of both Houses. If the House subsequently accepted the Joint Committee's Report then the bill was deemed to be passed. If it disagreed the bill was deemed to be withdrawn. If the Government, at least twelve months after the rejection of a bill by the Senate, and in a subsequent session, reintroduced the bill,

---

[1] Compare the number of sitting days of the Legislative Council of 1960, 66 days; 1961, 60 days; 1962, 42 days. The National Assembly sat 51 days in 1963; 91 days in 1964; 96 in 1965; and 99 in 1966.

and the House passed it, and it was sent to Senate at least one month before the end of the session, although the House might not before the end of the session agree to any amendments proposed by the Senate at this stage, the bill was passed.[1]

The procedure whereby Senate amendments were dealt with by the House was therefore complicated and involved. The Senate's power of delay was not unlimited, but it was important, and experience suggested that the Senate, for its part, was not always aware of the consequences to the Government of its actions, since most of its amendments which did hold up legislation were of minor importance.

The relationship between the two Houses became more difficult during 1965, not least because with the abolition of regionalism the original *raison d'être* for the Senate disappeared. The Senate was conceived of in the first place as a reviewing House: its function to review (as well as to initiate) legislation with particular consideration to any possible implications of discrimination against either a tribal or a racial minority. It was for this reason that the Senate was given a vital role in the amendment process: any amendments to the constitution that touched upon the then 'entrenched' clauses (all of which related to fundamental rights and the position and powers of the then Regions) required a 90 per cent majority in the Senate.[2] The constitutional amendments passed between October 1964 and April 1965, however, not only abolished regionalism and the powers of the then Regional Authorities; they also changed the amending process itself, so that any amendment to any part of the constitution now required only a two-thirds majority of each House.[3] The Senate, on the other hand, which might be regarded as a relic of regionalism, was not abolished; so that the question remained as to what its role would in fact be in the future; and whether it could under the new constitution, fulfil a useful function as a second chamber.[4]

The most significant fact about Parliament as it entered its third session was that the House of Representatives had become a public

---

[1] The Kenya Independence Order in Council 1963, Schedule 2, The Constitution of Kenya, s. 61.

[2] Ibid. s. 71.

[3] Act No. 14 of 1965, The Constitution of Kenya (Amendment) Act 1965 First Schedule, s. 71.

[4] It might be argued that with the abolition of regionalism, and within the one-party state, the Senate's reviewing function became more, not less important, as a protection for minority groups in the country. The Senators were still representatives of *districts*, as opposed to the constituencies of the Lower House. For a further discussion of the Senate see J. H. Proctor, The Role of the Senate in the Kenyan Political System in *Parliamentary Affairs*, Vol. XVIII, No. 4, Autumn 1965, pp. 389–415. The Senate was finally merged with the House of Representatives in December 1966. See below, Chapter 6.

forum where the representatives of the people fully exercised their right to debate critically the actions of the Government. Debate was usually vigorous and lively. It was often exceedingly humorous; it was also frequently very tense. M.P.s were not afraid to express their views on any subject including internal party conflicts. As a result, emotions often ran high, members often went close to forgetting the controls laid down by parliamentary practice, and the influence of the Speaker was a vital factor in containing several stormy and tense debates. Many M.P.s remained unfamiliar with the possibly unnecessarily complicated Standing Orders. They still rose on doubtful (sometimes fraudulent) points of order in order to evade the Speaker's rulings on debate. As elsewhere they often gave the impression of being concerned more with the picture they presented to the public eye – especially to the eyes of their own constituents – than with changing the minds of Members of the House. Ministers often complained of the tendency of M.P.s to leave the House immediately after they had spoken. M.P.s had none the less made the House a lively debating forum in which they insisted upon their right, as the representatives of the people, to speak on matters of public policy. 'This thing should be brought here and aired openly in this House', one Assistant Minister said of a major issue in September 1964; and this expressed the feeling of a majority of Members.[1] Many alleged that Ministers did not give enough time to the House.

No M.P. tabled a private bill before 1967; and one question suggested that some Members were originally unaware of their right to do so. On the other hand M.P.s made full use of Question Time. In 1959 Members of the Legislative Council asked 262 questions; in 1961, 258. In 1963–4 Members of Parliament asked 786 in the House and 225 in the Senate and in the (unusually long) session December 1963 to October 1965, 1617.[2] They also used private motions extensively to raise district and personal issues as well as matters of national importance; in 1965, 320 such motions were tabled and 68 debated in the House; 114 tabled and 72 debated in the Senate.

A Private Member's motion did not necessarily offer the M.P. a very satisfactory way of pressing courses of action on the executive: debate on such motions is strictly limited, and Private Member's business comes on Friday mornings, when attendance in the House fluctuates considerably. On the other hand, members obviously valued their

[1] *Official Report*, House of Representatives, Vol. III, Part II, Second Session, 18 September, 1964 col. 2579. The matter at issue was the proposed new Republican constitution which had then been published, and was subsequently submitted to a lengthy debate.
[2] Of these, 1533 were answered. Compare the situation in the Uganda National Assembly. See G. Engholm, *International Journal*, 1964.

right to raise such motions, and reacted strongly when it appeared that the Government wished to limit this right or kept embarrassing motions off the agenda.[1]

Members also used the adjournment debate extensively, to raise particular issues and generally to criticize members of the Cabinet. Again, an adjournment debate since it is limited to half an hour at the end of the day's proceedings, offered the M.P. only the briefest of opportunities to state his case. None the less it gave him a further chance to raise his grievances and especially to tackle the Government on an issue that he considered had not been dealt with satisfactorily in Question Time, and M.P.s made full use of this opportunity. Members took full advantage of the Budget debate, the debate on Supply, and the debate on the Speech from the Throne – later the Presidential address – to speak generally on Government policy, as well as on specific issues. Finally there was usually vigorous debate on most bills when they were before the House.

Until November 1965 the House of Representatives met in the former Legislative Council Chamber, in which the M.P.s were crowded close together, in a chamber built for a much smaller member-ship. This small chamber, especially after the dissolution of the Opposition (when Members became free to sit where they chose, on either side of the House), engendered a much greater intimacy of debate than did the new, and much larger one; but although something of the intimacy of the debate may have been lost, the vigour and intensity was by no means diminished.

Question Time was usually, as one might expect, the liveliest part of each day's proceedings. M.P.s' performance in ordinary debates suffered from their general lack of information on a wide variety of subjects (especially details of economic policy) as well as from their inability to use parliamentary procedure advantageously. Parliament in its early years therefore produced few polished parliamentarians; although the style of debate noticeably improved after a time. It did,

[1] See, e.g. *Official Report*, House of Representatives, Vol. IV, Second Session, 17 February 1965, col. 98. Since this was written the revision of Standing Orders made at the beginning of 1966, at the commencement of the third session, provided for a change in procedure on Private Members Motions. Hitherto an M.P. gave notice of a motion in the House, after which he had to wait until such time as his name was drawn in the weekly ballot made by the sessional Committee, who allocated time for those M.P.s whose names were drawn. Under the Revised Standing Orders the M.P. now hands his motion to the Speaker for approval; after such approval is given his motion is displayed on the notice board in Parliament Buildings. His name is then included in the weekly ballot at the Sessional Committee. If his name is drawn, he then puts his motion. If an M.P. has submitted more than one motion he must simply choose which one he wishes to put forward. This new procedure does not necessarily restrict the M.P.s' right to put forward such motions; it does mean they receive less publicity in the process of giving notice.

however, produce a significant group of men who refused to be a rubber stamp for the Executive. As a result, all the major issues that faced Kenya in her first two years of independence were aired in the National Assembly, some of them matters that the Government would have preferred to have had less publicly debated. The House of Representatives was the scene of some memorable occasions when M.P.s and Ministers clashed both over specific Executive actions as well as over the larger policy issues that faced the country; and this debate was conducted in the hearing not only of their fellow M.P.s but also of the public, for on most days there was a packed public gallery.[1]

The evidence suggested that Cabinet Ministers would certainly have preferred to be free from some of this criticism and that they attempted in the early months after independence to keep the National Assembly in recess as much as possible. Thus the Assembly was not called from March until 9 June 1964, in spite of backbench pressure for a meeting, and although Standing Orders then provided that the Budget should be presented each year before 7 June. Furthermore, Ministers for the most part failed to make use of the Ministerial Committees set up in 1963 with the intention of providing a bridge between Executive and Legislature.[2] Nevertheless, they were unable to keep their Legislature quiet and submissive.

Members of Parliament expressed their disapproval of the Government's delay in reassembling the National Assembly, in 1964, when the Standing Orders were amended to meet the situation created by the delayed introduction of the Budget.[3] They subsequently continued to publicize any suspected attempt by the Government to rule without Parliament. Furthermore at the end of 1964 a specific timetable and schedule of business for the 1965 session, which laid down the rule of fortnightly meetings of the House, was drawn up by the Vice-President's Office (which is responsible for National Assembly matters) and circulated to members in advance.[4] This concession by the Executive

---

[1] In the former Legislative Council Chamber there was seating for a maximum of 196 to 190 visitors in the Public Gallery and the Speakers' Gallery. In the new House of Representatives there is seating for a maximum of 600, although actual seating accommodation on ordinary days is 500.

[2] These Ministerial Committees were established soon after Parliament began its first session in 1963. There is a Ministerial Committee for each Ministry, composed of the Minister and ten M.P.s (both Senators and Members of the House). The intention was that each Minister would hold discussions with M.P.s on general and particular issues concerning his Ministry at regular intervals, and that M.P.s would through this discussion acquire a more specialized knowledge of some aspects of government.

[3] *Official Report*, House of Representatives, Vol. III, Part I, 10 June 1964, cols. 45–70,

[4] See Circular to all Members of National Assembly from the office of the Vice-President, 30 March 1965.

was a major victory for the M.P.s in their battle to gain recognition of the right of the National Assembly to review Executive actions.

The numerical weakness of the KADU Opposition in the House of Representatives in 1964 suggested that this decision was not made because of the existence of a formal opposition in the National Assembly. While the KANU Government respected the parliamentary conventions concerning the position of the Opposition in Parliament, they did not pay any great heed to the KADU Opposition during 1964. What they could not ignore, while the two-party system operated, was possible parliamentary opposition from M.P.s of their own party. A reading of the debates in 1964 suggested that it was this possibility of KANU opposition that forced Cabinet Members to concern themselves more with attitudes expressed in the Legislature. Although KADU had several able and experienced M.P.s, it was never KADU that provoked the real battle between Executive and Legislature, or the criticism that the Executive could not afford to ignore. It was always members of the backbench of KANU itself who were able to insist on debate, and who refused to be dictated to by the Executive. In the Budget debate in 1963, for example, a number of the KADU M.P.s expressed their dissatisfaction with the Government's use of the term 'African Socialism', which they urged them to define more clearly. The Government refused to be drawn. In 1965, however, faced with similar challenges from members of their own party (in what was now a one-party House), they felt constrained to attempt a definition, which led to the major statement of government policy in the Sessional Paper No. 10 on African Socialism.

The Government's decision to amend the constitution so as to introduce a Republic and abolish regionalism on the first anniversary of independence was made known in August 1964. Given the then constitutional requirements for any such amendment – it had to be passed by a 75 per cent majority in the House and a 90 per cent majority in the Senate – the Government's concern at opposition from their own backbench was the more understandable.

It is not difficult to trace the emergence of a group of independently minded KANU backbenchers within Parliament. When the National Assembly first met in June 1963, KANU formed its Parliamentary Group, which consisted (as their Party constitution provided) of the President, Mr Kenyatta (then Prime Minister) as Chairman, and all KANU Members of Parliament. The Parliamentary Group was envisaged as the place where KANU M.P.s would discuss proposed legislation with the Ministers before it came to the floor of the House: as the place where they could argue with their Government, the place where the Government would persuade members of the rightness of

Government proposals and perhaps take disciplinary action to ensure that members would vote with them. The Parliamentary Group did not however prove a very satisfactory meeting place between Ministers and ordinary M.P.s. Ministers were extremely busy, they tended not to attend Parliamentary Group meetings and they tended not to consult the M.P.s on proposed legislation. By mid-1964 KANU M.P.s were openly alleging that the Government ignored them and therefore did not give the Party a chance to put the Party view.[1]

The first open clash between backbenchers and the Cabinet arose over the question of East African Federation. In April 1964 the KANU Parliamentary Group set up a Working Committee on East African Federation, issued invitations to their fellow parliamentarians in Uganda and Tanzania to a joint meeting in Nairobi to discuss federation, and sent envoys to visit the Uganda and Tanganyika Governments. The reception all this received from their own Government made it clear that these actions did not have the blessing of the Cabinet, and made this disagreement public. Then in June, when the House reassembled, a KADU M.P. introduced a Private Member's motion 'That in view of the fact that all the people in Kenya were promised East African Federation immediately after Kenya's independence, this House calls upon the Government to accelerate the machinery for this purpose.' The Government was obviously embarrassed that the question of federation should be raised in this way. Hoping perhaps to disarm opposition as well as to dispel doubts as to their positive support of the federation movement, they gave priority to the motion at the busiest time of the year, notwithstanding that it was an Opposition Motion, and actually accepted it as it stood. The Prime Minister opened the debate for the Government, to insist that he and his Cabinet were doing all they could to bring federation into being: the major obstacle to be overcome before any such federation could be established was the regional constitution of Kenya – once they had got rid of regionalism in Kenya, he insisted, they could move forward to East African Federation. Mr Mboya, a member of the Kenya delegation to the East African Federation Working Party set up by the three Governments in 1963, justified the delay in the terms of the practical problems which had to be overcome. Mr Odinga, then Minister for Home Affairs, added his support for this argument and denied any suggestion that the Kenya Government was no longer concerned about federation. KANU backbenchers, nevertheless, supported KADU criticisms of the Government's attitude, and successfully moved an amendment to the motion which was passed (against

[1] E.g. *Official Report*, House of Representatives, Vol. III, Part 1, 10 June 1964, col. 49.

Government wishes) on a division and which insisted that federation must be introduced by 15 August 1964.[1]

East African Federation was in mid-1964 a popular but embarrassing issue to the Kenyan Government, who were fully aware of the issues involved and the difficulties militating against its immediate introduction. Why KADU introduced their motion at that particular time was not clear; what was clear was that the KANU backbench group, believing that the Government was neglecting KANU policy, used this issue to challenge them openly; and also that the outcome was to strengthen the position of the backbench element in KANU *vis-à-vis* the Government. In the two-party House in 1964 the Government could not ignore a group of backbenchers who might vote against them. This was the more important in view of the Government's announced intention of amending the constitution; with twenty-one M.P.s in the KADU Opposition, the support of KANU backbenchers was vital to securing this required majority. Backbenchers recognized their strong bargaining position, as their more open criticism of the Government during the second half of the year made plain. They had by that time established themselves formally as a group, with Chairman, Secretary, and other officers. They achieved a certain degree of unity among themselves in their attack on the Cabinet in the latter months of 1964, and established themselves as a group with a definite point of view.

This backbench view could be summed up under three main heads. First they challenged what they regarded as the oligarchic tendencies of the Cabinet, which they insisted must not become all powerful and indifferent to their views. Second, they insisted that in doing this and in criticizing Government policy, they were neither being disloyal nor opposing the Government in any fundamental sense; they remained loyal to the Government because it was their Party Government. Third, while loyal to their party government, they were nevertheless carrying out their duty by criticizing its policy, because as the representatives of the people they were the watchdogs of the public interest. Members of the Cabinet denied that backbenchers could arrogate this role to themselves: they insisted that all Members of Parliament were members of the Government, and it was the Government and the Party who were the watchdogs of the people. This argument did not persuade backbench M.P.s to change their minds as to the special role they had to play in Parliament. Nor did the advent of the one-party state lead them to change this view. After the

[1] *Official Report*, House of Representatives, Vol. III, Part I, **17** June 1964, cols. 253–97 and 18 June 1964, 322–52, for the debate.
The division on the amendment was carried by 59 votes to 28.

dissolution of KADU the new and enlarged backbench group continued to insist that they were the legitimate critics of the executive; and, within a one-party Parliament, the conscience of the Government.

In criticizing the Government's proposals for the Seven Forks Hydro Electric Scheme in February 1965, one of the backbenchers put it very plainly.

'We do not say,' he insisted, 'that we do not have confidence in the Minister, or in the government, but where the Government is wrong, where our Minister is wrong, we are entitled to correct the Minister; and of course if we are wrong too we ask to be corrected. So we are trying to suggest to the Minister so that we do not have a tug of war, voting No or voting Aye, so that we speak with one voice. This thing ought to be sent back to the parliamentary group so that we discuss it nicely, clause and clause . . .'[1]

Backbench opposition to the composition of the new Sessional Committee as proposed by the Government in February 1965 clarified this attitude further. Standing Orders provide for a Sessional Committee appointed at the beginning of each session whose function was to 'consider such matters as may from time to time arise in connection with the business of the House'.[2] This committee was responsible for deciding the order of business in the House. It was normally chaired by a Senior Government Minister; and the Government had final control of the way in which the time of the House shall be used. By convention the Sessional Committee included members of the Opposition party when such a party existed as well as Government backbenchers. The new committee proposed in February 1965, also included backbenchers; but not, as far as the backbenchers were concerned, a sufficient proportion. They therefore rejected the Government's proposal. 'It is not the Government's job to dictate the Committee,' one M.P. insisted. 'The committee should represent the interest of the whole country and this can be done only if more backbenchers are in it.'[3]

The backbench did not restrict itself to criticism of matters of detail in legislation; on the contrary they challenged the Government on major issues of policy such as land, nationalization, education: all matters that suggested their anxiety to establish their public image not only as the watchdogs of the people who safeguard their rights as well

[1] *Official Report*, House of Representatives, Vol. IV, Second Session, 17 February 1965, col. 120, cf. above p. 39.
[2] Standing Orders of the House of Representatives, s. 147.
[3] *Official Report*, House of Representatives, Vol. IV, Second Session, 17 February 1965, cols. 81–97.

as their interests, but also as the true radicals. This was evident in views expressed, for example, on the Supplementary Estimates in February 1965 (which backbenchers tried to turn into a major policy debate);[1] on the Agriculture (Amendment) Bill[2] and in their initial opposition to the Third Constitutional Amendment Bill.[3] As a result, few Bills were allowed an easy passage through the House.[4] Members also forced public statements from the executive on matters of general concern, such as allegations of subversion and the smuggling of arms, which might otherwise not have been forthcoming.

KANU backbenchers' insistence/upon their right publicly to criticize the executive was not simply the outcome of their desire to see the critical function of parliament established. There was much to suggest that many would in fact have preferred to see this debate held in private, and kept within the Party itself. Furthermore some backbenchers obviously did not easily accept or perhaps understand the principle that a government must be free to govern and the fact that their criticisms did not lead to major changes in policy or legislation clearly frustrated a good number of them. They used the House to criticize the Government not so much out of a belief in the virtues of parliamentary government and the relationship between legislature and executive within such a system, as because they had been unable to raise their criticisms or to control the executive within the organs of the Party itself.

The problem which a one-party state usually faces is that of transferring 'democracy' from organs of the Party to organs of the Government. One difficulty in this process is that whereas discussion within the Party is private debate in Parliament, for example, is public. The danger is that such elements of democracy as characterized the party will not be transferred to the Government organs. Moreover, the party itself might suffer. This is the problem which Tanzania was trying then to solve. In Kenya, the party represented an amalgam of different interests and was organizationally weak; KANU was always a loosely knit national movement in which the somewhat rudimentary central party organs exercised only a limited control upon the branches, and the branches still less upon the centre. Since independence, however, the central party institutions had scarcely functioned at all. Neither the Governing Council nor the National Executive of the party met during

---

[1] *Official Report*, House of Representatives, Vol. IV, Second Session, 17 February 1965, col. 78, 23 February 1965, Ibid., col. 188.
[2] Ibid., 3 March 1965, col. 487.
[3] Ibid., 23 March 1965. cols, 690–8. Also 24 March 1965, cols. 745–823.
[4] Compare the situation in the National Assembly in Tanzania. See William Tordoff, 'Parliament in Tanzania', in *Journal of Commonwealth Political Studies*, Vol. III, No. 2, July 1965, p. 92.

1964 or 1965 and the National Conference had not met since 1962.[1] As a result, members of the party had been unable to voice their disagreements with the Cabinet Ministers within the party itself. Many of the issues raised in Parliament in 1964 and 1965 were thus issues that might more appropriately have been fought out behind closed doors. Parliament, in other words, provided an alternative to the Party. The loose organization of the party, and the fact that differences of opinion on party policy existed at Cabinet as well as at backbench level, also meant that the Government was unable to enforce strict discipline upon its members and prevent them from raising these issues in the Assembly. Paradoxically therefore it was the weakness of party organization that was the most significant factor in establishing Parliament as a public forum for national debate; and thus in laying the foundation of a tradition of free, public criticism of the executive within the legislature.[2]

In Kenya therefore the typical problem of a one-party state was reversed: the Government was embarrassed because there was too much debate in the governmental organs and virtually no debate at all within the party. Kenya's problem was therefore to revitalize the organs of the party and so siphon discontent into party channels. The increased use made of the Parliamentary Group in 1965 was an early move in this direction.

President Kenyatta emphasized the importance of the M.P. as a bridge between the people and parliament. It was, he insisted, the M.P. who had to interpret the policies and decisions of the Government to the people.[3] This gave him, the M.P., a significant role in his own community and it also drew public attention to Parliament and its activities. It was not unnatural that M.P.s might appear in their speeches in Parliament to be thinking more of their public image than the particular issue in hand: they were aware that their own future depended to a large extent on the kind of reputations they created for themselves in Parliament as the representatives of the people. This was one reason why they challenged any Government measure that touched upon issues such as land or trade. These were issues on which there was bound to be a public response.

Very few Members of Parliament had, however, undisputed leadership in their constituencies: on the contrary, they faced several rivals. There were other elected leaders: the Senator for the district within which the constituency was situated, the elected members of the

---

[1] A National Conference was held on 12 and 13 March 1966.

[2] Debates in the House received extensive press coverage. A summary of each day's proceedings when the National Assembly is sitting is also usually given on the radio. Attendance in the public galleries is always good.

[3] See, for example, his address at the State opening of Parliament on 14 December 1964. *Official Report*, House of Representatives, Vol. IV, Second Session, cols. 3–10.

Provincial Advisory Council and the elected County Councillors, all of whom could claim to be popularly elected and so have a share in leadership. They might, in addition, find themselves challenged by Party officials. The fact that a KANU branch was organized on a district and not a constituency basis meant that the M.P. was not necessarily the local Party leader. In several districts M.P.s were in 1964 ousted from the district leadership by other party members (not always themselves M.P.s). The development of this conflict at local level made the M.P. even more concerned to establish a reputation for himself in the National Assembly. It made it more difficult, however, for the M.P. to fulfil his role as the party's link between Parliament and the people.

KANU backbench criticism of their own Government did not force the Government to make any major changes in its legislative programme; and it did not lead before 1966 to any Cabinet crisis. While the Government might have been inhibited from certain actions by parliamentary opposition which it acknowledged must be listened to, it had not been defeated. Backbenchers might challenge individual Ministers, and they might threaten to demand a change of government, but they could not take action. The Cabinet was able to carry on Government in spite of parliamentary criticism.

Two factors help to explain why this was so: first, the frictions among Members of Parliament which reflected the debates within KANU itself; and second, the role played by the President, and the loyalty given by all M.P.s to him. During 1964 KANU backbenchers achieved a degree of unity in their criticisms of the Executive primarily because they had a common objective, the desire to control the Executive, and the presence of the Opposition put them in a strong bargaining position. Beyond this objective of controlling the Government they were not united. They held differing views on many public issues, and had no agreed alternative policy. These differences of opinion became more apparent in 1965, after the dissolution of KADU and it became clear that there were two groups among backbenchers. The dissolution of KADU, and the inclusion of KADU M.P.s in KANU changed the balance between these two groups in favour of the Conservatives and, as the change of Party Whip in July 1965 showed, increased the friction. Such divisions weakened the bargaining powers of the legislature *vis-à-vis* the Executive.

A more important consideration was, however, the loyalty of members to the President, and the careful way in which the President, as the executive, acted: the careful way in which first as Prime Minister, and then as President, Mr Kenyatta handled disagreements between his Members of Parliament and his Cabinet Ministers so as to prevent any defeat of the Executive.

139

The fact that the party member was able to find an outlet for his views in Parliament rather than within the party rendered highly significant the President's membership of the National Assembly. This was an unusual constitutional provision, the effect of which was to enhance the standing of Parliament within the Governmental system. More important, it reinforced the position of the President in relation to his Cabinet. For the President's authority was enormously increased by the fact that he alone was able to contain dissident backbenchers.

In his address at the State opening of Parliament in December 1964 President Kenyatta said,

The constitution has provided as a matter of vital consequence that the Head of State should also be the Head of Government. In addressing this Parliament therefore I am addressing an institution of which I am also a vital part. The whole apparatus of the State becomes personified when I step down to join you. This process of so stepping down is not only a valuable personal right but also a significant Presidential obligation.[1]

The constitution provides, as we have seen, that the President as an ordinary M.P. and as Head of a Cabinet, was free to debate in the House. But in fact Mr Kenyatta rarely stepped down to participate in the debate in the legislature. During 1964 when he was Prime Minister he rarely took part in debate in the House of Representatives. On each of the few occasions that he visited the House after he assumed office as President he did so in his Presidential role, sitting in his Presidential Chair, and remaining outside the debate.

The President's absence meant that there was no acknowledged Head of the Government in the House to answer debate. In this respect the ambiguity surrounding the Vice-President's position is relevant. The Constitution provided that he should be the principal assistant of the President; but this was not interpreted to mean that he was Leader of the Cabinet in the President's absence. When in the House he was certainly acknowledged as the Senior Minister present. But in the absence of the President he was not the acknowledged Leader of Government business in the House. Questions directed to the office of the President were answered by the Assistant Minister.[2] Each Minister spoke for his own Ministry. Where a Government statement had to be made, it might come from any one of them, including the Vice-President. Although the Cabinet was in the House and

[1] *Official Report*, House of Representatives, Vol. IV, Second Session, 14 December 1964, col. 4.

[2] In the Cabinet reshuffle in December 1965, the Assistant Minister, Mr Nyamwea, became Minister of State in the Office of the President. In his new capacity he continued to answer questions asked of the President's Office. In 1966 he became Leader of Government Business. In 1968 Mr Arap Moi, as Vice-President, assumed this office.

collectively responsible to the National Assembly, it sat there consequently without its Chairman. Responsibility was thus difficult to make effective.

On the other hand the President's absence from the Chamber meant that the Executive (as distinguished from the Cabinet) did not come into open conflict with the Legislature; the Executive was therefore much safer. M.P.s appeared to make a distinction in their minds between the Cabinet as Government and the President as the Government. They freely attacked members of the Cabinet and demanded their individual resignations; and on occasion threatened to demand a change of Government. But this change of Government obviously meant a change of Cabinet Ministers, not of the Executive; and it did not represent a challenge to the President. Exactly what implications this had for the principle of Cabinet responsibility it was difficult to see. It did, however, mean that the President was able to assert his influence independently of the Cabinet, to persuade M.P.s to accept what was essentially a Cabinet policy, to which they might earlier have indicated their opposition. As a result of such intervention the President (after the federation motion in 1964) prevented open disagreement between Ministers and backbenchers from leading to a major Government defeat, but without restricting the freedom of debate.

In 1964, after the backbenchers' success on the federation motion, the Prime Minister (as he then was) called a private meeting of all M.P.s, at which, it seems, they discussed the basic grievance of backbenchers (i.e., that they were being ignored by the Cabinet) and some greater degree of co-operation was agreed upon.[1]

On 17 February 1965, at the beginning of the new sitting, the backbenchers again clashed with the Government, first on the question of the composition of the Sessional Committee,[2] and secondly (and more significantly) on the question of the Supplementary Estimates which they threatened to block. The following day, at the beginning of the afternoon's business, the Vice-President moved that the House adjourn in order to meet the President privately. The Members, after some debate, agreed, and after the adjournment all went across to the President's Office to talk with him.[3] Since this discussion was private, no account of what actually happened can be given; but Members afterwards publicly agreed that it had been very useful in establishing a better rapport between themselves and the Cabinet. They were also pleased that the President had agreed that he would in future meet all

[1] *East African Standard*, 26 June 1964.
[2] See above, p. 136.
[3] *Official Report*, House of Representatives, Second Session, 18 February 1965, col. 131.

M.P.s as a group for private talks at the beginning of each month.[1] The House subsequently agreed to a second Government proposal on the membership of the Sessional Committee which added two more back-benchers to the original list and thus, apparently, met their earlier criticism that the Committee as first proposed had been unduly dominated by Ministers.[2]

The next occasion on which a dispute between backbenchers and the Cabinet was settled in private was in the March 1965 debate on the proposed Agricultural (Amendment) Bill. On this occasion the President did not come publicly into the picture. This Bill, designed to enable the Government to establish more rapid means for the recovery of advances from defaulting settlers, gave the Government the power not only to act more directly against defaulters through the Courts but also to resume control of land from Africans on the settlement schemes. It was strongly opposed by many backbenchers, and at least one Assistant Minister, on the grounds that it was unjust. The back-benchers moved to have the Bill read in six months' time, which would have effectively killed it. The Ministries of Lands and Settlement and of Agriculture, concerned to keep the Revolving Loans Fund in action, were naturally anxious to avoid such a defeat. After a heated debate the House agreed by 49 votes to 23 to a motion by the Vice-President to adjourn the debate for a week to enable discussions to take place privately between Members and the Minister concerned.[3] Once again it was impossible to establish precisely how members were won around. When the debate was resumed, however, the Bill was passed without a division and the Vice-President thanked members 'for actually being able to see eye to eye with us on this particular, very important amendment'.[4]

The President's intervention also overcame opposition to a major Government bill on the occasion of the Third Constitutional Amendment Bill, in March 1965. When the second reading of the debate began, the bill was strongly attacked by several M.P.s who challenged the Government's opinion that it was simply a technical measure that provided for changes consequential upon the first amendment.[5] Mr Ngala (Member for Kilifi South) questioned the provisions for the

---

[1] *East African Standard*, 19 February 1965.

[2] *Official Report*, House of Representatives, Vol. IV, Second Session, 3 March 1965, cols. 454–61.

[3] *Official Report*, House of Representatives, Vol. IV, Second Session, 3 March 1965, col. 487–97, and 4 March 1965, cols. 522–50.

[4] *Official Report*, House of Representatives, Vol. IV, Second Session, 22 April 1965, cols. 1417–21.

[5] The Second Reading of the Bill was introduced by the Attorney General on 23 March 1965. *Official Report*, House of Representatives, Vol. IV, Second Session, col. 690.

control of land; Mr Kaggia (member for Kandara) the provisions that extended the period during which the Government could maintain a State of Emergency without going to parliament; Mr Anyieni (member for Majoge-Bassi) the amendment to the amending process itself.[1] All these were in fact significant constitutional changes on which M.P.s might legitimately raise questions. It was reported in the press that at a meeting of the Parliamentary Group M.P.s were pressing for the withdrawal and redrafting of the Bill.[2] At a second meeting of the group, however, attended by the President, a majority of members agreed to support the bill and no further objections were made. It was passed without difficulty, but not without a lengthy debate.[3]

By such personal intervention the President withdrew the debate from the public view, and in doing so prevented the tensions between M.P.s and Government reaching such a pitch that they might destroy the parliamentary system. The conflict was resolved outside the system; the argument between legislature and executive was in the last resort private. At the same time a significant convention concerning the nature of consultation between executive and legislature could be seen emerging.

The President intervened in a different sense in July 1965, when he suggested that the backbench group as such should be disbanded, as unnecessary within a one-party Assembly. In spite of an earlier refusal to consider such a suggestion, M.P.s on this occasion agreed to his proposal that the backbench group should be dissolved, and that there should be only one group, the Parliamentary Group, chaired by the President of the Party, which would meet monthly to discuss legislation with the Cabinet from the party point of view.[4]

The personal influence of the President was therefore vital in maintaining a working relationship between the Executive and the Legislature. Members agreed to act upon his suggestions not simply because he was the Executive, and could presumably threaten to dissolve the House and go to the country, but also because as Mr Kenyatta he had their full loyalty. His prestige and personality and his leadership role made it difficult for M.P.s to oppose him. Kenya therefore had a parliamentary opposition in the English sense although it did not necessarily have an alternative Government.[5]

[1] Ibid. and 25 March 1965, col. 823, *et. seq.*

[2] *East African Standard*, 27 March 1965.

[3] *Official Report*, House of Representatives, Vol. IV, Second Session, 27 April 1965, col. 1521.

[4] *East African Standard*, 22 July 1965.

[5] The emergence of the Official Opposition in March 1966 meant, of course, that Kenya did now, once again, have a possible alternative government.

6

Epilogue:
The Dominant
Party State 1966-8

The formation of the Kenya People's Union constituted a significant watershed in independent Kenya politics. It heralded the return of the two-party state. It presented a direct challenge to both KANU and Kenyatta. And it opened up the possibility of a new kind of inter-party debate in which economics assumed a greater prominence than personality or ethnic loyalty. Yet in the two years after the little general election it was not the Opposition which determined the direction of the political debate. The initiative still lay with the Government which dictated both the terms of the debate and the arena within which it should take place. Moreover, although a considerable attention was focused upon the renewed inter-party contest this was not in fact the fundamental issue under debate. The central conflict in Kenya politics in the two years after the formation of the KPU was in fact the continued conflict between the idea of the 'administrative state' and the heritage of a powerful, broadly based rural party politics. The issue was who should control the state: the bureaucracy or the party.

Faced with a new opposition party the KANU Government acted as many African Governments have done[1]: it challenged the legitimacy of opposition and narrowed the arena within which the KPU might function. As the arena within which political debate could take place was progressively restricted, members of both parties found it increasingly difficult publicly to register dissent. Under these circumstances Parliament continued to occupy a crucial role as a platform for public debate; and its Members continued to use it to publicize all the major political issues. This in turn meant the continued dominance within KANU of the parliamentary caucus and the continued rivalry

[1] See M. Kilson, 'Authoritarian and Single-Party Tendencies in African Politics'. *World Politics*, January 1963.

144

for control of that body. KANU itself remained internally divided by the same cleavages that had disturbed the party in the past, focused on personal rivalry and ethnic divisions rather than on the policy issues that had emerged in 1965 and 1966. Parallel to this party weakness was the further centralization of governmental power. Constitutional and administrative developments gave the Executive a greater degree of independence of its legislature, culminating in the passage of the tenth constitutional amendment which altered the method of presidential election and succession and therefore the rules of the political game.[1] In this final chapter these developments must briefly be considered.

KANU leaders had given ample hints during the little general election of the attitude that the party might adopt towards any KPU candidates returned to Parliament. At a major rally the President had employed a traditional Kikuyu curse to consign the Opposition to oblivion.[2] A KANU statement released immediately before the election results were known declared that Kenya would remain a *de facto* one-party state even though a 'handful of political rejects' had run away from KANU to set up a splinter group.[3] Mboya, immediately after the results had been announced, jubilantly suggested that the Opposition, because of their small numbers, might not be recognized.[4] It was not therefore surprising when, in the new two-party state, both the Government and KANU challenged the very legitimacy of opposition itself and portrayed KPU as having betrayed Kenyan unity. They went further to question the party's loyalty to the state, on the grounds that it represented, they claimed, only one tribe and because of its alleged subversive intentions. Such allegations, reminiscent of the debate of 1965, reached a climax with the strange appearance in March 1968 of a booklet produced under official cover and intended for 'restricted circulation' which sought to prove these allegations. A number of statements made by Opposition Members of Parliament were quoted, but out of context, to show that the Members were using the National Assembly 'to undermine democracy and stability by

[1] Between May 1966 and June 1966 the constitution was further amended five times, by Act No. 18 of 1966, which provided for increased security powers; Act No. 40 of 1966 which established a unicameral legislature; Act No. 4 of 1967 which removed doubts raised by the fifth amendment; Act No. 16 of 1968 which removed Provincial Councils and district and provincial boundaries from the constitution; and Act No. 45 of 1968 which *inter alia* altered the method of presidential election. These will be referred to here respectively as the sixth to tenth amendments. Finally in November 1968 the Government published a new constitutional documen tincorporating all ten amendments which was finally passed as Act No. 5 of 1969. See Appendix.
[2] Rosberg and Nottingham, op. cit., p. 275. The curse was Kura Na Miiri Ya Mikongoi, literally translated 'to be lost in the roots of the Mikongoi tree'.
[3] *East African Standard*, 24 June 1966.
[4] Ibid., 28 June 1966.

seditious means'.[1] Talk of this kind and allegations of communist sympathies among members of the Opposition at times created an atmosphere similar to that of the period of crisis in 1965.[2]

KPU was nevertheless recognized as an Opposition party. In the House of Representatives they formed a small band of seven seated on the Speaker's left. They did not have sufficient numbers to be recognized under Standing Orders as the Official Opposition; and this meant that they lost special privileges, including a salary for Mr Odinga as Leader of the Opposition. They were however accorded the status of a parliamentary party and unofficial opposition, and by a gentleman's agreement in the Sessional Committee given certain other privileges. Mr Odinga became Chairman of the Public Accounts Committee and Opposition motions received priority every third Private Members' day.[3]

While accorded this parliamentary position and registered as a party by the Registrar-General, the Opposition functioned outside Parliament only under great difficulties. A number of their officials (but none of their Members of Parliament) were detained in 1966 under the Preservation of Public Security Act.[4] Kaggia was arrested early in 1968 and charged with holding an illegal meeting for which he was imprisoned for six months.[5] Party officials also found it difficult to build any organization at district level. Some of the branches already opened were refused registration, and with the possible exception of Central Nyanza no sub-branches appear to have been set up. Others faced official restrictions upon meetings.[6] How much support or sympathy the new party aroused it was difficult to assess; but open support became all the less probable in the face of legislation passed early in 1967 which extended to local authorities the provision that any Councillor who changed his party must also resign his Council seat.[7]

[1] The circumstances of the release of this document were never explained, nor its authorship. See *Daily Nation*, 14 March 1968, *East African Standard*, 16 March 1969 and *Official Report*, The National Assembly, First Parliament, Sixth Session, Vol. XIV, 14 March 1968, col. 890, and 15 March, col. 933. The booklet, entitled *The Parliamentary Record of the KPU Opposition*, was laid on the table.

[2] See above, Chapter 2. Anonymous circulars prophesying the downfall of the Government and critical of Government Ministers also continued to appear.

[3] *Official Report*, The National Assembly, First Parliament, Sixth Session, Vol. XIV, 27 February 1968, col. 45. An official Opposition had to have a minimum of thirty members.

[4] See below for the passage of the constitutional amendment. For the detentions see the *East African Standard*, 25 July, 5, 8, 12 and 28 August and 5 November 1966.

[5] Ibid., 18 March 1968.

[6] *Official Report*, The National Assembly, First Parliament, Fifth Session, Vol. XI, 4 April 1967, col. 1902 for one discussion of the position of KPU branches under the law.

[7] Act No. 11, 1967, Local Government (Amendment and Special Provisions) Act 1967. The Rift Valley Provincial Advisory Council had in July 1966 expelled three members for KPU sympathies.

The party was also subjected to a good deal of localized violence which the Government deplored but could not prevent. On two occasions a Cabinet Minister was involved in a KANU attack upon a KPU office.[1] In December 1967 Kaggia was attacked when visiting Thika.[2] Police had to take action against KANU Youth Wingers both in Nyeri and at the Coast when on other occasions they attacked KPU supporters.[3] There was therefore a good deal of sporadic violence which could not fail to influence public support or obstruct the activities of the Opposition.[4]

KPU complained increasingly of official refusals to issue them with permits to hold public meetings, a matter which they raised in Parliament more than once. Soon after the little general election KPU had held a rally at Mombasa at which Odinga had addressed a large crowd; but they held no other meetings in the following two years.[5] While the Minister for Home Affairs denied the existence of any ban on meetings the Office of the President on more than one occasion acknowledged their refusal to allow a particular meeting on security grounds. The Government's control over meetings, exercised through the Provincial Administration, was in fact on their own admission applied against KANU as well as KPU officials and Members of Parliament. They argued that all meetings were licensed in the name of the individual, not the party; and that each had to be considered on merit in terms of the security situation of the moment. Nevertheless Executive control over meetings was undeniably a powerful advantage since it enabled the Government to determine the scope of the conflict and the extent to which the inter-party debate should take place in public. During this period the open inter-party debate was progressively restricted to the parliamentary arena.

Under these circumstances Opposition leaders resorted to alternative tactics to obtain a public hearing. In Nyanza, where seven of the nine Members of Parliament were on home territory, they adopted the habit of attending traditional funeral ceremonies, which they were alleged to use for political propaganda.[6] Self-help meetings called by

---

[1] *Daily Nation*, 3 and 15 July 1967, and 13 November 1967.

[2] *East African Standard*, 14 December 1967.

[3] Ibid., 4 and 27 November 1967, 18 June 1968.

[4] See ibid., 31 August 1967 for a press conference by Odinga at which he alleged thuggery and arson against his party. KANU denied these allegations. KPU also raised the subject in Parliament on a number of occasions.

[5] This subject was also raised on a number of occasions in Parliament. See for example *Official Report*, The National Assembly, First Parliament, Fifth Session, Vol. XIII, Part III, 3 November 1967, col. 1678.

[6] Ibid., Fifth Session, Vol. XII, Part I, 25 May 1967, col. 186, or ibid., Fifth Session, Vol. XIII, Part I, 9 November 1967, col. 1937. There seems little doubt that they did use funerals for such purposes; but so also did their KANU opponents, including Mboya.

local groups to obtain support for a particular project offered a second non-political occasion at which they could appear. Odinga and other party officials held press conferences to ensure publicity for their views as well as to complain about the treatment of the party and the restrictions upon their movement. Odinga spoke to student gatherings in Nairobi and at the University Colleges in Kampala and Dar es Salaam. His efforts to secure an international platform were, however, defeated when he was refused permission to leave the country.[1] Even with these opportunities, the party was unable to sustain the kind of inter-party debate that might have established a clear public image of what the Opposition stood for.

In the face of progressive restrictions upon their movements KPU turned increasingly to Parliament, which became their major public platform. They used the National Assembly to protest against Government restrictions, to challenge Government policies and to articulate their views. Their recognition as a parliamentary party was therefore crucial for their survival. Their position in the National Assembly was however extremely vulnerable. With only seven (and in a combined House nine) Members they faced the constant danger of losing recognition if any of their group crossed the floor.[2] Moreover, they were no threat to the Government in a combined House of over a hundred-and-fifty Members. Although they distributed responsibility for different subjects between themselves to ensure that there was an Opposition spokesman on all business that came to the House it was not easy to sustain debate on every issue. While they therefore undoubtedly articulated an Opposition viewpoint the extent of the inter-party debate was limited.

The significance of Parliament in these two years was not, however, derived solely from the fact that it provided a platform for inter-party debate. What made Parliament of crucial importance was that KANU backbenchers continued, as they had done before the Limuru conference, to use this platform to challenge their own Government. Members of Parliament had generally by this time grown more adept at manipulating parliamentary procedure to ensure a hearing for their own views. As a result the tradition, established between 1963 and

[1] *East African Standard,* 21 March 1968. Also *Official Report,* The National Assembly, First Parliament, Sixth Session, Vol. XIV, 29 March 1968, col. 1297. This refusal, made on the grounds that it was the planting season, aroused a good deal of ironical amusement in Nairobi. See *Sunday Nation,* 1 April 1968.

[2] And understandably KANU did not hesitate to seek to woo some of their opponents across. Two returned to KANU, and were re-elected as KANU candidates in the middle of 1968: Mr Kioko from Machakos and Mr Oduya from Busia. Under the National Assembly Remuneration Act 1968 and the National Assembly's Standing Orders, a party with fewer than seven Members would not be accorded recognition as an Opposition party. Its Members would therefore have to sit as independents.

1965, of using parliament as a platform for the KANU party debate was maintained. On a number of occasions between 1966 and 1968 KANU backbenchers forced through the House Private Members' motions that challenged Government policies and must have caused official embarrassment. They passed a motion in July 1967, for example, calling for the Africanization (not Kenyanization) of commerce and thus challenged not only the Government's promises of equal treatment for all Kenyan citizens regardless of race but also the constitution itself.[1] They were also prepared to question the behaviour of the Executive and in many respects kept executive behaviour under review. They initiated two inquiries into alleged police brutalities, first in Mombasa and second in Kisii.[2] They challenged the actions of civil servants, particularly the Provincial Administration, including chiefs, whose powers they believed to be excessive.[3] Opposition Members were also quick to raise matters of this kind; but it was clearly the KANU backbench rather than the Opposition which was the more able to obtain a hearing.

Similarly it was KANU backbenchers who won a number of concessions from the Government on different Bills. In November 1966 they persuaded the Government to refer a major Bill, the Dairy Industry Bill, to a committee of inquiry, notwithstanding the fact that one such commission had already been carried out and the matter was of some urgency.[4] The Graduated Tax Bill, which had been withdrawn in the face of backbench pressures in January 1966, was replaced in September of the same year by a second Bill that conceded backbench demands, particularly on fines for non-payment of taxes.[5] In a heated debate in November 1967 the backbench defeated the Government's proposal (contained in the Land Control Bill 1967), to allow the sale of land under special provisions to approved enterprises in which non-Kenyans would be permitted to participate.[6] They also won significant concessions in the local government legislation of April 1968 which prohibited any non-party candidates from standing

---

[1] *Official Report*, The National Assembly, First Parliament, Fifth Session, Vol. XII, Part II, 7 July 1967, cols. 1962–88.

[2] The Mombasa Inquiry, generally known as the Makupa Affair, can be followed in National Assembly, *Papers Laid* No. 61 of 1966, 25 October 1966. The Kisii Inquiry had not been published at the time of writing.

[3] See, for example, *Official Report*, The National Assembly, First Parliament, Fifth Session, Vol. XIII, Part II, 28 November 1967, col. 2529 for a question about a chief arresting people who had failed to attend his baraza (meeting).

[4] Ibid., Fourth Session, Vol. X, Part II, 23 November 1966, cols 1902–31.

[5] Ibid., Fourth Session, Vol. X, Part I, 12 October 1966, col. 722.

[6] Although on this particular point their victory was due more to front-bench ineptness in the committee stage than to back-bench strength. In the second major conflict on this Bill the back-bench was soundly defeated. See Ibid., Fifth Session, Vol. XIII, 27 November to 7 December 1967.

F

for election.[1] Finally it took the Government three months to obtain agreement to the tenth constitutional amendment passed in June 1968.[2] The KANU backbench was not therefore entirely unsuccessful as a lobby.

An analysis of the debate on these and other issues suggests that KANU backbenchers were willing to challenge the Government on at least two kinds of issues. First were those that affected their own political position, such as changes in constituency boundaries and electoral procedure or in the basis of representation. Second were those that appeared to deny the rapid African social and economic progress promised during the days of the nationalist movement. These might involve the sale of land to non-Africans or the imposition of higher taxes or harsh sanctions for the non-payment of taxes. They were also intensely concerned at the place of Africans (including themselves) in the modern sector of the economy.[3] The record suggested that the Government was less likely to make concessions on the first category than on the second; but that if they overlapped they were more likely to seek a compromise, particularly if the issue was one in which the grass roots population might become involved.[4]

The Government did not therefore ignore parliamentary criticism; and Parliament in Kenya continued to fill a significant role in the political system. Nevertheless the most striking characteristic of these two years was the continuing trend towards Executive dominance. This could be seen in the Government's relationship not only with the Opposition but with its own backbench. The monthly consultations between the President and the Parliamentary Group, initiated in 1964, became less frequent. Once again the President tended to intervene only at points of crisis. On these occasions criticism was still transferred from the floor of the House to the privacy of the Parliamentary Group; but the impression gained from backbench comments, particularly in the House, was that the President now tended less to mediate than to arbitrate between his Ministers and his backbenchers. Consultations between Ministers and Members were also less frequent and Ministers became less attentive to Parliament. On more than one occasion backbenchers registered a vigorous protest against empty front benches and their speeches demonstrated

[1] See below, pp. 62–3.
[2] See below, pp. 154–5.
[3] There is an interesting glimpse into KANU Parliamentary Group discussion on this subject in the debate on a Government proposal to guarantee financial support to the Kenya Canners Ltd, in the course of which a Minute of a Parliamentary Group Meeting was laid on the table. See *Official Report*, The National Assembly, First Parliament, Fifth Session, Vol. XII, Part II, 26 July 1967.
[4] I have discussed this at greater length in 'The Role of Parliament in Kenya', *East Africa Journal*, October 1968.

the old fears of government by Cabinet oligarchy.[1] The Government's determination to proceed with stated policies was put clearly by the Assistant Minister for Agriculture during the debate on the Land Control Bill when he rejected the proposal from the backbenches to alter the composition of the proposed Land Control Boards, which were to control land transfers:

... Mr Deputy Chairman, Sir, the question of this amendment cannot be accepted by us on the Government side ... This was clearly stated at the (Parliamentary Group) meeting by the Minister himself, that it was a Government decision ... therefore this amendment contradicts the wishes and decisions of the Government ...[2]

The Government certainly overruled the backbenchers more often than they conceded their point.

One reason for this was the weaker position of the backbenchers, following the withdrawal of the Radicals into KPU, within the Parliamentary Group as a whole. Members were inhibited by the potential disciplinary effects of the fifth amendment as well as by the implications raised by the power of the Executive to detail without trial. They were demonstrably alarmed in 1967 by the knowledge that Members of Parliament enjoyed no statutory immunity against detention without trial, notwithstanding Mr Moi's assurances, as Vice-President, that no Member would be detained on account of statements made in the House.[3]

KANU backbenchers were also less united as a group. Not all the Radicals had followed Mr Odinga into Opposition; but those who stayed in KANU were few in numbers and less likely to influence the Parliamentary Group as a whole on policy issues. The continuing disagreements about land, and especially the question of the introduction of a ceiling on the amount an individual might own, was a clear indication of this.[4] Although the old alliances between Members from the less developed areas reasserted themselves on occasions Members were also more divided by regional antagonisms, particularly those between the Central Province and the rest. They were therefore less able to act effectively together.

An additional and important influence upon Government-backbench relations was the weaker parliamentary position of the KPU as

[1] E.g. *Official Report*, The National Assembly, First Parliament, Fifth Session, Vol. XI, 21 February 1967, col. 190.
[2] Ibid., Fifth Session, Vol. XII, Part II, 4 December 1967, col. 8213.
[3] Ibid., Fifth Session, Vol. XIII, Part II, 21 November 1967, col. 2175. Members' fears had been aroused by the detention of Mr John Keen, then a Kenyan Member of the Central Legislative Assembly. Mr Moi had succeeded Mr Murumbi as Vice-President in December 1966.
[4] See, for example, the debate on the Land Control Bill in November 1967, ibid., Fifth Session, Vol. XIII, Part II, 27–29 November, cols. 2485–2654.

compared with the former KADU Opposition. On the one hand the presence of an Opposition made it easier for the Government to discipline its members. On the other KPU's numerical weakness made it more difficult for KANU backbenchers to exploit their pivotal position as they had in the two party House in 1964.

The scope of the authority of the Executive was also increased by the continuing process of constitutional amendment. The sixth amendment of May 1966 enlarged the President's powers in matters of security. This amendment, and the amended Preservation of Public Security Act, allowed the President, if he considered it necessary in the interest of the security of the state, to invoke wide powers including detention without trial without nullifying the constitutional provisions on fundamental rights. The power which received most publicity was that of detention without trial; but others included general restrictions on movement and strict censorship and control of the press.[1] Regulations made under this Act had to be renewed by Parliament every eight months; and Parliament retained the power, as the Attorney General emphasized during the debate, to revoke such regulations at any time they saw fit. Nevertheless a Member's ability to exercise his control depended very much upon party dispositions in the House. The weakness of Parliament, in this respect, was demonstrated by the manner in which the Security Regulations were renewed in November 1967. On that occasion Members received no prior indication that the question was to be raised. Notice was given on a supplementary order paper issued on the day on which the Regulations would otherwise have expired; and the National Assembly agreed to their renewal the same afternoon.[2] The requirement of parliamentary approval for their renewal was itself abolished by the tenth constitutional amendment in June 1968.[3]

During these two years Parliament also agreed to changes in the statutory law which further enlarged the Executive's powers of control. The Public Order (Amendment) Act, 1968, for example, prohibited the display of all 'political flags, banners and emblems' in Kenya (and incidentally created a problem at the time of future elections which was

[1] The Sixth amendment is Act No. 18 of 1966. This amendment was passed within two days of publication of the Bill. It aroused strong public attention, and a good deal of public opposition in the press. The Act was published on 7 June; *Kenya Gazette*, Supplement No. 50 (Act No. 7). Part III of the Preservation of Public Security Act, which provided for detention without trial, was brought into operation on 20 July. *Kenya Gazette*, Supplement No. 66, Legal Notice No. 211. Regulations made under this section for detention and restriction were published on 16 August; *Kenya Gazette*, Supplement No. 73, Legal Notice No. 240, Part II, which provided generally for public security measures was brought into operation on 6 September 1966.

[2] *Official Report*, The National Assembly, First Parliament, Fifth Session, Vol. XIII, Part II, 20 November 1967, col. 2119. See also the Order Paper for the day (mimeo).

[3] See below, p. 154.

not immediately foreseen). The Societies Act, passed at the end of 1967, gave the Executive, through the Registrar-General, a much greater control over all associations and societies. Some backbenchers, and more particularly the Opposition, challenged the implications of the Bill, but it was nevertheless passed without difficulty.[1]

The process of constitutional amendment was continued with the amalgamation of the Senate and the House of Representatives to form a unicameral legislature in December 1966.[2] KANU leaders had always been unhappy at the creation of an Upper House and this amendment brought the parliamentary institutions into closer accord with their original ideas about the proper structure of a strong central government. The Senators agreed to this amendment only after hard bargaining; and they won important concessions in the process. Each Senator was given a House of Representatives constituency which in turn led to detailed bargaining over constituency boundaries. It was also agreed that the life of Parliament should be extended from 1968 to 1970, to take into account the position of those Senators who would otherwise have retained their seats until 1972.[3] Once passed, however, this amendment removed a specific constitutional restriction upon the actions of the Executive, since it removed a House whose importance had lain in its right to delay legislation for specific reasons. The merger of the two Houses also altered the political balance in favour of the front bench, for it further weakened any cohesion in the KANU back-bench and gave the Government the advantage of numbers in the enlarged single chamber.

The Executive acquired an additional freedom with the ninth amendment, passed in April 1968, which finally abolished the Provincial Advisory Councils and removed the definition of provincial and district boundaries from the constitution.[4] Up to that date the boundaries of districts and provinces recommended by the Boundaries Commission of 1962 had been entrenched in the constitution. This had meant that any alteration of those boundaries had to be passed in Parliament and with a special majority. The ninth amendment of the constitution removed this requirement; boundaries would in future be altered by an ordinary Act of Parliament. To the extent that the entrenchment had been withdrawn, this gave the Government a greater

---

[1] Public Order (Amendment) Act, Act No. 12 of 1968. Societies Act, Act No. 4 of 1968. For the debate see *Official Report*, The National Assembly, First Parliament, Fifth Session, Vol. XIII, 19 and 26 October 1968.

[2] Act No. 40 of 1966.

[3] This bargaining was alluded to in the debate on the Amendment. See *Official Report*, The House of Representatives, First Parliament, Fourth Session, Vol. X (Part II), 21 December 1966, cols 3028–3084.

[4] Act No. 16 of 1968. This should be considered in conjunction with the Districts and Provinces Bill.

freedom of movement in legislating for boundary changes. This in itself was perhaps of less significance than Members thought, in view of the fact that the Government had already changed three district boundaries by administrative decisions, which were only later taken to Parliament.[1]

The constitutional amendment that carried the greatest implications for the relationship between the Executive and the legislature was, however, the tenth, passed in June 1968, which altered the method of presidential election.[2] The creation of a presidential republic in 1964 had not, it might be argued, involved a radical departure from the independence constitution, in so far as the President, as Head of Government, had remained responsible to Parliament. The parliamentary system of government had thus been preserved.[3] This had in fact been one of the factors on which Mboya, then Minister of Justice, had claimed a unique quality for that constitution. The importance of Parliament had moreover been ensured by the direct involvement of the House of Representatives in the election of the President, and particularly their responsibility, as electoral college, for the election of a successor on the occasion of the death or resignation of a President in office. The tenth amendment, however, radically altered the role of Parliament by providing that in future the President would be chosen by direct election by the people in a national poll. The presidential candidates would be chosen by their parties; they would still require for nomination the support of a thousand people, and they would still also be required to stand for a constituency seat. The candidate who, having been elected as a constituency member, also won a majority of the votes as presidential candidate, would be declared President. The election of the President was in this way taken out of the hands of the Parliamentary Group (of KANU) and transferred to the party. To the extent that the President became dependent upon a national electorate he increased his independence of the legislature. While he remained constitutionally responsible to

---

[1] These were the division of Central Nyanza into Siaya and Kisumu Districts; the abolition of Thika as a separate administrative district; and the alteration of Laikipia District boundary to transfer Thomson's Falls from the Rift Valley to the Central Province. See Memorandum of Objects and Reasons, Districts and Provinces Bill 1968: *Kenya Gazette*, Supplement No. 28 (Bill No. 6), 5 April 1968. The debate on this Bill began on 17 June 1968, but was subsequently adjourned.

[2] Act No. 45 of 1968. This Act, in addition to the changes in the presidential election, provided also for presidential succession at times other than a general election; prohibited independent candidates from standing for election to the National Assembly; removed the requirement that Regulations made under the Preservation of Public Security Act must be renewed by Parliament every eight months; and tied the election of the constituency member more closely to that of the President. These changes are discussed below.

[3] See above, Chapter 5.

Parliament he became politically more independent of it, since he was no longer necessarily dependent upon the Members for his election.

The amendment went further, for it also took responsibility for the succession on occasions other than a general election out of the hands of the National Assembly. In the event of the death or resignation of the President a presidential election now had to follow within ninety days. In the meantime the Vice-President automatically succeeded to office, although he was restricted in his exercise of executive power.

Finally the election of the Member of Parliament at the time of a general election became more dependent upon that of the President. Not only were all candidates required to signify their support for their party's presidential candidate; their names now appeared on the same ballot paper, and the two votes were cast together. In this manner the constituency election in a real sense became subordinate to that of the President. Since independent candidates were also prohibited, this provision subtly subordinated the constituency candidate to the President as leader of his party, and provided a possible means of central discipline over party candidates.

The prohibition of independent candidates, which was introduced also (and discussed first) for local authority elections, was of considerable significance not only for the position of Parliament but also for the relationship between the Government and its own party. Over these two years events had suggested that the party enjoyed very little control over the Government; and that the relationship remained very much as in the years immediately after independence, when the Radicals in KANU had complained that the party was not accorded its proper place in the political system. At the same time, however, the branches had continued to resist headquarters control; so that in this respect also the situation had not altered. KANU, moreover, as a party, remained functionally weak. Although Kenyatta launched a new membership drive in December 1966 there was little evidence that KANU greatly enlarged its paid-up membership or improved its organization as a result. Provincial party conferences were held in 1967, but in many cases branch officials failed to follow them up with recruitment drives. The branches came to life only at the time of their elections for party officials; and KANU leaders at district and lower levels turned to other organizations (particularly government committees) to obtain influence and patronage. The party continued therefore to play a limited role at district level.[1] At the national level its institutions functioned only intermittently. The National Executive met on seven occasions

[1] This varied, of course, from one district to another. In Nairobi, for example, where the branch was much more active, KANU officials and followers played an important communication role. The party élite was also, it appears, generally more active in Central Province than elsewhere.

during 1967, but the National Governing Council was not called from the time of the Limuru Conference until April 1968.[1] The Parliamentary Group therefore remained the only continuously active body within the party; and Parliament continued to be used as the organ for the party debate. Members of Parliament continued to provide a major link between district and the centre.

The party was at district level still subject to the same kind of internal conflicts that had divided it in the past. This could be seen in the intense struggle that took place at the time of branch elections, which were the occasion of deep conflict which in some places ended in violence. They were in many cases followed by claims and counter claims against the results, even when (as was in some instances the case) the contest might have been brought to an end by the recognition by the Registrar-General of one group as the legitimate party officials.[2] This party conflict grew more intense as the possibility first of local authority and then national elections grew closer. By the end of 1967 factionalism was once more open and admitted; the branches were deeply divided,[3] particularly in Nakuru, Nairobi, Kakamega, Machakos and Mombasa.

This factionalism was primarily a continuation of the factionalism that had divided KANU in the period of the *de facto* one-party state and earlier. It was symptomatic of the same cleavages that had existed at that time. This was most clearly indicated in Machakos and Muranga, where the Members of Parliament, each with his own following behind him, were ranged against each other as much as against KPU.[4] In Mombasa and Nakuru there was much of the old KANU–KADU rivalry to be discerned in the contest for office, and particularly in the intense battle that developed around Ronald Ngala.[5] The rivalries in the branches also reflected the earlier challenge, now grown more pronounced, to the Members of Parliament, from KANU men who wanted to find a way to the centre: in Nakuru, Nyeri, Kakamega and Laikipia, for example, Members of Parliament were unseated from branch office in 1967.[6] In other districts they held their own.

This conflict between those in office and those outside was particularly intense in Central Province where the various groupings among the Kikuyu who had been unable to obtain office in 1962 and

---

[1] *Minutes of KANU Governing Council* held at State House, Mombasa, 26–27 April 1968 (mimeo).

[2] See, e.g. *East African Standard*, 7 August 1968.

[3] Ibid., 7 January 1968. A good deal of this party conflict was regularly reported in the press over this period.

[4] See, for example, on Muranga, *East African Standard*, 14 June 1968, and for Machakos, ibid., 24 August 1968.

[5] E.g. ibid., 23 July 1968.

[6] Ibid., 8 July 1967; 26 July 1967; *Daily Nation*, 22 August 1967.

1963 were now seriously reaching out for power. This was graphically demonstrated in the elections for the Nairobi branch in January 1968, when the former Mayor of Nairobi, Alderman Rubia, making a bid for a place on the national political scene, defeated the Member of Parliament for Mathari, Dr Waiyaki, for the office of chairman.[1] Rubia and Waiyaki, in terms of their past records and associations, represented two different groupings among the Kikuyu. Waiyaki had belonged to the 'Ginger Group' of the pre-independence days. He had stood against Mboya (almost certainly with Odinga's support) in the 1961 elections,[2] and he had been associated with the Radicals in the *de facto* one-party state. In a frank interview at the time of Odinga's resignation (when he had himself resigned his position as Assistant Minister but had remained in KANU as a backbencher) he had made clear his belief that only loyalty to Kenyatta held KANU together, and that the party had lost much of its original nationalist fervour.[3] His constituents included some of the poorest element in Nairobi; and although he now took a less public part in the continuing internal KANU debate he was still regarded as representative of the more radical element in KANU and among the Kikuyu. Rubia, on the other hand, had been a Nairobi City Councillor in the 1950s and then a nominated member of the Legislative Council between 1958 and 1960. He had become the first African Mayor of Nairobi in 1962. A leading Kikuyu businessman, he also held a large number of company directorships.[4] He stood therefore for the new Kikuyu business class which was surging upwards at this time and which clearly wanted a share in power.

The local rivalries within KANU's branches were also still linked, however, with the rivalries within the national leadership group which had not disappeared with Odinga's withdrawal from the party. In the conflict that had reached its climax with the Limuru Conference and Odinga's resignation, attention had been focused by events upon the rivalry between him and Mboya. That had not, however, been the only personal rivalry within the party; and soon after the little general election there were indications of those other rivalries within the Cabinet. Once again, as in 1965, party members began to attribute the party's difficulties to conflict within the national leadership. This was openly referred to in Parliament. Speaking in the debate on the presi-

---

[1] *East African Standard*, 29 January 1968 and 17 February 1968. Waiyaki and his supporters, who included at least two of the other Nairobi Members of Parliament, challenged the legality of the election and announced their intention of appealing to the President. Nothing further was heard of this, and Kenyatta recognized Rubia. See *Daily Nation*, 13 February 1968.

[2] Bennett and Rosberg, op. cit., p. 177.

[3] *Sunday Nation*, 23 May 1966.

[4] *Who Rules Industry in Kenya?* Nairobi: East African publishing House 1968.

dential address in February 1968, for example, the Minister for Power and Communications, Mr Nyamweya, blamed parochial interests and personal ambition for the difficulties with which he believed the country was faced. 'Mr Speaker, Sir,' he said,

today the troubles we are having everywhere in this country and in this House are based on these personal ambitions and personal jealousies. It is our primary duty, Mr Speaker, to see that these things are removed from us . . .[1]

Although this was the subject of constant rumour and gossip rather than substantial reporting, the increasing public references, especially in Parliament, suggested that the Cabinet was once again divided within itself.

The alignments which followed these divisions within KANU's leadership ranks appeared more than once to shift and change. They were focused primarily, however, upon Mboya and his position within the party and the Government. As a result the rivalry at branch level and the contested elections were interpreted in terms of local alignments for or against Mboya. Alderman Rubia's victory in Nairobi, for example, was popularly interpreted as a defeat for Mboya and a challenge to his position in Nairobi. The opposition to Ronald Ngala at the Coast was interpreted similarly, particularly after the return to KANU of Alderman Kombo, formerly Mayor of Mombasa, who had moved to KPU in 1966.[2] Such factional arrangements were discussed in terms of alleged associations rather than open and acknowledged alignments; but early in 1968 one Member of Parliament brought the question to the floor of the House, when he announced that he had been challenged over a particular vote by a member of the Government who 'was telling me that: you are one of Mboya's supporters and we have known you, including some other members, and with the list we are going to have you out . . .'[3] Odinga's resignation from KANU had not, it appeared, brought the opposition to Mboya from within his own party to an end. Although he had survived the challenge to his position at the Limuru conference (when one of the Luyia leaders, Masinde Muliro, had contested against him for the post of Secretary General) the opposition to him from inside KANU's ranks had not come to an end. KANU politics appeared to a large extent to be an attempt to isolate Mboya.

It is necessary therefore to look a little more closely at Mboya's own position at this point. First he still stood as the most able member of

[1] *Official Report*, The National Assembly, First Parliament, Sixth Session, Vol. XIV, 29 February 1968, col. 225. See also 4 March 1968, col. 307.

[2] See for example *Daily Nation*, 6 August 1968.

[3] *Official Report*, The National Assembly, First Parliament, Sixth Session, Vol. XIV, 28 February 1968, col. 134.

Kenyatta's government, unrivalled in his organizational skill and his ability to argue his case either in parliament or at a public meeting. It was he more than any other member of the Government who could argue with the Opposition and who also won backbenchers round by sheer parliamentary skill. It was frequently he who defended a difficult Government position. As the most able parliamentarian with a decade of experience, he could not be defeated in the House, a fact that did not always endear him to members of his own party. He had built up the Ministry of Economic Planning and Development, notwithstanding inter-departmental difficulties, into a significant part of the central government machine. As the Minister for Planning he stood at the centre of debate about economic development.

Second it was Mboya who maintained the KANU challenge to Odinga and KPU in Nyanza, where he sought to build a local party branch and to erode Odinga's base. He did not, in the middle of 1968, appear to have achieved any great success in this objective; and some of his own supporters believed he had adopted the wrong techniques. He enjoyed a more secure position in South than in Central Nyanza, where all the Members of Parliament remained with KANU; but here also his base was not completely secure. Perhaps one problem was that he was unable to bring into Nyanza those short-term benefits that might have persuaded more people of the advantages of support for the Government.

In Nyanza and in Nairobi it was commonly alleged that Mboya was husbanding South Nyanza as a safeguard against the possible loss of his Nairobi constituency. But this interpretation of his role both ignored a number of elements in the situation and was also almost certainly an oversimplification of the position. He was seeking not only to enlarge his own political base but also to overcome Luo conservatism and to persuade them to come forward and participate in development. Thus his efforts to win support from Luo elders were an attempt to win over not just the most politically influential sector of the community but also the men who had in the past determined reactions to agricultural change.[1]

Third, notwithstanding his activities in Nyanza, Mboya still stood as a non-tribal leader: a completely national figure without an ethnic base. His national position was demonstrated above all by his position as Secretary General of KANU. This image was not destroyed by the constant questions raised in local discussions about his ability to retain a Nairobi seat in a city now predominantly Kikuyu.

[1] This conclusion is based on discussions with different Nyanza leaders, and with the late Mr Mboya himself, as well as attendance at representative meetings over this period.

Mboya's critics still challenged him as being too 'pro-West'; a challenge carried right on to the floor of Parliament by one of the Opposition Members in July 1967 with a motion calling for his dismissal on the grounds of alleged associations with CIA.[1] To label him merely 'pro-West' was however to miss the real point of his policy position. As the Minister for Economic Planning, by 1968 Mboya stood essentially for a rational economic development as opposed to any short-term policies that might benefit one group at the future expense of the country as a whole. He argued explicitly for broad limits of planning within which the politics of influence must be contained. This could be seen in the development plan and in policy statements from his Ministry. It implied a challenge to any one group that wanted immediate benefits at the cost of future development, and was likely in particular to arouse opposition from a burgeoning economic class.

The tensions within KANU were linked also with the question of the political succession. Mr Odinga's withdrawal from the party had not resolved that issue, although it had narrowed the party's field. While the question was not publicly discussed it was implicit in much of the political debate; and clearly much of the factional manœuvring within KANU was linked with the question of succession. This was demonstrated by the debate over the tenth amendment, which altered the rules for the presidential election. The intention to alter the method of election was announced unexpectedly in November 1967, when a motion to draw up rules to govern the procedure followed by the National Assembly as an electoral college was brought to Parliament. Instead of proceeding with this question the Government announced, through the Vice-President, without any prior notice, that it intended to alter the constitution to provide for popular election of the president.[2] The matter then disappeared from public if not private debate until the end of March 1968 when, again without any prior warning, the Government published a Bill to alter the constitutional provisions concerning the office of President. This ran into considerable difficulty, evidenced by its withdrawal by the Government and the production

[1] *Official Report*, The National Assembly, First Parliament, Fifth Session, Vol. XII, Part II, 14 July 1967, cols. 2244–77.

[2] No rules had been drawn up in 1964 when the presidential republic had been established. A Sessional Committee reviewing Standing Orders in 1967 had therefore drafted rules for such occasions, and proposed their discussion. Although the Speaker had explained clearly that no amendment of the constitution was involved, Members of Parliament and some Ministers obviously took alarm; and one of the local papers, the *Daily Nation*, used the occasion to raise the whole question of presidential election and to argue that this was not a task for Parliament. See *Daily Nation*, 25 November 1967. Also Final Report of Select Committee Reviewing Standing Orders, National Assembly, 20 November 1967 (mimeo).

subsequently of a second and then a third draft.[1] The ensuing debate, which took place intermittently over the following three months, was focused primarily upon the sections of the Bill that concerned the succession on the occasion of the death or retirement of the President. The other changes introduced by the Bill, which significantly affected the position of the Member of Parliament, were challenged by the Opposition and by a small group of KANU backbenchers; but it was the provisions for succession that aroused the most sustained debate and on which the Government significantly shifted their position. Whereas in the first draft Bill the Vice-President automatically succeeded to the office for the remainder of the life of Parliament, the provision as finally passed provided for an election within ninety days and left the Vice-President (who temporarily succeeded to office) very much restricted in his position as interim President. The debate made it clear that a large number of Members feared that whoever assumed office would quickly and unconstitutionally entrench himself in power. The debate on the succession was essentially an internal KANU debate; and it was in no way concerned with Kenyatta. Kenyatta's position was secure and unchallenged; what Members feared was his successor and a possible misuse of power at the time of any change of office.

The debate suggested however that few Members appreciated the implications for the future of Parliament of the introduction of a popular presidential election, which widened the arena within which the succession would be decided and thus took it out of their hands. They failed also to elicit an answer to their questions as to which element of the party would control the selection of the presidential candidate; although this now became the crucial issue in any succession debate.

The debate over the tenth amendment took place against a background of increasing KANU conflict at branch level precipitated by the announcement early in 1968 that local authority elections would take place in the middle of the year. All KANU (and KPU) leaders were bound to seek some influence in the Municipal and County Councils in their areas, since these controlled a wide range of services at district level and were a major source of both development and patronage. Members of Parliament in a country where representatives were largely viewed in terms of what they brought to their constituents[2] needed access to these resources to secure for their consti-

---

[1] *Kenya Gazette*, Supplement No. 26 (Bills No. 5), 29 March 1968. The second draft was published in *Kenya Gazette* Supplement No. 40 (Bills No. 8), 10 May 1968; and the third in *Kenya Gazette*, Supplement No. 50 (Bills No. 12), 17 June 1968. It was the third draft which became Act No. 45 of 1968, The Constitution of Kenya (Amendment) (No. 2) Act 1968. This procedure was made necessary by the requirement that a Bill for the amendment of the Constitution could not itself be amended in the Committee stage but must be passed (or rejected) as it stood.

[2] Cf. attitudes expressed during the little general election, see above, Chapter 4.

tuents the local developments which they expected. This in turn meant access to Councillors prepared to support their areas, and sympathetic to their needs; and this implied a share in the selection of party candidates. For this reason the conflict for control of the party branch (which controlled the party nominations for local authority candidates) became intense.

This struggle for power at district level carried with it at this point, however, implications for the political position of KANU as the Government in power; for a divided KANU branch at district level raised the possibility that the party might lose control of the County, or Municipal, Council to the Opposition, which had announced its intention of contesting all local authority seats. This was openly admitted when the disappointed faction within the Nakuru branch announced in April 1968 that KANU members might be forced to vote for KPU in the forthcoming local government elections.[1] The National Organizing Secretary also admitted the possibility that disappointed KANU candidates refused a party nomination might stand as independents.[2] Yet Independents might split the vote and give KPU the victory; or having been elected then join the Opposition and give them a majority.

KANU Independent candidates were an established tradition in Kenyan politics; they had in the past demonstrated the independence at district level felt by party adherents, and the difficulties encountered by the central party organization in imposing party rulings on branches. In the *de facto* one-party state of 1965 this had not presented a serious threat to the Government itself; but with a new Opposition party it raised great difficulties which the KANU Executive could resolve only if it were able to discipline its own members more successfully in the past. The internal factional disputes within the party however made this difficult. It may have been with this situation in mind that the decision to legislate against independent candidates was made in April 1968. This decision not only altered the basis of representation; it established a new relationship between the branch and the centre and ushered in a new phase in local central relations within KANU.

The Local Government Regulations (Amendment) (No. 2) Bill 1968 provided that no independent candidate should stand for election to any local authority.[3] Published without any prior public discussion it obviously took Members (including it appeared some members of the Cabinet) and the public by surprise. It was published on the same day as

---

[1] *East African Standard*, 3 April 1968.
[2] Ibid., 27 March 1968.
[3] *Kenya Gazette*, Supplement No. 26 (Bills No. 5) 29 March 1968.

the first Bill for the tenth constitutional amendment (discussed above), which prohibited independents for national elections also, and the debate which followed was therefore concerned with the principle in general and not restricted to the question of local government candidates. There was a good deal of public reaction against the proposal as the columns of the local Press indicated. Members of Parliament were immediately hostile; and showed their intention of challenging the Government when they refused to allow them to go ahead and debate the Bill immediately.[1] They agreed to allow it to come to the House a week later. In the intervening period the President not only held a Parliamentary Group meeting but also called all KANU branch chairmen to a meeting at State House in Nairobi, where it appeared that some agreement about the legislation was reached.

In spite of these private party meetings the Bill quickly ran into difficulties when the second reading began on 9 April, in a hostile House and before crowded public galleries where a good many County Councillors were listening. A second meeting of the Parliamentary Group the following morning did not overcome backbench hostility; and that afternoon (10 April) Mboya, who had spoken at length in an attempt to overcome backbench criticism, sensing the feeling in the House proposed an adjournment of the debate. A week later the Bill came back to Parliament again, and was passed, still not without difficulty, and only when Mboya, who had assumed the role of Government spokesman on the issue, had promised that a number of amendments would be introduced at the committee stage to meet backbench objections.

These amendments, which owed a great deal to Mboya's drafting,[2] were of considerable significance for the law and the practical conduct of elections in the future. The provision that abolished non-party candidates was retained; but the procedure for party nomination was much more precisely defined in the Act itself. The Bill had originally prescribed that no one might stand for election as a Councillor unless 'his nomination is supported by the leader of a political party'. The law as finally passed laid down a detailed nomination procedure that all political parties must follow. It also provided for the right of appeal to the courts by any aggrieved candidate whose appeal to his own party had been set aside. These were therefore important concessions, and they were made directly in response to backbench fears that the process

---

[1] The debate on this issue is contained in *Official Report*, The National Assembly, First Parliament, Sixth Session, Vol. XIV, over the period 1–19 April 1968. The Act, Act No. 31 of 1968, is in *Kenya Gazette*, Supplement No. 39 (Acts No. 8), 10 May 1968.

[2] This conclusion must be drawn from an analysis of the debate and the events surrounding the successive party meetings.

of party nomination would be open to manipulation by a small clique either at district or at national level.

Given the pattern of KANU branch conflict between Members of Parliament and branch officials and other would-be local leaders, the abolition of independent candidates was bound to have implications for both groups. The former particularly could not afford to accept a nomination procedure that might be open to manipulation at a time when they were strongly under attack. This could affect Ministers in the same way as backbenchers. It seems unlikely, given the temper of the House, that Members would have passed the Bill as it originally stood; and the amendments on nomination and appeal were a specific concession to the House. It is doubtful however whether they were a complete victory for the Members of Parliament. The nomination procedure remained under the supervision of branch officials. But the clearest indication that the Members of Parliament might have lost the day was the fact that on this occasion, for the first time since the Limuru Conference, the President had called in other members of the party to debate a matter of legislation. A meeting of the National Executive with all district branch chairmen had met under Kenyatta's chairmanship on 3 and 4 April, before the Bill went into the House. Kenyatta therefore had deliberately widened the scope of the debate, as he probably could not avoid on an issue that so obviously affected everyone in the party. Since twenty-three of the forty-one branch chairmen were still Members of Parliament[1] the latter were still able to hold their own. Although no official account of the substance of the discussions was released it appeared by all reports that Kenyatta had overcome the objections of various members by a careful arbitration between the two groups, Members of Parliament and party officials. Nevertheless the dominant position of the parliamentary caucus had been breached, with important implications for future party debate.

A more significant change in the party arena followed soon afterwards, however, at a second major party meeting of the Governing Council called by the President at Mombasa at the end of the same month. At that meeting the party constitution was amended in three ways. First the nomination procedure for candidates for Local Authority and National Assembly elections was incorporated into the constitution. Second the composition of the Annual Delegates Conference (still the ultimate authority in the party and still responsible for the election of party leaders) was altered. Whereas in the past each district had sent six delegates to the conference it was agreed that

[1] See the *Kenya Gazette*, Special Issue, 31 May 1968, for a list of KANU District Branch Chairmen, issued in the Madaraka Day Honours List, in which all were awarded the Order of the Burning Spear, Class II.

in future each district would send six delegates from each constituency (in addition to all members of the National Executive and all Members of Parliament). Third KANU Members of Parliament were to be included in the district Executive Committee of the area in which their constituency was situated. And finally representation on the National Governing Council was altered to a constituency instead of a district basis. In future each constituency would have one representative on the Governing Council.[1] These changes altered the balance between ethnic groups within the new and enlarged party institutions. They also significantly moved the emphasis away from district (and ethnic) representation to the constituency, and so potentially improved the position of the Member of Parliament within the party. It remained to be seen however whether the new structure would enable KANU not only to solve its organizational problems but also to resolve the factional conflicts from which it suffered.

The agreements reached in Nairobi and Mombasa did not prevent further fierce internecine fighting within KANU branches over the nominations for local government candidates. In the following two months there was a continued battle for party nomination carried on in full view of the public and fully reported in the local Press. In Nyeri, branch nominations had to be abandoned after an outbreak of violence and were subsequently held under police guard.[2] In Nairobi a crowd of Kikuyu from one ward held up the former Vice-President, Mr Murumbi's car in protest against their ward branch's nominations; and another crowd marched to the Office of the President to protest against another set of nominations.[3] In Machakos the conflict led to an open fight between two Ministers who were finally separated by the police.[4] In Mombasa the conflict was resolved only by the personal intervention of the President, who finally brought both factions together and arbitrated an agreement.[5] In spite of these bitter disputes, there were however few appeals against the party's nominations. The outcome in Machakos suggested that in fact the factional rivalry had not yet been resolved, for the events left one group in charge of the party branch and the other in charge of the County Council. The long

[1] Minutes of KANU Meeting at Mombasa, April 1968 (mimeo). See also a statement issued on these meetings by Mr Mboya as Secretary General, 9 May 1968 (mimeo). These changes were reminiscent of proposals for party reform that Mboya had raised in an article in *Pan Africa*, 21 February 1964, but which had subsequently disappeared from sight.

[2] *Daily Nation*, 5 July 1968 and *East African Standard*, 13 July 1968.

[3] *Daily Nation*, 14 July 1968.

[4] *East African Standard*, 2 and 3 July 1968. For graphic pictures of this incident see *Daily Nation*, 2 July 1968.

[5] *East African Standard*, 15 August 1968. A detailed analysis of the conflict within the major branches contributes a great deal to an understanding of KANU alignments and I hope to pursue this elsewhere.

party battle was brought to a halt when the official nominations for the County Councils took place. In one district after another KPU (which had suffered no problems in selecting its candidates but had faced serious difficulties in getting them all to the Returning Officers) found its candidates disqualified on technical grounds. All KANU candidates were therefore returned unopposed, and in August 1968 KANU had full control of every Local Authority in the country.[1]

The wholesale disqualification of Opposition candidates caused considerable public speculation and brought an outright charge from Mr Odinga of Government victimization of his party. The disqualifications, he alleged, were 'illegal and irresponsible'.[2] The Government denied the allegations; and speaking from Mombasa four senior Ministers (Mr Moi, Mr Mboya, Mr Kibaki and Mr Mackenzie) issued a detailed rebuttal of each of Odinga's points. They placed the responsibility for the disqualification on KPU itself. The Opposition had been unable, they argued, organizationally to ensure that all its candidates had properly filled in their nomination papers. And they pointed out that it was open to the KPU to appeal against the Returning Officers' decisions.[3] Although the Opposition announced its intention of doing so, the party did not in fact pursue this action; and there the question remained. All KANU Councillors were duly gazetted; the Councils proceeded to elect their chairmen (not without renewed party difficulties) and to settle themselves in for a four-year term of office.

Although the intense debate over the outcome of the local government nominations moved out of the public focus the lesson had not in fact been lost: for the whole sequence of events had demonstrated, in a dramatic fashion, the dominant position of the Executive. It had also brought into greater prominence the Provincial Administration, whose officers had, as Returning Officers, been in charge of the election procedure.

The bureaucracy, and particularly the Provincial Administration, had played a crucial part in the centralization of power that had enlarged the scope of the Executive since independence. One of the most marked developments in the period from 1963 had consequently been the gradual expansion in the authority of the Provincial Administration. This had begun when responsibility for the Administration was transferred to the Office of the President in December 1964. During

---

[1] The exception was in Lamu where elections were held for six Township seats. For the disqualifications see especially *East African Standard*, July and August 1968. Kisumu County Council, which had earlier been suspended, was not involved in these elections.

[2] *East African Standard*, 8 August 1968.

[3] Ibid., and *Daily Nation*, 8 August 1968.

1965 many of the powers that the Administration had lost at independence were restored to it, so that by the end of that year Administrative Officers occupied a position very similar to that of their colonial predecessors[1]. Their authority derived essentially from their position as the Agent of the Executive and the personal representatives of the President in the field. The Provincial Commissioner was restored to the position of head of the administration in his province and recognized as the overall co-ordinator of governmental activities at that level, responsible directly to the President. As the Office of the President described his role in 1968,

Within the limits of his area a Provincial Commissioner is the principal executive officer of the Government, responsible for the peace and good order of the Province and the efficient conduct of public business. . . .[2]

By 1968 the scope of the Administration had been greatly enlarged by the progressive transfer to it of additional responsibilities. Its duties covered the key areas of the assessment and collection of graduated personal tax; chairmanship of the Boards responsible for the selection of settlers for the settlement schemes; of the Land Control Boards which controlled all land transfers; of the Provincial and District Agricultural Committees which had significant powers (especially at district level) on local agricultural matters; of the District Joint Trade Loans Board, which was responsible for advising the Ministry of Commerce and Industry on loans for small traders. They had also assumed a greater role in self-help organization, having in many districts become chairmen of the co-ordinating committees set up under the Community Development Department to control self-help projects and to distribute Central Government funds. As a result the Government had retained in their control much of the resources available at district level. The Administration had also been assigned the major role in the Development Committees set up by the Ministry of Economic Planning. Administrative Officers were expected to play a prominent part in development and to act as a 'mobilizing agent' at all levels. It was therefore the Administrative Officer rather than the party official who became the major link between the Government and the people in the country at large.

The decision to emphasize the role of the Administration as the Agent of the Executive accorded with the predeliction for strong centralized government held by KANU leaders; for the Administration was a centralizing agency that in the past had ensured the

[1] See above, Chapter 2.
[2] *Government Manual*, Nairobi, 1968.

dominance of the central government throughout the country.[1] At the same time it challenged the role of the party. The power of the Provincial Administration was therefore questioned by many KANU Members of Parliament and party officials as inappropriate in the independent state.

The root cause of the friction that developed between Administrative officers and party officials and Members of Parliament was the fundamental question of leadership: for the decision to use the Provincial Administration as the agent of the executive meant that there were two groups of men in the country each of which believed could legitimately claim to lead the people. On the one hand the Administrative Officers saw themselves, on behald of the President, as leaders of the people, a role the President had explicitly assigned them.[2] And they believed themselves much more able to assume that responsibility than the politicians. On the other, the Members of Parliament were the popularly elected representatives of the people and therefore considered themselves as their political leaders. Parliamentarians challenged the authority of the Administration and the tendency of Officers to assert themselves at their expense. They also resented the manner in which elected unofficials were replaced by the Administration as chairmen of various local boards, particularly the District Agricultural Committees, which played an important role in the community. Finally they objected deeply to the fact that the Administration was not responsible to Parliament.

The resulting conflict between administrators and politicians at district and provincial level led the Government to attempt a definition of the relationship between party and civil service. This was attempted first in December 1965, when a Development Seminar was held in Nairobi for both Administrative Officers and Members of Parliament. At that seminar the President and the Minister for Economic Planning placed the responsibility for co-operation equally upon both groups, each of which was urged to recognize the legitimacy of the role the other had to play. At the same time the President made a careful distinction between their roles. 'The politician,' he said:

is the instrument through which the people make their voices heard in the legislative body of the country. He is chosen by the people and he speaks for them in parliament and elsewhere. But as a member of parliament he has some responsibility to accept and advance the decisions of parliament on national programmes. It is perfectly correct that he should advance the interests of his constituency . . . but . . . he should not attempt to use

[1] See above, Chapter 1.
[2] See, for example, *East African Standard*, 13 March 1965.

his position of influence to bully civil servants into deviating from national programmes. It must be understood that civil servants are responsible to their ministers and cannot accept instructions from politicians. District and Provincial Commissioners are responsible to me.

The role of the civil servant is that of the professional. He is employed by the Government to get things done. There are not many of us, I hope, who would presume to tell a doctor how and where to operate on a sick person. We should apply the same restraint in our dealings with other professionals . . . I do not expect civil servants to advise the Government on political feelings in the country . . .'[1]

At the Limuru Conference in March 1966 the President emphasized the need to retain a politically neutral civil service, and rejected the idea that civil servants should become party members. There was too great a danger he argued, if civil servants were to become active members of the party, that in the division of interests between politics and professionalism the efficiency of the service would suffer.[2]

The attempt to establish a greater harmony between party and Administration was demonstrated by the manner in which the President reacted to conflict over the position of chiefs, the lowest rank in the administrative hierarchy. The chief, responsible for law and order in his location, occupied a crucial position in the administrative structure. The post was for a variety of reasons a coveted one at the local level, and also one of considerable power, based upon the Chiefs' Authority Act which followed closely the earlier Native Authority Ordinance of colonial days. Appointments lay with the Office of the President, to whom Provincial Commissioners forwarded their recommendations. In 1965, however, President Kenyatta, faced with pressures from party officials, agreed that they and Members of Parliament should participate in the selection of these officers, notwithstanding their position as civil servants. It was decided that applications for the post of chief should in the first place be considered by a local committee, which would include the District Commissioner, the County Councillor for the area, the district branch chairman of KANU, the Senator for the district and the constituency member of the House of Representatives. This committee selected three applicants, for whom the people of the location then voted at a public meeting. The name of the successful candidate was then sent to the Office of the President.

The formation of the new opposition party, however, and the return to a two-party state put the Government in a dilemma. The popular

[1] *Speech by His Excellency the President* at the Kenya Institute of Administration, 15 December 1965. Kenya News Agency Handout No. 768.
[2] *Points made by His Excellency the President Mzee Jomo Kenyatta*, KANU Delegates Conference, March 1966, Nairobi: Government Information Service.

election of a chief might well bring a man sympathetic to the opposition into the office; but the chief, once appointed, was assumed to be a civil servant. Not surprisingly, the procedure was altered and the selection returned to the Administration (responsible to the Office of the President) which was not bound to consult local political leaders.[1] The KANU Members of Parliament, particularly from Central Province, objected strongly; but their objections were overruled.

This change symbolized the enlarged authority and assertiveness of the Administration in the new two-party situation. While the principle of a neutral civil service was maintained nevertheless after the middle of 1966, the role of the Provincial Administration, as the personal agent of the Executive, became more clearly political. Notwithstanding assertions to the contrary political control assumed the dominant place in their functions. This brought them into conflict with Opposition Members of Parliament, not least over the question of public meetings. It also brought them into conflict with County Councillors, who jealously guarded the independence of their Councils.[2] But the men who most vigorously challenged the new assertiveness of the Administration were KANU Members of Parliament, who objected to the apparently subordinate role to which they were relegated. As on many other issues the strongest objections were voiced by KANU backbenchers from Central Province, one of whom remarked in November 1967: 'It seems as if the Minister in Nairobi and the top civil servants no longer trust the politicians.'[3] KANU backbenchers maintained a steady barrage against the Administration in Parliament, where they raised questions about their powers and their behaviour.[4] They objected to the fact that the Administration was not responsible to Parliament, and to the manner in which this enhanced the independence of the Executive. These objections reached a climax in November 1967 in the backbench opposition to the Government's decision to make the Administration chairmen of the new Land Control Boards, set up under the Land Control legislation, which assumed control of all land transfers.[5]

It was therefore the KANU backbench rather than the Opposition

[1] *Official Report*, The National Assembly, First Parliament, Fifth Session, Vol. XIII, Part I, 7 November 1967, col. 1798. It remained open to a District Commissioner to hold a public election for the post of chief if he considered it desirable, and in certain districts such elections were still held in 1968.

[2] There is not room here to discuss the growth of Central Government authority over the local authorities which developed in these two years, but see in particular *Report of the Seminar on Local Government*, Kenya Institute of Administration, December 1967 (mimeo).

[3] *Official Report*, The National Assembly, First Parliament, Fifth Session, Vol. XIII, Part II, 28 November 1967, col. 2529.

[4] Ibid.

[5] See ibid., for this debate.

that maintained the strongest objections to the role of the Administration. Branch chairmen also brought their objections to the President at the meetings he convened in Nairobi and Mombasa in April 1968. In the face of this party protest the President intervened to provide a new statement of the respective roles of party and civil service. This was given on the occasion of a joint meeting of Provincial and District Commissioners and KANU branch chairmen held under Kenyatta's chairmanship in Nakuru in July 1968.[1]

The President was reported to have told this meeting that 'no ruling party can effectively exist without the Administration' and to have urged the two groups to work together. But the most significant fact of this meeting was that it clearly and openly associated the Provincial Administration with the party, and therefore implicitly rejected the concept of a politically independent service. The Provincial Administration remained responsible directly to the President, not the party. But while civil servants were not, it appeared, to become members of the party, the service and the party were now much more politically fused. This was symbolized soon afterwards by the attendance of the Coast Provincial Commissioner at President Kenyatta's meeting with the two KANU factions in Mombasa.[2] Other events suggested that if the Administration and Party had been brought closer together it was the former that would occupy the dominant position. This was implied, for example, in the subsequent intervention of the Administration in the KANU branch elections in Machakos, which were held under their supervision.[3]

By the middle of 1968 the Executive in independent Kenya enjoyed a position very similar to that of the Executive during the days of colonial rule. The President occupied a position very much akin to that of the Governor, both in the scope of his powers and in the manner in which he could call upon the Administration to ensure Central Government control. This control had enabled the Government to ensure that Kenya remained a dominant party state; but it had left KANU, as the dominant party, in a weak position. The administrative and legal framework inherited from the colonial years had been turned effectively to the use of the new state. But the other inheritance of a weak party machine had also survived. The extent to which KANU leaders recognized this emerged clearly out of a heady, boisterous debate in Parliament at the end of June 1968, when both Ministers and Members used an adjournment motion to attack their own KANU administration for its inadequacies. The structural changes introduced

[1] See *East African Standard* and *Daily Nation*, 29 July 1968.
[2] *East African Standard*, 15 August 1968.
[3] *Official Report*, The National Assembly, First Parliament, Sixth Session, Vol. XV, 28 June 1968, Adjournment debate, *passim.*

171

at Mombasa had not yet taken effect. Members, apprehensive perhaps at the then impending local government elections, did as they had for five years: turned to Parliament to reassert their dissatisfaction with the state of their party. Their attack was not on Kenyatta; KANU Members continued to make the distinction between Kenyatta and the Government that they had made in 1965; and to object to his Ministers without making any challenge to him. The debate was conducted therefore around and below him without any challenge to his role. The questions were directed at the Cabinet.

While the political debate was primarily concerned in these two years with questions of personality and power it was not entirely unconcerned with policy. The Opposition took the issues that had led to their withdrawal from KANU in 1966 as the beginnings of an inter-party debate on policy and emphasized the need for a more egalitarian society. Although they succeeded in articulating their general views on the dangers of a class society[1] they failed, however, in this period to produce alternative policies. They were also restricted in their opportunities to develop an inter-party debate. It was therefore the disagreements within KANU that dominated the policy debate.

The KANU debate was conducted within the terms of reference successfully laid down by the Government in 1965 and incorporated in Sessional Paper No. 10. KANU Members were therefore concerned primarily not with fundamentals but with the questions of the allocation of resources. Accepting the overall policy of a mixed economy and a development policy that emphasized the need for individual effort they were consequently concerned as to which group would benefit from that development. The allocation of resources was equally the concern of the Opposition; but it was KANU backbenchers rather than KPU spokesmen whose attacks upon the Government were the focus of this debate. This emerged clearly in the debates in 1967 on the Government's crucial policies for the Kenyanization of the business and commercial sector of the economy which at this time assumed a growing prominence in their programme.[2] It was demonstrated most clearly however in the continuing debate on land, and in questions about the future of that sector of the former European Highlands that had not yet been transferred to African ownership. In particular it was seen in expressions of fear from Kalenjin that they would be excluded

[1] See for example *Official Report*, The National Assembly, First Parliament, Fifth Session, Vol. XIII, Part II, 18 December 1967, cols. 3227–30, in the debate on civil service salaries.

[2] For the Government's new trade licensing and immigration control decisions which were the basis of this policy, see *Official Report*, The National Assembly, First Parliament, Fifth Session. Also Act No. 25 of 1967, The Immigration Act 1967, and Act No. 37 of 1967, The Trade Licensing Act 1967.

from those Rift Valley lands that had not yet been transferred to African ownership. This was the cause of the long struggle between the KANU backbench and the Government on the question of chairmanship of the new Land Control Boards.[1] The KANU debate was therefore still primarily concerned with property.

This debate was conducted in terms of regional and therefore ethnic interests; and it resulted in the expression of fears of Kikuyu domination. These fears were expressed generally, and so went beyond KANU. The debate in the National Assembly was the parliamentary expression of a growing national concern. Between 1966 and 1968 the fears of Kikuyu control of the civil service and the economy that had emerged in 1966 assumed an increasingly prominent position in the public and especially the KANU party debate. So pronounced did allegations of specific Kikuyu dominance become in Parliament that a point was reached when the Speaker ruled that further references to this subject would be out of place.[2] There was therefore a good deal of talk of 'tribalism' in the political debate.

'Tribalism' however, if it represented anything, represented fears of economic neglect. The antagonism expressed towards the Kikuyu was not merely or even primarily a tribal legacy rooted in divergent loyalties of the past. It was closely related to concern for the present. It was the contemporary issues and conflicts directly related to Kenya's economic development that raised these fears of dominance by one tribe in all aspects of Kenya's life: in government, commerce and business.

Finally this political debate highlighted two crucial developments that distinguished the Kenya of 1968 from the Kenya of 1963. First the economy was generally in a stronger position, more buoyant and more diversified. The Government continued to face major economic problems, but the evidence suggested the ability to tackle them. Second, the Government stood in a much stronger position *vis-à-vis* both party and Parliament. The progressive centralization of power since 1963 had put the executive more firmly in control; and in the process the country had moved closer to the concept of an administrative state.

---

[1] The debate on this Bill was an excellent example of the kind of struggle that could take place between the Government and its own back-bench. For other expressions of Kalenjin fears of Kikuyu assumptions of land in the Rift Valley, see for example *Official Report*, The National Assembly, First Parliament, Sixth Session, Vol. XV, cols. 542–50 for an Adjournment debate moved by a Member from Kericho District on the Transfer of a European farm for which two rival African groups, one predominantly Kalenjin and one including Kikuyu, were competing.

[2] Ibid., Sixth Session, Vol. XIV, 28 February 1968, col. 153. The occasion was the debate on the presidential address.

Appendix

CONSTITUTIONAL CHANGES IN KENYA 1964–9
The ten amendments to the Kenya constitution passed between the middle of 1964 and April 1969 are listed below, with the major changes introduced, and the date of publication of each Act. These amendments were finally brought together in a new constitutional document, Act 5 of 1969. For a full discussion of the Kenya constitution reference should be made to Yash Ghai and J. P. W. B. McAusland, *Public Law and Political Change in Kenya* (forthcoming).

1st Amendment Act, Act 28 of 1964, Published 24 November 1964.
Established a republic with an executive President, who became Head of State, Head of Government and Commander of the Armed Forces. The first president would be the man holding office as Prime Minister immediately prior to the establishment of the Republic. Future presidents would be elected at the time of a general election. A candidate for the presidency had to be a candidate for the House of Representatives, and his nomination had to be supported by 1,000 registered voters. All candidates for the House of Representatives had to indicate their support for a presidential candidate. The presidential candidate who, having won his constituency seat also received a majority of votes of the number of Members of Parliament was declared elected. At times other than a general election (i.e. on the death or resignation of the President) The House of Representatives, acting as an electoral college, would elect a successor by a procedure laid down in the constitution. Removed all except specially entrenched powers from the Regional Assemblies by amending Schedule1. Other changes included the provision for a Vice-President appointed by the President from among the elected members, to be 'principal assistant of the President in the discharge of his duties' but not automatically to succeed him.

2nd Amendment Act, Act 38 of 1964, published 17 December 1964.
Amended certain specially entrenched clauses concerning the Regions, e.g. on the financial relations between the Centre and the Regions, and the method of alteration of regional boundaries.

174

3rd Amendment Act, Act 14 of 1965, published 8 June 1965.
Altered the parliamentary majority required for approval of a declaration of a state of emergency from 65 per cent to a majority. Also provided that the period after which a parliamentary resolution must be sought should be extended from seven to twenty-one days. Decreased the parliamentary majority required for a constitutional amendment to 65 per cent in both Houses.

Abolished the special entrenchment of certain sections of the constitution.

Abolished those sections of the constitution concerning the executive powers of the Regional Assemblies. Renamed those Assemblies Provincial Councils, and gave Parliament the power to confer functions upon them. Abolished the right of appeal to the Privy Council. Altered the title of the Supreme Court to High Court.

Removed the provisions concerning control of agricultural land transactions from the constitution. Declaration of emergency made valid for three months instead of two.

4th Amendment Act, Act 16 of 1966, published 12 April 1966.
Made Commonwealth citizens eligible for rather than entitled to citizenship.

Brought the constitution into line with trade union law.

Required that an M.P. who was sentenced to a prison sentence of six months or over should vacate his seat.

Required that any M.P. who failed to attend eight consecutive parliamentary meetings without permission of the Speaker should lose his seat, although it allowed the President to waive rule.

Gave the Speaker an original but not a casting vote.

President given power to appoint and dismiss from civil service.

Public service tenure at pleasure of President. President's powers to rule by decree in North-Eastern Region extended to Marsarbit, Isiolo, Tana River and Lamu districts.

5th Amendment Act, Act 17 of 1966, published 30 April 1966.
Required an M.P. who resigned from the party that had supported him at the time of his election, at a time when that party was a parliamentary party, to vacate his seat at the expiration of the session.

6th Amendment Act, Act 18 of 1966, published 7 June 1966.
This must be read in conjunction with amendments made at the same time to the Preservation of Public Security Act, cap 57.

Provided that fundamental rights of, *inter alia*, movement, association assembly and expression would not be contravened if, under the provisions of the Preservation of Public Security Act, the President exercised his special powers including detention without trial.

7th Amendment Act, Act 40 of 1966, published 4 January 1967.
Provided for the merger of the Senate and House of Representatives to establish a unicameral legislature, the National Assembly.

8th Amendment Act, Act 4 of 1967, published 31 March 1967.
Removed doubts on the interpretation and effect of section 42A of the constitution concerning the resignation of members under the fifth amendment, by act by making it retrospective.

9th Amendment Act, Act 16 of 1968, published 19 April 1968.
Abolished the Provincial Councils and deleted from the constitution all references to the provincial and district boundaries and alteration thereof.

10th Amendment Act, Act 45 of 1968, published 12 July 1968.
Altered the method of presidential election. In future the president would be directly elected by the national electorate at the time of a general election. All candidates for a general election should be nominated by a political party. At the time of a general election every political party taking part in the election would be required to nominate a presidential candidate. At the poll the ballot paper would pair the presidential candidate and the parliamentary candidate belonging to the same party.

Altered the provisions for succession. If the office of president became vacant other than at the time of the dissolution of Parliament an election for President should be held within ninety days. In the interim period the Vice-President would exercise the functions of the office, but on certain matters including the preservation of public security and the appointment and dismissal of Ministers would act only in accordance with a resolution of the Cabinet.

Removed the requirement that the National Assembly should every eight months reaffirm its support for an order bringing Part III of the Preservation of Public Security Act (which provides *inter alia* for detention without trial) into force.

Altered the composition of the National Assembly by substituting the twelve Specially Elected Members who were elected by the elected members of the House of Representatives twelve nominate members appointed by the President.

Act 5 of 1969, published 18 April 1969, brought all these amendments together in a revised constitution. Certain additional amendments were also made, including the alteration of the membership of the Electoral Commission, all of whose members would now be appointed by the President. (Formerly the Speaker had been Chairman.)

176

Index

Adeno, Paul, 112
African Elected Members' Organization, 15
Africanization of the economy, 52–53; party positions towards, 84–88
Agar, E. O., 43
Akumu, Denis, 66, 85, 87
Anyieni, Z., 39, 43; moved motion on control of land, 49, 68, 75, 143
Argwings-Kodhek, C. M. G., 15 n., 75 n.
Ayodo, S., 116

Bala, Okuta, 108 n., 109, 113
Baring, Sir Evelyn, Governor, 22, 23, 25

Chiefs, retirement of, 1964, 33; method of selection, 169–70
Chilo, Ondiek, 108 n., 109, 119
Civil service, expansion of in colonial period, 22; dominant position in colonial period, 27–29; under independent government, 29, 33, 166; role of after independence, 168–9; relationship with party, 169, 171
Cliffe, Lionel, 83 n.
Communism, fears of, 64–68, 69, 88, 146; tactical use of in election, 68
Constitutional amendments, first, 34, 125; third, 35, 142; fifth, 76–78, 145 n.; sixth, 152; seventh, 153; ninth, 153–4; tenth, 154–5, 160–1; Appendix, 174–6
Corner Bar Broup, 53, 70 n.

District, as a basis for political support, 8; and competitive politics, 73; as a base for national leadership, 16
District Associations, 8

Elgeyo, 9
Executive, during colonial period, 20 seq.; relationship with legislature, 28, 34, 40, 125 *seq.*, 153, 154–5; powers of, 35, 152

Foreign policy, debate on, 51–52, 57, 87

Gachago, J., 49
General Service Unit, 23
Gichoya, K. N., 75
Gichuru, J. S., 56, 87 n.
Governor, authority of, 28

Hyden, Goran, 83 n., 94 n.

Independence constitution, 12, 33, and n.

Kaggia, Bildad, and KANU Backbench, 45; land policies, 45–46, 48; contest for district leadership, 61; association with Lumumba Institute, 63, 64; views on communism, 66; deputy leader of KPU, 73, 75; views on representation, 77, 79; and 1966 by-election, 82, 83, 90–91; arrested, 146, 147
Kalenjin, 3 n., 9, 10, 47, 55, 66, 91–92, 93–94, 172

179